Sources Of
American Spirituality

Early New England Meditative Poetry

ANNE BRADSTREET AND EDWARD TAYLOR

Edited by Charles E. Hambrick-Stowe

PAULIST PRESS

New York ◊ Mahwah

Grateful acknowledgment is made for permission to reprint material from *The Poems of Edward Taylor,* edited by Donald E. Stanford. Copyright 1960 by Donald E. Stanford. Reprinted by permission of Donald E. Stanford.

Library of Congress Cataloging-in-Publication Data

Early New England meditative poetry.

(Sources of American spirituality)
Poems by Anne Bradstreet and Edward Taylor.
Includes indexes.
1. Christian, poetry, American—New England.
2. American poetry—Puritan authors. 3. American poetry—Colonial period, ca. 1600–1775. 4. Spiritual life—Poetry. I. Hambrick-Stowe, Charles E.
II. Bradstreet, Anne, 1612?–1672. III. Taylor, Edward, 1642–1729. IV. Series.
PS595.C47E27 1988   811'.1'08   88–25400
ISBN 0-8091-0416-4

Published by Paulist Press
997 Macarthur Boulevard
Mahwah, N.J. 07430

Printed and bound in the United States of America

CONTENTS

GENERAL INTRODUCTION

Fifty years have passed since Perry Miller with his patient scholarship and stylistic flair overturned many of the myths that twentieth-century Americans had come to harbor about their Puritan forebears. Thanks to him and the school that followed him there are not many, at least in the halls of academia, who still cling to images of Puritans as ice cold prigs whose lives were devoid of passion and creativity.

Miller showed us how the Puritans drew on and interpreted some of the great philosophical and theological traditions, adapting them to their situation in the New World. Yet, even he did not realize the extent to which a similar process was occurring with the Puritan practice of piety. That realization and the very apt articulation of it has been the contribution of the editor of this volume, Charles Hambrick-Stowe.

In this volume, he continues his efforts to present an examination of Puritan piety in the context of a comprehensive study of the Reformed *and* Catholic traditions that shaped it. Arguing that English Puritan and Continental Catholic spirituality flowered simultaneously, drawing on many common nutrients, he opens our eyes to the common ground on which Protestant and Catholic piety stood, even in the bitter Post-Reformation age. Yet, to his credit, he does not overstate his case to the point of neglecting the real differences between the two spiritual traditions. In fact, by showing their similarities, he is able to highlight more deftly their unique features.

All this is done via the study of two New England poets, Anne Bradstreet and Edward Taylor. The choice to study spirituality through poetry, rather than through the sermons of Taylor or the catechism that Bradstreet was reared on, is important, for it challenges us to consider how genre affects spiritual expression. In analyzing the language of poetry we are led by force to look for new tools, well aware that those that worked so well for dogmatic theology or even for comparative religion might not work here.

1

We are also led to the relation between aesthetics and religious expression. Something of the Puritan sense of beauty and taste for God was conveyed in this poetry that seldom was seen in the official church statements or even in the sermons of the clergy.

In the poetry of these two Puritan sages, we are given a glimpse of the immediate moment when their imaginations searched for ways to express their grief, their joy, their search for God, and their faith in his real, though often inscrutable presence.

John Farina

PREFACE

"I believe in . . . the communion of saints."

For many Protestant Christians this affirmation from the Apostles' Creed has remained an unfathomed mystery. The Reformers in the sixteenth century and Protestants ever since have rejected as superstitious and oppressive the Roman Catholic "cult of the saints" with its notion of heavenly intermediaries and its official canonization procedures. Rightly insisting that the biblical word "saint" refers not only to great names in the faith but to every ordinary believer, we have emphasized the koinonia of membership with one another in the church. At other moments we have focused our understanding on that precious fellowship of the saved in heaven spoken of by Jesus Christ and the Book of Revelation. But we have known little, indeed have been highly suspicious, of any experienced connection between the two. The traditional Catholic system, whatever its abuses and its tendency to divert attention from Christ as sole mediator, preserved the wondrous mystery of life in the Body of Christ in, over, and beyond time. Now as Protestant Christians are once more being drawn to the spiritual disciplines, perhaps we may receive instruction and inspiration through the examples of men and women who knew Christ long ago and now enjoy Christ together in heaven. In some sense, best left undefined, we may enjoy spiritual communion with our forebears in Christ and, through study of their experience of grace, receive ourselves the grace of God. "Wherefore seeing we also are compassed about with so great a cloud of witnesses, let us lay aside every weight, and the sin which doth so easily beset us, and let us run with patience the race that is set before us" (Heb. 12:1).

The New England Puritans of the seventeenth century are among the most important witnesses in the formation of an "American spirituality." Their deeply personal piety, together with the covenantal congregational-

3

ism of their doctrine of the church and commonwealth, became a major source for the American self-concept as it emerged in the nineteenth and twentieth centuries. For this reason, no specialty in the study of American history has flourished like Puritan studies. In the history of spirituality, the Puritans are of great importance for another reason. With one foot in the medieval and the other in the modern world, they are a vital link with the dynamic spiritual movements of the late Middle Ages. For Protestants as well as Catholics, the sixteenth and seventeenth centuries were an explosively creative period in the history of spirituality. The early New Englanders brought these devotional traditions with them to America beginning in the 1620s and 1630s.

We may know something about the Puritan practice of piety by reading their sermons, devotional manuals, and other officially published materials. Early New Englanders were also great keepers of journals and diaries, writers of spiritual autobiographies, and composers of devotional poetry. Through such personal records of devotion we glimpse their inner world. The meditative poetry of Anne Bradstreet (writing from the 1640s through the 1660s) and Edward Taylor (writing from the early 1680s until 1725) represents not only the best in colonial American literature but the bared souls of two saints. Bradstreet and Taylor were distinctively American writers and no doubt contain the germ of the "American spirituality" for which this series of books seeks the sources. Their American spirit derived from their struggle to come to terms with what it meant to live not in Europe but in a new land and on a frontier. Deeper than this provincial spirit, the sympathetic reader encounters the Holy Spirit in their meditations, and therein a spirit that is universally Christian. Although separated from us by three centuries, the struggles and spiritual longings of Bradstreet and Taylor can, in our own meditations and prayers, illumine the path of our modern pilgrimage.

The texts are taken from previously published but now out of print editions. Some of Anne Bradstreet's poems were published in her lifetime as *The Tenth Muse Lately Sprung Up in America* (London, 1650). An enlarged and revised edition, *Several Poems* (Boston, 1678), appeared posthumously. The complete, definitive edition of all the extant poems and writings was the work of John Harvard Ellis, *The Works of Anne Bradstreet in Prose and Verse* (Charlestown, Mass., 1867). A facsimile of the seventeenth-century editions was published by Josephine K. Piercy, *The Tenth Muse* (Gainesville, Fla., 1965). Jeannine Hensley's edition of *The Works of Anne Bradstreet* (Cambridge, Mass., 1967), with its complete modernization of spelling, punctuation, and capitalization, loses the original spirit of the poems and even distorts the true meaning of some lines. Robert Hutchinson, ed., *Poems of Anne Bradstreet* (New York, 1969), based on the Ellis edition, was of great usefulness, although its arrangement of the poems by theme rather than chronology was somewhat idiosyncratic. Recently, Joseph R. McElrath, Jr., and Allan P. Robb published an important critical edition of *The Complete Works of Anne Bradstreet* (Boston, 1981), based on painstaking analysis of the available copy-texts and complete with 300 pages of editorial apparatus setting forth variant readings. McElrath and Robb have been criticized for their decision to adopt the 1650 text of *The Tenth Muse* poems instead of the 1678 text from which Ellis worked. Their thesis that the earlier edition more nearly reflects the author's own intention is highly debatable since *The Tenth Muse* was published without her knowledge or consent and she refers in several places to her later efforts at revision. In any case, their monumental volume is a resource for scholars, not general readers. The present work derives its text from the Ellis edition. I have modernized the letters ''s'' and ''u,'' spelled out abbreviations, and replaced the ampersand with ''and,'' but, with Ellis, have retained the original spelling, capitalization, and punctuation. The publishing history of Edward Taylor is much simpler and, except for a few lines, is entirely modern. Taylor as poet was essentially discovered by Thomas H. Johnson, who published *The Poetical Works of Edward Taylor* (Princeton, N.J., 1939). Johnson presented some of the Preparatory (or, as he called them, Sacramental) Meditations, but this was nevertheless far from a complete edition. That had to wait another twenty years until the masterful work by Donald E. Stanford, *The Poems of Edward Taylor* (New Haven, 1960). The poems selected for the present volume appear here with his kind permission, for which I express deep gratitude. *The Poems of Edward Taylor* is, sadly, now out of print. The present volume does not simply re-present selections from that indispensable edition, however. My annotations for the Bradstreet and Taylor poems—and especially those for Taylor—here make these spiritual writers accessible to a wider range of readers.

I wish to express my appreciation to three groups of persons who have contributed to my spiritual and intellectual understanding both of the Puritans and of myself: my professors and academic colleagues; the people of the churches and church-related institutions I have served in Japan, Massachusetts, Maryland, and Pennsylvania; and my family, immediate and extended, but especially my wife Elizabeth. The book is dedicated to my parents, Edwin G. and Florence M. Hambrick, and to my children, Anne Pilgrim, Thomas Wait, and Charles Gift Hambrick-Stowe.

INTRODUCTION

1. SPIRITUALITY IN THE REFORMED TRADITION

The meditative poetry of two New England Puritans, Anne Bradstreet (1612?–1672) and Edward Taylor (1645?–1729), brings us into the world of Reformed spirituality. It is a world about which we have known little; indeed, until recently it was hardly thought to exist. Calvinism may have created a new tradition of scholastic theology and sparked cultural and political revolutions. But how could its granite doctrines—the utter spiritual inability of sinners, the omnipotent sovereignty of God, God's selectivity in the salvation of the elect—provide a context within which believers would seek God's divine embrace? Yet, as the poems of Bradstreet and Taylor show, orthodox Puritans who carried Calvinism to the New World did seek God in the systematic ways we associate with Catholic masters such as Francis de Sales, Jeanne de Chantal, and Augustine Baker. The doctrine of sanctification, as a reading of the poems suggests, enabled Puritans to understand God not only as Judge but as Redeemer and even Lover of souls.

Protestant and modern Catholic spirituality were born in the European devotional revival of the sixteenth and seventeenth centuries. While Roman Catholics by nature cultivate tradition, Protestants are not so careful and forget they once meditated and prayed according to methods they now think of as Catholic. Spiritual theology and practical spirituality have re-emerged as fresh undertakings for Protestants, as new as Roman Catholic appreciation of Protestant spirituality. These new appreciations have flowered in the last decade, although the roots of the new scholarship can be traced earlier. Current interest in Reformed spirituality stems from developments over the twentieth century in the fields of Catholic and Protestant scholarship and in the secular study of history and literature.

7

The Catholic reappraisal of Reformed piety associated with Vatican II actually predates the Council by a few years. Vatican II's recognition of Protestants as "separated brethren" made official a new scholarly view. The shift is apparent in a comparison of Pierre Pourrat's classic four-volume *Christian Spirituality* (1922–1955), and the three-volume work by Louis Bouyer and others, *A History of Christian Spirituality* (1960–1965; Eng. ed. 1963–1969). Pourrat had nothing to say about Protestant spirituality; the notion was a contradiction in terms. Luther and Calvin, "Manichaean Quietists," negated the need to pray. Protestantism was "egoistic and altogether anthropocentric. The whole plan of redemption is brought down to man's salvation. Do not ask this kind of mysticism for acts of pure love. It is incapable of them. To pay to Jesus the homage of praise and love, to which he is entitled by his divine perfection, is far from its practice." Of the English Reformation Pourrat wrote, "There was no spiritual writing in England at this time."[1] By contrast, Bouyer devoted most of an entire volume to a positive assessment of Protestant spirituality. While not uncritical of Reformation theology, he found much that was traditional—and hence true—in its spiritual thought and practice. His loftiest evaluation, astonishingly, was of "the great spiritual writers of Puritanism" who carried Calvin's key doctrine of sanctification to its warmest experiential conclusion "with an evangelism still very much tinged with a late medieval love of Christ—evocative of Gerson and the *Imitation*." With "vehement mystical feeling for Christ," Puritans "were closer to many aspects of the Jesuits and Visitandines of the period than were the traditional Anglicans." Bouyer even suggests the Puritan origin of the French Catholic cult of the Sacred Heart. Thomas Goodwin's *The Heart of Christ in Heaven towards Sinners on Earth* (1652) presented "a synthesis of the devotion to the Sacred Heart which irresistibly reminds us of Paray-le-Monial . . . but a good half-century before Margaret-Mary Alacoque." Just as English Puritans read Catholic spiritual works, evidence exists that French clergy knew some Anglican writings. Were they "incapable of also reading the Puritans? It is not self-evident." Bouyer was undoubtedly incorrect in putting forth a causal link between Puritan and Catholic spiritual theology, but his more cautious conclusion is full of truth: "Agreements of this kind in spiritual works of roughly the same period are at least a sign of the community of religious thought and culture that went much further than people have hitherto realized."[2] Re-publication of Bouyer's volumes by Seabury Press in 1977 and

---

1. Pierre Pourrat, *Christian Spirituality*, vol. III (New York, 1927), 64–66, 70; vol. IV (Westminster, Md., 1955), 436.

2. Louis Bouyer, *Orthodox Spirituality and Protestant and Anglican Spirituality* (New York, 1969), 134–142.

cross-fertilization of Catholic and Protestant thought at seminaries and re-treat centers have furthered Catholic interest in the history of Protestant devotion and opened the field of spirituality to Protestants in a new way.

Protestants have not written books like Pourrat's because no Protestant academic discipline existed to call them forth. Catholic theology consisted of three or four branches: dogmatic, moral, and spiritual theology. The study of spirituality was divided between ascetic and mystical theology, either as separate disciplines or parts of a single discipline. Ascetic theology was the study of the ordinary believer's purposeful and regular practice of meditation and prayer. Mystical theology studied the extraordinary, God-inspired spiritual states of saints like St. John of the Cross and St. Teresa of Avila. The three "Ways" of ascetic theology to be practiced by all Christians—the Purgative, Illuminative, and Unitive—shaded into mystical theology, often clouding the boundary between the two. If Louis Cognet paid little explicit attention to these distinctions, using instead the new term "spiritual ideas," his explanation was traditional. " 'Spiritual ideas' . . . are not, strictly speaking, the speculations of theologians, yet ideas which seem to be purely theological often have profound effects on the most practical aspects of Christian life." His concern for "the thought and conduct of the Christian, in so far as they form part of his devotion, his personal relations with God, his interior life" was the work of a well-established academic discipline. But when Protestants outlined the theological curriculum they abandoned this discipline of spirituality. Protestant seminaries, established in the nineteenth century, replaced ascetic and mystical theology with practical theology, encompassing liturgics, homiletics, the care of souls, and so on.[3]

Protestants had developed a new vocabulary of "religious experience" and sanctification to describe the work of the soul, instead of the Catholic concept of spirituality. Early Reformed theologians analyzed the scheme of salvation in intricate detail. Scripture suggested a doctrine of sanctification between justification through God's sheer grace and glorification with Christ in heaven. Sanctification made possible the grace-filled life of the Christian while still on earth. A saint—a believer undergoing sanctification—practiced the spiritual disciplines of reading (especially of the Bible, but also sermons, devotional manuals, and other religious books), meditation, and prayer and was graced with various religious experiences, some-

---

3. F. L. Cross, ed., *The Oxford Dictionary of the Christian Church* (New York, 1974), s.v. "Ascetical Theology." Louis Bouyer, *The Spirituality of the New Testament and the Fathers* (New York, 1963), vii–ix. Louis Cognet, *Post-Reformation Spirituality* (New York, 1959), 7–8. Washington Gladden discusses the Protestant practical theology curriculum in *The Christian Pastor and the Working Church* (New York, 1898), 1–22.

times ecstasy of a high order. In Puritan theology sanctification was a dynamic process of spiritual growth; saints expected to progress toward perfection and be prepared for glory at the hour of death. Numerous Puritan devotional manuals (such as John Downame's *A Guide to Godlynesse,* 1622), journals and meditative poetry (such as that of Anne Bradstreet and Edward Taylor), and spiritual biography and autobiography (exemplified by Jonathan Edwards' *An Account of the Life Of the Late Reverend Mr. David Brainerd,* 1749) expressed this spirituality of progressive sanctification through spiritual discipline. Puritan writings are certainly within the field of spirituality. Protestants were not without those qualities and practices that Catholics have so systematically studied. But Protestants rejected much of the language of Catholic spirituality even as they retained traditional exercises. ''Mysticism'' called to mind supposed corruptions of monastic life and a false elevation of solitary celibacy over communal responsibility and fellowship. ''Spiritual exercises'' evoked the superstition of candles and beads. American revivalism and anti-Catholicism emphasized biblical study and only the first step of the Christian life, conversion, to the exclusion of anything that smacked of being Catholic. Bouyer argued that the neo-orthodox theologians deepened Protestant antipathy to spiritual theology by classifying mysticism as neo-paganism. Without an academic discipline devoted to it, study of Protestant spirituality languished.[4]

Protestant interest in the field of spirituality survived through the work, not of theologians, but of philosophers and psychologists in the late nineteenth and early twentieth centuries. Josiah Royce and William James are the best known of the scholars who undertook a new scientific study of ''religious feelings and religious impulses.'' James' *The Varieties of Religious Experience* (1902) exercised influence until our own time. Baron Friedrich von Hugel's massive work, *The Mystical Element of Religion as Studied in Saint Catherine of Genoa and Her Friends* (1908) focused the scientific study of spirituality on a single figure and (though the author was Catholic) introduced academic Protestants to classical Catholic mysticism. Evelyn Underhill approached the subject in a uniquely persuasive way, most comprehensively in her widely read *Mysticism* (1911). An Anglican, she wrote as a spiritual practitioner and director, but related her subject to the fields of psychology and philosophy.

Few Protestant church historians recognized the centrality of religious experience and devotional practice. Geoffrey F. Nuttall's *The Holy Spirit in Puritan Faith and Practice* (1946) and Gordon S. Wakefield's *Puritan Devotion* (1956) were exceptions that proved the rule. The Quaker scholarship of Rufus Jones insisted on the primacy of experience over doctrine

4. Bouyer, *Orthodox Spirituality and Protestant and Anglican Spirituality,* 57–58.

and delved into the medieval Catholic roots of Quaker inner light mysticism. Jones' books, such as *New Studies in Mystical Religion* (1927) and *The Flowering of Mysticism: The Friends of God in the Fourteenth Century* (1939), attracted the attention of some liberal Protestants. These works, influential as they were, did not lead Protestants to see spirituality as anything but a sidelight. They did not constitute an organized field of study. There was little effort to uncover the history of Protestant spirituality until post-Vatican II ecumenical cooperation began to bear fruit. Such projects as *The Westminster Dictionary of Christian Spirituality* (1983) and the series in which this volume appears would not have been undertaken until the 1980s. Wakefield writes, " 'Spirituality' is a word very much in vogue among Christians of our time. French Catholic in origin, it is now common to evangelical Protestants also."[5]

Developments in the study of early American history and literature have also contributed to the flowering of spirituality. Perry Miller, in his seminal work, *The New England Mind* (1939), devoted his first two chapters to the Augustinian tradition and the Puritan practice of piety. That initial nod in the direction of spirituality was offset by the remainder of the book which achieved his real purpose, the recovery of Puritan theology's intellectual grandeur. In the intervening years, in spite of Alan Simpson's gemlike *Puritanism in Old and New England* (1955), which saw religious experience as "the essence of Puritanism," Puritanism was usually studied as an intellectual or social movement. Recently, however, the concept of popular mentality, including religious ritual and experience, has bridged intellectual and social history. New biographical studies of key figures sympathetically discuss their spiritual experiences. Edmund S. Morgan writes, "The level of scholarship dealing with [the Puritans] has reached a point where it can address the human condition itself. In recent years the focus has shifted from theology to experience, from doctrine to devotion, and the results have been rewarding."[6]

A similar development has taken place in the field of literature. Louis L. Martz opened the way with *The Poetry of Meditation* (1954, rev. 1962). Martz discovered the pervasive influence of Catholic methods of medita-

---

5. Gordon S. Wakefield, ed., *The Westminster Dictionary of Christian Spirituality* (Philadelphia, 1983), v.

6. Alan Simpson, *Puritanism in Old and New England* (Chicago, 1955), 2. Edmund S. Morgan, "Heaven Can't Wait," *New York Review of Books,* May 31, 1984, 33. See, for example, David Levin, *Cotton Mather: The Young Life of the Lord's Remembrancer, 1663–1703* (Cambridge, Mass., 1978); David D. Hall, "The World of Print and Collective Mentality in Seventeenth-Century New England," in John Higham and Paul K. Conkin, eds., *New Directions in American Intellectual History* (Baltimore, 1979) and "The Mental World of Samuel

tion, outlined in the Ignatian *Exercises* and other manuals, on Anglican poets like Donne and Herbert and on Puritan Richard Baxter. Martz extended his analysis to the American poetry of Edward Taylor in his "Foreward" to the complete edition of Taylor's poems. Since Taylor's entirely secret poetry was discovered only in 1937, critical reaction is an index of the emerging literary interest in spirituality. Working from the 1939 partial edition of his poems, scholars felt Taylor to be sui generis, unorthodox, an Anglican sympathizer, maybe a crypto-Catholic. No Puritan could write as he did. Martz and others published their studies of meditative poetry prior to the 1960 complete edition, preparing the way for a mature reading of Taylor's poetry in the light of classical spirituality and Puritan covenant theology. Karl Keller interpreted the poems convincingly as the products of Taylor's spiritual exercises, even revelatory of Taylor "in the process" of meditation. Barbara Lewalski has shown that English Protestant meditative poetry need not be explained simply by tracing Continental Catholic roots. Poets from Donne and Herbert to Taylor shared an English, Protestant, Pauline, biblical spirituality independent of direct Ignatian influence. Scholars have identified Edward Taylor as the finest practitioner of Protestant meditative poetry in early America. While critics are interested in his poetry for its literary merits, those interested in spirituality are far more drawn to what the poems reveal of Taylor's soul and of his relationship with God.[7]

Anne Bradstreet scholarship has been dominated by a debate over the relationship of her religion and her art. One side devalued her poetry on the grounds that Puritan theology was inimical to inspiration; the other praised her poetry as artistic rebellion against orthodoxy. Robert Daly laid the dispute to rest by demonstrating "that Puritan orthodoxy was conducive to the production of poetry, and that Bradstreet's poetry is illuminated by an understanding of the theology which structured the experiences her poetry expressed." Her poems "were prayers, religious acts." Daly echoes Bouyer's dictum on the inextricable relation of dogmatic and spiritual theology: "Christian spirituality is distinguished from dogma by the fact that,

<hr />

Sewall" in David D. Hall, et. al., eds., *Saints and Revolutionaries* (New York, 1984); Charles E. Hambrick-Stowe, *The Practice of Piety: Puritan Devotional Disciplines in Seventeenth-Century New England* (Chapel Hill, N.C., 1982); Patricia Caldwell, *The Puritan Conversion Narrative* (Cambridge, Mass., 1983); Kenneth Silverman, *The Life and Times of Cotton Mather* (New York, 1984); Charles Lloyd Cohen, *God's Caress: The Psychology of Puritan Religious Experience* (New York, 1986).

7. Thomas Johnson, ed., *Poetical Works of Edward Taylor* (New York, 1939). Donald E. Stanford, ed., *The Poems of Edward Taylor* (New Haven, 1960). Karl Keller, *The Example of Edward Taylor* (Amherst, Mass., 1975), 92. Barbara Kiefer Lewalski, *Protestant Poetics and the Seventeenth-Century Religious Lyric* (Princeton, N.J., 1979). Karen E. Rowe, *Saint and Singer: Edward Taylor's Typology and the Poetics of Meditation* (New York, 1986).

instead of studying or describing the objects of belief as if it were in the abstract, it studies the reactions which these objects arouse in the religious consciousness.''[8]

The enthusiasm of discovering an ecumenical classical spirituality could lead one to ignore the violent separation of seventeenth-century Protestants from Catholics. If Puritans and Visitandines engaged in similar devotional acts, then dogmatic differences should not have mattered so much to them. Perhaps, as cynics are wont to say, dogmatic theology is destructive of humanity's common spiritual bonds. The separation was undeniable. How, then, can we best compare the spiritual exercises and experiences of Reformed Protestants and Roman Catholics?

One approach takes that in Reformed spirituality which fits the Catholic rubric and evaluates it by Catholic tools of scholarship. The Puritan contemplative was graced in ways that comport with this model. If Teresa of Avila wrote, "In this state . . . I saw close to me toward my left side an angel in bodily form," New England's Cotton Mather also saw and received messages from angels. In 1693 Mather recorded in his diary (in Latin, to honor the experience and conceal it from unlearned eyes), "After outpourings of prayer, with the utmost fervor and fasting, there appeared an Angel, whose face shone like the noonday sun." In 1718–1719, during a period of personal turmoil, the visitations returned. Instead of the angel descending to him, now Mather felt his soul ascending: "The flights, which I thus took among the holy Angels. I find my Pen unable to write the Things, and the Terms, to which my Soul mounted up as with the Wings of an Eagle." Other ministers and some laypeople wrote of similar experiences.[9]

Edward Taylor, perhaps more than any other New England Puritan, knew what it was to yearn for the soul's unitive state with Christ as mystic Lover, which we associate with Teresa or John of the Cross. The first of his "Preparatory Meditations before my Approach to the Lords Supper," written on a Saturday night in July 1682, is focused on the "Matchless Love" of God in Christ: "What Love is this of thine, that Cannot bee / In thine Infinity, O Lord, Confinde." God has "Marri'de our Manhood, making it its Bride." After confessing "my Lifeless Sparke! / My Fireless Flame! What Chilly Love, and Cold?" Taylor pleads, "Lord blow the Coal: Thy Love Enflame in mee" (I:1, ll. 7, 1–2, 6, 15–16, 18). His is an in-

---

8. Robert Daly, *God's Altar: The World and the Flesh in Puritan Poetry* (Berkeley and Los Angeles, 1978), 82–88, 127. Bouyer, *The Spirituality of the New Testament and the Fathers,* vii.

9. Kieran Kavanaugh, O.C.D. and Otilio Rodriguez, O.C.D., trans., *The Collected Works of St. Teresa of Avila* (Washington, D.C., 1976) vol. 1, 193. C.W. Ford, ed., *Diary of Cotton Mather* (New York, 1957), vol. 1, 86–87; vol. 2, 578; quoted in Silverman, *Life and Times of Cotton Mather,* 127–128, 311–312.

tensely personal prayer for the Bridegroom's lips to kiss or blow upon his heart. Over the 43 years Taylor composed and recorded his meditations in poetic form he grounded his devotions in a passage from the Song of Solomon (or Canticles, as he and others called it) more often than in any other book of the Bible. Even when meditating on another source the love theme was strong. He makes Isaiah's vision of an avenging Redeemer-Judge ("Who is this that cometh from Edom . . . glorious in his apparel," 63:1) into a lover's dream:

> Pluck back the Curtains, back the Window Shutts:
>   Through Zions Agate Window take a view;
> How Christ in Pinckted Robes from Bozrah puts
>   Comes Glorious in's Apparell forth to Wooe.
>   Oh! if his Glory ever kiss thine Eye,
>   Thy Love will soon Enchanted bee thereby. (I:12, ll. 25–30)

Taylor concludes,

> Oh! let thy Beauty give a glorious tuch
>   Upon my Heart, and melt to Love all mee.
> Lord melt me all up into Love for thee
>   Whose Loveliness excells what love can bee.
>   (I:12, ll. 45–48)

In the poems from Song of Solomon Taylor employs suggestive love-making imagery. He pleads to Christ that "these thy Lips poure out this myrrh on mee" (II:121, l. 37), and "I being thus, become thy Vallie low. / O plant thyselfe my lilly flower there" (II:160, ll. 13–14).

Parallels between Anne Bradstreet and Teresa of Avila (1515–1582), gifted women a century apart, are fascinatingly close. Bradstreet's too-brief autobiographical sketch, "To my dear Children," describes an early pilgrimage of faith similar to that presented in Teresa's volume, *The Book of Her Life.* Both women wrote for "the Glory of God" and for a human audience, Teresa's being her spiritual fathers, Bradstreet's her children. The accounts are similar in their confession of "sitting loose from God," succumbing to the "vanity and follyes of youth" as teenagers, and of God shaking them from natural impulses through illness. Teresa wrote that God "sent me a serious illness" to "prepare me for the state that was better for me." Bradstreet recalled, at 16 "the Lord layd his hand sore upon me and smott mee with the small pox. When I was in affliction, I besought the Lord, and confessed my Pride and Vanity and he was entreated of me, and again restored me.''[10] Both women were literate and enjoyed the world of books. When Teresa turned to spiritual authors, she went so far as to say, "my fondness for good books was my salvation." Bradstreet read the Protestant devotional manuals that corresponded to the _Letters of St. Jerome,_ Osuna's _The Third Spiritual Alphabet,_ and Augustine's _Confessions_ which guided Teresa. Teresa had to abandon the chivalric romances she enjoyed with her mother, but young Anne Bradstreet seems not to have been interested in the easily available English "penny merriments" that Puritan households abhorred. She later saw no reason to give up the serious writers she adored, Sir Philip Sidney, Sir Walter Raleigh, and Guillaume Du Bartas as translated by Joshua Sylvester. Secular poetry by reliable Protestants was not without its uses, the encouragement of virtue and the reinforcement of an English Reformed worldview.[11]

Teresa and Bradstreet experienced dryness following their initial periods of illness, with subsequent cycles of deeper renewal, even renewed conversions. Teresa took the habit and entered the convent; Bradstreet married and crossed the ocean to "a new world and new manners." Teresa immediately experienced "great happiness at being in the religious state of life," while Bradstreet balked at first in New England: "my heart rose." But she "submitted to it and joined the church at Boston." Illness continued to play a role in the women's spirituality. In the convent, Teresa wrote, "the change in food and life-style did injury to my health. . . . My fainting spells began to increase, and . . . heart pains." In New England, Bradstreet "fell into a lingering sicknes like a consumption, together with a lamenesse." Teresa prayed that God "would give me the illnesses by which He would be served." Bradstreet rejoiced: "Among all my experiences of God's gratious Dealings with me I have constantly observed this, that he hath never suffered me long to sitt loose from him, but by one affliction or other hath made me look home, and search what was amisse . . . and these Times (thro' his great mercy) have been the times of my greatest Getting and Advantage, yea I have found them the Times when the Lord hath manifested the most Love to me."[12]

As women of spiritual depth, both knew the frustration of not being understood. The men who arranged for the publication of Anne Bradstreet's poetry in London without her knowledge or final editing expressed patronizing wonder at her ability: "The Auth'ress was a right Du Bartas girl. . . .

10. Kavanaugh and Rodriguez, trans., _Works of St. Teresa,_ vol. 1, 32–39. Robert Hutchinson, ed., _Poems of Anne Bradstreet_ (New York, 1969), 179–180.
11. Kavanaugh and Rodriguez, trans., _Works of St. Teresa,_ vol. 1, 35, 40, 43.
12. Kavanaugh and Rodriguez, trans., _Works of St. Teresa,_ vol. 1, 41–42, 46. Hutchinson, ed., _Poems of Bradstreet,_ 180.

I muse whither at length these girls will go.'' Teresa lamented that for ''twenty years . . . I did not find a master, I mean a confessor, who understood me, even though I looked for one.'' Further, both knew the political risks of female endeavor. Teresa recorded: ''His Majesty began to give me the prayer of quiet very habitually—and often, of union—which lasted a long while. Since at that time other women had fallen into serious illusions and deceptions caused by the devil, I began to be afraid.'' She was referring to *alumbrados* like the illuminist Francisca Hernandez whose antinomianism led to her arrest by the Inquisition. Bradstreet recalled how New England was beset with ''Blasphemy, and Sectaries, and some who have been accounted sincere Christians have been carried away with them. . . . I have remembered the words of Christ that . . . the very elect should bee deceived.'' She alluded to New England's other public Anne, Anne Hutchinson, the Puritan illuminist banished as an antinomian by the ministers and magistrates. Teresa and Bradstreet, in spite of their orthodoxy, could not be sure they were immune from danger. Bradstreet wrote, ''Upon this Rock Christ Jesus will I build my faith; and if I perish, I perish. . . . I know whom I have trusted, and whom I have believed.'' Bradstreet knew her experience was true because it was rooted in the Bible: ''If ever this God hath revealed himself, it must bee in his word, and this must bee it or none. Have I not found that operation by it that no humane Invention can work upon the Soul?'' Teresa, who seems not to have even had a Bible, knew the truth of her experiences intuitively and directly: ''I know through experience that what I say is true and that what can be said is the least of what You do, Lord, for a soul You bring to such frontiers.'' She knew what she experienced was true because she experienced it.[13]

Bradstreet assessed her spirituality modestly. ''I have often been perplexed that I have not found that constant Joy in my Pilgrimage and refreshing which I supposed most of the servants of God have; although he hath not left me altogether without the wittnes of his holy spirit, who hath oft given mee his word and sett to his Seal that it shall bee well with me.'' Still, she wrote, ''I have sometimes tasted of that hidden Manna that the world knowes not . . . against such a promis, such tasts of sweetnes, the Gates of Hell shall never prevail.'' She used the imagery of love to describe her relationship with Christ. Surveying the ashes of her destroyed house, Bradstreet considered how she would no longer hear the ''bridegroom's voice'' while meditating there by candlelight. In a preparatory meditation on her own death, she recorded that voice. When she prayed, ''Come deare brid-

13. Kavanaugh and Rodriguez, trans., *Works of St. Teresa*, vol. 1, 43, 152, 177. Robert Hutchinson, ed., *Poems of Anne Bradstreet* (New York, 1969), 183. Jeannine Hensley, ed., *The Works of Anne Bradstreet* (Cambridge, Mass., 1967; rev. 1981), 4.

grome,'' she heard Christ say, ''Come away'' (''As weary pilgrim,'' l. 44). Bradstreet's experience of Christ as bridegroom was the product of numerous sermons and her own study of Scripture. Teresa, with an astonishingly tentative grasp of Scripture, wrote in the same tradition. When ''the Lord in His goodness desired that I should see and showed Himself to me in a rapture,'' she likened the experience to that of ''two persons here on earth who love each other deeply and understand each other well.'' In her divine vision she and Christ were like ''two lovers [who] gaze directly at each other, as the Bridegroom says to the Bride in the *Song of Songs*—I think I heard that it is there.''[14]

Bouyer's approach in *Protestant and Anglican Spirituality* was to analyze Protestant spirituality according to the Catholic rubric. This is a productive avenue of study, as there are many similarities. Bouyer, as a Catholic, perceived in Puritan spirituality a re-Catholicizing process. ''We can find nothing in these works to contradict, or even to disagree with, Catholic faith. We must go further: whatever their individual doctrine on other points, when these Protestants were dealing with spirituality they expressed a faith whose substance had become Catholic again.'' By this evaluation, having discovered the existence of the Puritan contemplative we would be led to identify Anne Bradstreet and Edward Taylor (married and in the world) as would-be tertiaries who retreated as best they could for periodic communion with God.[15]

Bradstreet, Taylor, and other Puritans would not fare well if we pressed this line of comparison. For all the similarities, Bradstreet was no St. Teresa. Her experience of Christ inviting her to ''Come away'' to heaven does not compare with Teresa's ecstatic transverbation. Taylor's meditative poems often reveal more of a yearning for ecstasy than ecstasy itself. Karl Keller suggests that the seeming mystical eroticism is ''not so much ecstatic transcendence'' as it is Taylor's passionate use of ''a metaphor for his desire to be godlike.'' The poems show Taylor's ''intense yearning to be beloved,'' his imaginative entering-into a spiritual realm that he ''desperately hopes'' can transform him from a dirt ball into a bride.[16] This is not to suggest that Taylor's meditations were not spiritually satisfying to him; they were truly for him means of saving grace. But within Taylor a spiritual struggle continues to rage between this world and the next. Puritan contemplatives flew with the angels in what can be described as unitive states, but did not feel the sweet agony, continuing in Teresa for

14. Hutchinson, ed., *Poems of Anne Bradstreet*, 181. Kavanaugh and Rodriguez, trans., *Works of St. Teresa*, vol. 1, 177. Hambrick-Stowe, *Practice of Piety*, 13–19.

15. Bouyer, *Orthodox Spirituality and Protestant and Anglican Spirituality*, 143.

16. Keller, *Example of Edward Taylor*, 215–217.

days on end, of the angel's spear plunged into the heart. Taylor's and Brad-street's devotions, and Puritan piety generally, would fall within the first stage or two of traditional Catholic ascetic theology. The exercises as we have them in Puritan diaries and devotional manuals largely describe Teresa's hand-dipped bucket or hand-turned water-wheel. The unitive states in which Bradstreet, Taylor, Mather, and others experienced Teresa's third stage of heavenly rain probably were, according to the Catholic system, the highest rung of ascetic, not mystical, theology. There was no mysticism, strictly defined, in Puritanism.

Mystical theology describes the spiritual states of persons whose med-itations and prayers are removed from daily human life. God elevated Ter-esa to spiritual states "often without [her] being able to avoid it" in ways unknown to Puritans. Teresa distinguished herself from other spiritual writ-ers by insisting that only the most advanced should completely "turn aside from corporeal things," and protested that many who seek union with God directly without means are "left floating in the air" helplessly. "It is an important thing that while we are living and are human we have human support." But what she meant by "human support"—meditation on the humanity of Jesus and reception of the Sacrament—is quite different from what the Puritans meant by means of grace. Puritan spirituality at every stage was rooted in the earth of church fellowship, civil society, family re-lations, and personal trials.[17]

Without resorting to the "novel insistence on [plural] Christian spir-itualities" which Bouyer criticizes, and negating the commonality which is so plain, we must remember that dogma helps shape spirituality. Bouyer rejects the penchant of comparative religion scholars to dissolve the bound-aries between Christian and non-Christian mysticism. It is "impossible . . . to set up a serious comparison between spiritualities without taking account of the dogmas presupposed by each. . . . Dogmatic theology, therefore, must always be presupposed as the basis of spiritual theology."[18] It follows that dogmatic distinctions between Reformed Protestants and Roman Cath-olics were bound to produce differences in spirituality. Chief among the theological differences was the new shape of Protestant anthropology. While Catholic spiritual theology was based on the faithful's ability to stir up the uncorrupted spark of the soul to seek God, in Protestant thought no part of the person's being was unmarred by the Fall. God became human in order to save sinners whose faculties were totally incapable of reaching

17. Kavanaugh and Rodriguez, trans., *Works of St. Teresa*, 144–152.

18. Bouyer, *The Spirituality of the New Testament and the Fathers*, vii–viii. See also Steven T. Katz, ed., *Mysticism and Religious Traditions* (New York, 1983), esp. the chapter by Robert M. Gimello, "Mysticism in Its Contexts," 61–88.

up to God. Protestants based spirituality on God's justification and sancti-
fication of corrupted humanity, as opposed to the Catholic concept of lifting
one's soul to God, albeit through the gift of grace, by the strength of one's
still pure inner spark. Theological differences require that Puritan spiritu-
ality must also be considered apart from the traditional Catholic rubric.

Reformed Protestants transformed classic spirituality by applying it to
a new worldly setting, while retaining traditional language, methods, and
manuals. Puritan contemplatives and ordinary faithful alike looked to the
stuff of daily life as the starting point and catalyst of meditation and prayer.
Theirs was a spirituality not of would-be monks and nuns but of house-
holders—husbandmen and housewives. As householders, Puritans would
not leave behind the people and things they loved, nor did they believe God
wanted them to even if they could. There was no distinction here between
clergy and laity; all were called to sainthood and all lived and moved and
had their being in Christ and, sanctified, in the world. Ministers, therefore,
were no spiritual elite. The exercises they practiced were the very ones they
directed their flocks to undertake, although not surprisingly they did so with
greater zeal than many laity. Puritanism was a popular lay spirituality.

Two basic approaches toward the discipline of meditation prevailed in
Puritan spirituality. Barbara Lewalski, quoting Joseph Hall's *Arte of Divine
Meditation* (1606), refers to these as "extemporall" or "occasional" and
"deliberate." Puritans did not mean by occasional meditation that it was
undertaken "now and then"; rather by "occasional" they meant "occa-
sioned by outward occurrences offered to the mind," the spiritual appli-
cation of the intellect to the import of daily events and circumstances.[19]
"Deliberate" meditation, which I prefer to call "formal" since all medi-
tation is deliberately undertaken, is the regular and planned focusing of the
mind on an external and usually conventional religious object. This may be
a biblical text, an object suggestive of death, a scene in nature, a doctrine
or mental religious image, or even the sacramental elements. Anne Brad-
street and Edward Taylor composed meditative poetry after engaging in
both types of spiritual exercises, although much of Bradstreet's best poetry
resulted from her occasional meditations on the death of a grandchild, her
husband's absence, and on the destruction of her home by fire. Conversely,
while Taylor wrote a few extant occasional meditations, by far the majority
of his poems were the expression of his Saturday night formal meditations
on the next morning's sacrament and sermon text. The poems of these two
New Englanders, therefore, illustrate the ways Puritans sought for God in
meditation while yet living in the world.

Calvin's doctrine of sanctification played a key role in the develop-

---

19. Lewalski, *Protestant Poetics*, 150–151.

ment of Puritan spirituality. While the Catholic saint was an extraordinarily gifted mystic separated from the world by the cloister, the Puritan saint was an ordinary believer sanctified by God living and praying in the world. The English theologian William Ames, whose work guided New England thought, defined sanctification as "the real change in man from the sordidness of sin to the purity of God's image." The term could indicate "separation from ordinary use or consecration to some special use," but the theological doctrine implied not separation from the world but the salvation of the world. "The term is rather to be understood as that change in a believer in which he has righteousness and indweling holiness imparted to him." Moreover, "it pertains to the whole man and not to any one part." God sanctified people for life in this world, for proper creaturely enjoyment and fulfillment. Through God's Spirit, things and relationships even became means of grace. Sanctification was the doctrinal vehicle enabling a spirituality of the householder in which devotion began with the consideration of physical reality.[20]

This world, as any devout Puritan knew, was transitory and love of the creatures led to grief. Earthen vessels, created by God and sanctified for human use, were bound to crumble, to die and decay. Here is the crisis that underlay Puritan spirituality. Householders were subject to the grief of losing those persons and things with which God blessed their lives. One of Edward Taylor's most moving poems is his occasional meditation, "Upon Wedlock, and Death of Children," in which he swings into the comfort of the promises—"I thank thee, thou takst ought of mine, / It is my pledg in glory, part of mee / Is now in it, Lord, glorifi'de with thee" (ll. 28–30)— only to crash again to earth in grief when he remembers his child's death— "But oh! the tortures, Vomit, screechings, groans, / And six weeks Fever would pierce hearts like stones" (ll. 35–36)—and back to heaven again— "I piecemeale pass to Glory bright in them" (l. 40). Devotional acts sparked by grief became for Puritans the means of a deeper sanctification; they still did not abandon the things of this world but humbly offered them up to the transcendent God. Devotional guides cautioned the Puritan to travel this world as a stranger and a pilgrim, not to look for ultimate meaning in any created thing. As Anne Bradstreet wrote admiringly of her deceased father, former Massachusetts Bay Colony governor Thomas Dudley, "Upon the earth he did not build his nest, / But as a Pilgrim, what he had, possest" ("To the Memory of my dear and ever honoured Father Thomas Dudley Esq.," ll. 33–34).

---

20. Bouyer, *Orthodox Spirituality and Protestant and Anglican Spirituality,* 85–89, 143. William Ames, *The Marrow of Theology,* John D. Eusden, trans. (Durham, N.C., 1983), 167–169.

Language, the use of poetic metaphor, became for Edward Taylor the bridge between the world of the flesh and that of the spirit, between earth and heaven. Words could be, as they were in a sermon or in the institution of the sacrament, sanctified as means of grace. Much of Taylor's imagery could be considered sanctified because it was taken from Scripture, but many of his metaphors were also from everyday life. Moreover, God could make holy use of any words used to glorify him, even the crudest and earthiest. Taylor knew well the limitation of language; indeed, he spends many lines in his poems confessing his linguistic inadequacy. In a 1701 poem in particular, this finitude is the focus of meditation. "Words though the finest twine of reason, are / Too Course a web for Deity to ware" (II: 43, ll. 11–12). As in the Puritan approach to God generally, the first stage in spiritual regeneration here was penitence, or humiliation.

> Words are befould, Thoughts filthy fumes that smoake,
>   From Smutty Huts, like Will-a-Wisps that rise
> From Quaugmires, run ore bogs where frogs do Croake,
>   Lead all astray led by them by the eyes.
>   My muddy Words so dark thy Deity,
>   And cloude thy Sun-Shine, and its Shining Sky.
>
> Yet spare mee, Lord, to use this hurden ware.
>   I have no finer Stuff to use . . . (ll. 19–26)

The Puritans would not abandon, but embrace, words. After all, "We finde thee thus in Holy Writ definde" (II:43, l. 42). So Taylor offered God what words he could "To kiss thy feet, and worship give to thee" (l. 50). If God would redeem him, Taylor promised, then in heaven "I'le bring thee praise, buskt up in Songs perfum'de, / When thou with grace my Soule has sweetly tun'de" (ll. 53–54).

Puritanism, as New Englanders often said, was thus a spirituality of weaned affections, rooted always in this world but reaching toward the other world. This world's dynamic matrix of change and mortality was the setting for the Puritan life of prayer. Puritan spirituality is characterized by its effort to embrace finitude, the pain of loss, and seek in faithful prayer God's eternal word of hope. Although the Puritans are famous for scrutinizing the details of their lives, their intensely human spirituality did not leave them stranded in grim anxiety. Above all, the manner in which they approached the fundamental experiences of finitude created a spirituality that did not crush but often healed and uplifted the human spirit in communion with God. Theirs was a spirituality that began with sanctified love for the transient things of this world, a spirituality of the householder strug-

gling with loss, a spirituality that never abandoned but finally looked be-
yond this sanctified mortality to eternal glorification, a spirituality that
released the beloved creature to God in the sure hope that in God life was
not lost but renewed.

2. THE MEDITATIVE POETRY OF ANNE BRADSTREET

Anne Bradstreet was born in 1612(?), probably in Northampton, En-
gland, and grew up in the Tattershall Castle household of the Earl of Lin-
coln, where her father was steward or financial manager.[21] Her literary and
religious education was not obtained in any school but from her parents,
Thomas and Dorothy Dudley, and from the stimulating environment of the
household itself. Bradstreet described her mother in elegiac verse as loving
and obedient, kind to servants and the neighboring poor, and "A true In-
structor of her Family" ("An Epigraph On my dear and ever honoured
Mother Mrs. Dorothy Dudley," l. 7). Most significantly, she exemplified
the kind of Puritan piety Bradstreet herself sought to practice as an adult:

> The public meetings ever did frequent,
> And in her Closet constant hours she spent;
> Religious in all her words and wayes,
> Preparing still for death till end of dayes (ll. 9–12)

She remembered her father as a stern but pleasant man who served as
her "Guide, Instructor too" in faith as well as in letters ("To the Memory
of my dear and ever honoured Father Thomas Dudley Esq.," l. 5). In New
England, as governor of Massachusetts Bay Colony, he became "To Truth
a shield, to right a Wall, / To Sectaryes a whip and Maul" (ll. 73–74), and
Anne no doubt learned the tenets of Puritan orthodoxy at his knee. He was
also "A Magazine of History" (l. 75), imparting a sense of the past which
showed up later in his daughter's more formal poetry. Anne read Sir Walter
Raleigh, Sir Philip Sidney, Joshua Sylvester's translation of Du Bartas, and
possibly even Shakespeare.

The Earl of Lincoln's household itself provided an education for young
Anne Dudley. Puritan clergy and nobility often visited to discuss the polit-
ical and religious prospects of nonconformity. Among the regulars was the
Rev. John Cotton from nearby Boston who would soon become a leading
theologian in New England's Boston. These discussions led the Dudleys to

---

21. For the life of Anne Bradstreet, see the definitive biography, Elizabeth Wade
White, *Anne Bradstreet: The Tenth Muse* (New York, 1971).

join John Winthrop's great adventure to establish Massachusetts Bay Colony in 1630. But first, in 1628, Anne married Simon Bradstreet, another officer in the Earl's house. He held his bachelor's and master's degrees from the leading Puritan college at Cambridge, Emmanuel, center of the "Spiritual Brotherhood" of divines who erected the intellectual and interpersonal structure of the Puritan movement. Simon was twenty-five, Anne only sixteen, a startlingly young age for a Puritan marriage. From her later poems it appears the couple enjoyed the best of marriages, marked by loyalty and love. The young couple accompanied the Dudleys on the Arbella as it sailed in 1630. In a lay sermon delivered on board, they heard Governor Winthrop expound the commonly held vision of what God would require. Quoting Micah's admonition "to do justly, and to love mercy, and to walk humbly with thy God" (6:8), Winthrop stated that

> for this end, wee must be knitt together in this worke as one man, wee must entertaine each other in brotherly Affeccion, wee must be willing to abridge our selves of our superfluities, for the supply of others necessities . . . for wee must Consider that wee shall be as a Citty upon a Hill, the eies of all people are uppon us; soe that if wee shall deale falsely with our god in this worke we have undertaken and soe cause him to withdrawe his present help from us, we shall be made a story and a by-word through the world.[22]

Not that Anne Bradstreet was without qualms, for, as already noted, her "heart rose" at the "new world and new manners" which she found in America. But she saw the hand of God upon the colony and she soon joined the church. The Bradstreets lived, after brief sojourns in Charlestown/Boston and Newtowne (Cambridge), for a decade in Ipswich. Anne Bradstreet wrote only one extant poem from the Ipswich years, an occasional meditation "Upon a Fit of Sickness," in 1632. In the early 1640s they settled permanently in Andover (now North Andover), Massachusetts. It was in Andover, as her husband's activities in colonial politics increased and he was elected governor, that she found bits of time, often late at night, for her poetry. Since writing was considered unseemly for women, Anne Bradstreet thus opened herself to criticism: "I am obnoxious to each carping tongue / Who says my hand a needle better fits" ("The Prologue," ll. 25–26). But she was more generally known for her wisdom in managing household affairs and devotion to her family and to God. Anne Bradstreet died in 1672 at the age of 60, survived by her husband, seven of her eight chil-

---

22. John Winthrop, "A Modell of Christian Charity," in Perry Miller and Thomas H. Johnson, eds., *The Puritans: A Sourcebook of Their Writings* (New York, 1963), 198–199.

dren, and fifty-three grandchildren. Barring an unexpected discovery, no
one will ever know if other women also wrote such poems on political and
religious themes.

The writings of Anne Bradstreet have long commanded critical literary
attention, but only recently have some scholars recognized her as a religious
poet.[23] Bradstreet's work falls into two categories, her public and her pri-
vate poems. The former, so termed because of their public themes, included
classical and largely unimaginative treatments of "The Four Elements,"
"Of the four Humours in Mans Constitution," "Of the four Ages of Man,"
"The four Seasons of the Year," "The four Monarchyes," the English po-
litical crisis of 1642, Queen Elizabeth, and admired poets. A well-meaning
brother-in-law, the Rev. John Woodbridge, carried these poems to London
without her permission and found a publisher. The volume, *The Tenth Muse
Lately Sprung Up in America* (London, 1650), was both an embarrassment
and a source of pride to Anne Bradstreet. The second edition, published
posthumously in 1678, contained new poems prefaced: "Several other
Poems made by the Author upon Diverse Occasions were found among her
Papers after her Death, which she never meant should come to public view;
amongst which, these following (at the desire of some friends that knew her
well) are here inserted." Her extant papers contained other private poems
and writings that were edited and published in the complete edition by John
Harvard Ellis in 1867. Bradstreet's private poetry and her well-wrought
thirty-three stanza "Contemplations" establish her reputation as a fine
poet. Critics have described her works as love poems (e.g. "To my Dear
and loving Husband"), domestic poems (e.g. "In memory of my dear
grand-child Elizabeth Bradstreet"), and classical dialogues (e.g. "The
Flesh and the Spirit"), though some are undeniably religious meditations
by any standard (e.g. "What God is like to him I serve" and "By night
when others soundly slept"). The concept of Puritan spirituality as a lay
spirituality of householders shaped by the doctrine of sanctification and
sparked by the experience of loss, however, opens the way for a reading of
all of Bradstreet's private poetry as the expression of her spiritual life.[24]

Anne Bradstreet's continual confrontation with the experience of loss
is a theme underlying her private poems. We have already seen that she

---

23. See the excellent collection by Pattie Cowell and Ann Stanford, eds., *Critical Es-
says on Anne Bradstreet* (Boston, 1983).

24. Agnieszka Salska, "Puritan Poetry: Its Public and Private Strain," *Early American
Literature* (Fall 1984), 107–121. Eileen Margerum, "Anne Bradstreet's Public Poetry and the
Tradition of Humility," *Early American Literature* (Fall 1982), 152–160. Hensley, ed.,
Works of Bradstreet, xxix. These categories are the framework of Hutchinson, ed., *Poems of
Bradstreet.* Robert Daly reviews the traditional approaches to Bradstreet's poetry and argues
for a religious interpretation in *The World and the Flesh in Puritan Poetry,* chap. 3.

identified her loss of health as a spiritual catalyst. God seemed to chastise Bradstreet with afflictions "upon my own person, in sicknesse, weaknes, paines, sometimes on my soul, in Doubts and feares of God's displeasure, and my sincerity towards him, sometimes he hath smott a child with sicknes, sometimes chasstened by losses in estate." These times of loss were "the Times when the Lord hath manifested the most Love to me."[25]

Bradstreet wrote her earliest extant poem "Upon a Fit of Sickness" in 1632 on this crisis of finitude.

> Twice ten years old, not fully told
> Since nature gave me breath,
> My race is run, my thread is spun,
> lo here is fatal Death. (ll. 1–4)

Her amateurish attempt at verse concludes with an equally conventional Christian affirmation which nevertheless expressed a faith that was stronger for her survival of smallpox.

> The race is run, the field is won,
> the victory's mine I see,
> For ever know, thou envious foe,
> the foyle belongs to thee. (ll. 29–32)

As she matured as a poet, Bradstreet did not seek to avoid suffering by fixing on another world or religious formulas; she passionately engaged with her illness. "In my distresse I sought the Lord," she wrote. It was when "in sweat I seem'd to melt" that God appeared and said, "Live." After "sore fits" and "fits of fainting" she embraced her own weakness; the utter need of her "wasted flesh" yielded her praise to God.

> In anguish of my heart repleat with woes,
> And wasting pains, which best my body knows,
> In tossing slumbers on my wakeful bed,
> Bedrencht with tears that flow'd from mournful head,
> Till nature had exhausted all her store,
> Then eyes lay dry, disabled to weep more.
> ("Upon some distemper of body," ll. 1–6)

Only then was she able to "look . . . up unto his Throne on high, / Who sendeth help to those in misery" (ll. 7–8) and God "eas'd my Soul of woe,

---

25. Hutchinson, ed., *Poems of Bradstreet*, 180.

my flesh of pain" (l. 11). Loss of health was a sign of mortality, a memento mori. Bradstreet's last poem, "As weary pilgrim, now at rest," already commented upon, recorded her most advanced meditation on her illness and imminent death. She began by composing the image of the pilgrim arriving in heaven, reflected on her own sufferings—"By age and paines brought to decay" (l. 21)—and longingly cried, "Oh how I long to be at rest / and soare on high among the blest" (ll. 23–24). Meditation on the tomb of Christ, her own tomb, and the promises of Scripture opened her ears to the welcoming voice of Christ to "Come away" (l. 44).

Anne Bradstreet's loving relationship with her husband Simon was a source of spiritual joy. She felt in her husband the love of Christ and in her passion for him a foretaste of heaven. Her love also filled her with fear—fear of losing him. Her love poems outwardly expressed her prayers struggling with the finitude of their relationship. A poem "Before the Birth of one of her Children" came from a spiritual experience faced by most women, the dark side of anticipating a baby's birth: sober preparation to die in childbirth. Her general recollection that "All things within this fading world hath end" (l. 1) became personal.

> How soon, my Dear, death may my steps attend,
> How soon't may be thy Lot to lose thy friend,
> We both are ignorant, yet love bids me
> These farewell lines to recommend to thee. (ll. 7–10)

The farewell poem gave voice less to Bradstreet's fear of death or Simon's possible need to grieve than to her own anticipatory grief over losing *him* when she died. She was loath to face a time "when that knot's unty'd that made us one" (l. 11). Knowing that he would remarry, she grieved at the thought of losing him to another woman.

> Yet love thy dead, who long lay in thine arms:
> And when thy loss shall be repaid with gains
> Look to my little babes my dear remains.
> . . . .
> These O protect from step Dames injury. (ll. 20–22, 24)

Anne Bradstreet, in effect, lost her husband for long periods of time when he traveled on Massachusetts colonial business. She mourned his absence as a "loss," however temporary. "As loving Hind that (Hartless) wants her Deer . . . So doth my anxious soul, which now doth miss, / A dearer Dear (far dearer Heart) than this" ("As loving Hind," ll. 1, 5–6). Describing his absence as "this dead time" ("A Letter to her Husband," l. 13), she knew that their reunion would be temporary: "Let's still remain but one, till death divide" ("As loving Hind," l. 32).

The love poems paralleled Bradstreet's prayers for her husband's safe return. She shifted to addressing her poems as prayers directly to God in a series written in 1661 when Simon was in England negotiating with the new royal government. Since Bradstreet wrote these poems in hymn or psalter form, it seems likely that she sang them to God in her secret devotions. Some of these "spiritual songs" were simple petitionary prayers, as for example "Upon my dear and loving husband his goeing into England, Jan. 16, 1661":

> Into thy everlasting Armes
> Of mercy I commend
> Thy servant, Lord. Keep and preserve
> My husband, my dear friend.
>
> . . . .
>
> Lord, let my eyes see once Again
> Him whom thou gavest me,
> That wee together may sing Praise
> For ever unto Thee.
>
> And the Remainder of oure Dayes
> Shall consecrated bee,
> With an engaged heart to sing
> All Praises unto Thee. (ll. 5–8, 41–48)

Others expressed grief "In my Solitary houres in my dear husband his Absence" in more personal terms.

> O Lord, thou hear'st my dayly moan,
> And see'st my dropping teares:
> My Troubles All are Thee before,
> My Longings and my feares. (ll. 1–4)

She communed in meditation during her husband's physical absence with the Bridegroom of her soul, Jesus Christ, who was always present.

> And thy Abode tho'st made with me;
> With Thee my Soul can talk
> In secrett places, Thee I find,
> Where I doe kneel or walk.

Tho' husband dear bee from me gone,
Whom I doe love so well;
I have a more beloved one
Whose comforts far excell. (ll. 9–16)

Bradstreet sought compensation for Simon's abandonment of her from the
One who would never leave her side. In her journal she wrote that an illness
was more difficult to bear because "my husband was from home (who is
my chiefest comforter on Earth); but my God, who never failed me, was
not absent, but helped me, and gratiously manifested his Love to me."[26]
She prayed that as God had blessed her by her son's earlier return from
England, God would grant her husband's return. In other poems her hus-
band was an emblem of Christ; now her son's return evoked the resurrection
of God's Son from death.

O shine upon me, blessed Lord,
Ev'n for my Saviour's sake;
In Thee Alone is more than All,
And there content I'll take.

O hear me, Lord, in this Request,
As thou before ha'st done:
Bring back my husband, I beseech,
As thou didst once my Sonne. ("In my Solitary houres," ll. 29–36)

Biblical faith combined with personal experience—God did "bring back"
both His Son and "my Sonne"—to produce hope. Bradstreet completed
the cycle with a prayer of thanksgiving in poetic form when her husband
returned a year later. If Simon's return was a kind of resurrection, Brad-
street also saw their love as a means of grace. She concluded her beautiful
poem, "To my Dear and loving Husband": "Then while we live, in love
lets so persever, / That when we live no more, we may live ever" (ll. 11–
12).

Bradstreet's spirituality was shaped by the loss of offspring. Unlike
Catholic spiritual writers, she prayed and wrote as a housewife and mother.
The devotion of Cotton Mather and Samuel Sewall was fired by grief at
losing many children to death. Anne and Simon Bradstreet saw all their
children survive to adulthood. Nevertheless, as all mothers do, she lost
them to adulthood. Her "eight birds hatcht in one nest" grew up and flew

---

26. Hutchinson, ed., *Poems of Bradstreet*, 183.

off to make new families. Bradstreet was too wise to cling to them or to her own youth.

> My age I will not once lament,
> But sing, my time so near is spent.
> And from the top bough take my flight,
> Into a country beyond sight. ("In reference to her Children," ll. 73–
>   76)

Content that she had done well by them, she bid, "Farewel my birds, fare-wel adieu" (l. 93), and dedicated more time to meditation.

Far more difficult was the task of burying three grandchildren, including her namesake, who died in infancy. Bradstreet's inner turmoil at the death of three-year-old Anne bespoke the sense of crisis that generated Puritan spirituality, rooted as it was in this world.

> With troubled heart and trembling hand I write,
> The Heavens have chang'd to sorrow my delight.
> How oft with disappointment have I met,
> When I on fading things my hopes have set?
> Experience might 'fore this have made me wise,
> To value things according to their price:
> Was ever stable joy yet found below,
> Or perfect bliss without mixture of woe?
> ("In memory of my dear grand-child Anne Bradstreet," ll. 1–8)

Bradstreet was not saying her love for her grandchild was misplaced. Her love for her (like that for her husband) was an experience of "perfect bliss"—a "shadow," and hence a fleeting glimpse, of "stable joy" and eternal bliss "without mixture of woe." The child had been "lent" as an "impermanent" earthly blessing and so had to be released with a "Farewel dear child" (l. 15). She had been a blessing nonetheless, and her death pointed Bradstreet to the place where "Thou with thy Saviour art in endless bliss" (l. 18). Like King David (2 Sam. 12:23), Bradstreet wrote, "But yet a while, and I shall go to thee" (l. 16). In grief over another grandchild, she found comfort in the thought that Christ "will return, and make up all our losses" ("On my dear Grand-child Simon Bradstreet," l. 9). Yet her wounds were never fully salved by grace and some commentators perceive an angry bitterness at a God who would "eradicate" ("In memory of my dear grand-child Elizabeth Bradstreet," l. 12) young children. Her memorial to Elizabeth, from its opening—"Farewel dear babe, my hearts too much content"—until the final line, registers a controlled grief in its regular

iambic meter. The poem concludes with the affirmation—or accusation—
that death "Is by his hand alone that guides nature and fate" (l. 14). The
last jarring, irregular syllables bespeak a profound spiritual and emotional
disjunction within the poet's soul.[27] This tension between the comforting
strength of grace and the unyielding pain of life in the world fueled Puritan
spirituality.

Anne Bradstreet recorded her meditations on transiency and mortality
in three excellent poems, "The Flesh and the Spirit," "The Vanity of all
worldly things," and "Contemplations." These should be categorized as
formal meditations, whereas most of her private poetry was the product of
occasional meditation. The first appears to be based on Galatians 5:16–17:
"This I say then, Walk in the Spirit, and ye shall not fulfil the lust of the
flesh. For the flesh lusteth against the Spirit, and the Spirit against the flesh:
and these are contrary the one to the other." In the text the phrase "lust
against" suggests a desire to master or conquer, and in Bradstreet's med-
itation the internal forces, personified as "two sisters" (l. 3), "combate
with" (l. 41) each other in dialogue. Flesh, claiming that "Industry hath
its recompence" (l. 22), tempts Spirit with honor, wealth, and sensual plea-
sure. Renouncing Flesh as "unregenerate," Spirit refutes the claim that
meditation is "Notion without Reality" (l. 14). "I have meat thou know'st
not of. . . . Mine Eye doth pierce the heavens, and see / What is Invisible
to thee" (ll. 66, 77–78). Earth must be left behind for the eternal "City
pure," and the meditation ends on a note of determination: "If I of Heaven
may have my fill, / Take thou the world, and all that will" (ll. 105, 107–
108). In "Vanity," similarly, the way of the world is "labour, anxious care
and pain" (l. 10). But "There is a path, no vultures eye hath seen. . . . It
brings to honour, which shall ne're decay, / It stores with wealth which time
can't wear away" (ll. 35, 45–46).

"Contemplations" is a classic exercise of meditation in nature, but
frustrated by spiritual inability.

> Silent alone, where none or saw, or heard,
> In pathless paths I lead my wandring feet,
> My humble Eyes to lofty Skyes I rear'd
> To sing some Song, my mazed Muse thought meet.
> My great Creator I would magnifie,
> That nature had, thus decked liberally:
> But Ah, and Ah, again, my imbecility! (ll. 50–56)

27. Randall R. Mawer, " 'Farewel Dear Babe': Bradstreet's Elegy for Elizabeth,"
Early American Literature (Spring 1980), 29–41.

Why do human beings not sing to God as naturally as do the trees and birds? The answer lay in the biblical doctrine of sin. Shifting her meditation to the Genesis stories of the Fall and Cain's murder of Abel, Bradstreet stood by the riverside as one afflicted by the effects of sin. Without God's grace even the "losses, sickness, pain" (1. 199) of earthly life would not make people "deeply groan for that divine Translation" (1. 210). And the blessings God granted on earth in themselves were useless. The "fool . . . takes this earth ev'n for heav'ns bower" (1. 221). Time, "the fatal wrack of mortal things" (1. 225), brought all to naught. Bradstreet saw that she must look beyond both the blessings and losses of life here to the only abiding hope: "Only above is found all with security" (1. 224). The way "above," of course, was through Christ who would write the saint's name "in the white stone" of Revelation 2:17. Bradstreet knew that she would "last and shine when all of these are gone" (ll. 231–232).

Anne Bradstreet's Puritan spirituality trained her to live fully and lovingly in this world but with the eyes of her heart ready for the next world. The loss of beloved people and things and the impending loss of her own life were the crises within which she sought the Lord in impassioned prayer and found spiritual resolution. The loss of her home and the poem that she wrote on the occasion of its burning conform to this devotional pattern. In the poem, Robert Daly correctly observes, Bradstreet "compares her love for her house and her pain at its passing to Christ's love for man and His suffering on the cross; this comparison is a terribly powerful argument for the ultimate triviality of the house. It enables the speaker to achieve the perspective she seeks. . . . She finds 'above the sky' the promise of heaven, figured appropriately as a house." Every analysis of this poem, "Upon the burning of our house, July 10th, 1666," reads Bradstreet's loss as the physical things of her house and its furnishings. Critics find her tender domestic memories of the house particularly feminine. An understanding of the true nature of her loss will further illustrate the Puritan spirituality of the householder.[28]

When fire destroyed their Andover, Massachusetts, home, Anne Bradstreet sought the release of her emotional trauma and the consolation of God through prayer and poetry. As with other works, her poem gave voice and structure to her approach to God. "Upon the burning of our house" is a remarkable work, Bradstreet at her literary best. But we seek to learn not

---

28. Daly, *God's Altar,* 100–101. For comment on "Upon the burning of our house," see Josephine K. Piercy, *Anne Bradstreet* (New York, 1965), 82; Ann Stanford, *Anne Bradstreet: The Worldly Puritan* (New York, 1974), 107–109; Wendy Martin, *An American Triptych* (Chapel Hill, N.C., 1984), 74–75. Randall R. Mawer, " 'Farewel Dear Babe' ": Bradstreet's Elegy for Elizabeth," *Early American Literature* (Spring 1980), 29–30.

so much about her art as about the spirituality her art expressed. The poem lays bare the tension between love for creatures and Creator which fueled her life of prayer. It describes the moment when the stairway that she built between the one and the other—that is, the manuscripts of her devotional poetry—went up in flames with the house. Poems expressing prayers were divinely inspired, had lifted Bradstreet's soul above the created world. But even they had to be released. Love for them was no more permanent than love for any other thing or creature. Bradstreet knew what it was to be *almost* a "Fond fool [who] takes this earth ev'n for heav'ns bower." Her love for both the Creator and the creature (for things, indeed, co-created by God and her) led her once more into the crisis of human loss and, ultimately, her receipt of grace and hope.

The poem's title, added by her son who transcribed the poem from her manuscript, included the date of the event, "July 10th, 1666." The last three digits of the year were fearful to any biblically minded believer. The satanic beast of the last days described in Revelation 13 "maketh fire come down from heaven on the earth in the sight of men . . . and his number is Six hundred threescore and six." In contrast to the damned with the "mark . . . or the number of his name," Bradstreet had long felt assured that her name was "grav'd in the white stone," as she wrote in "Contemplations," and that her poetry was preparation to sing the "new song before the throne" of the Lamb. But in her poem on "The Four Elements" Bradstreet wrote that while fire was normally a domestic servant, it "by force, master, [its] masters can." Whole towns, the palaces of kings "in confused heaps, of ashes may you see." Fire humbled the proud. It also signified the coming Last Judgment from which none were exempt: "the world I shall consume / And all therein, at that great day of Doom."[29] The numbers three (symbolic of divinity) and six (symbolic of sin, judgment, and damnation) juxtaposed in her mind and provided a meditative structure. The fire was both judgment and grace. Bradstreet wrote the poem in three parts, each composed of three stanzas of six lines. The date of the fire, then, was no casual detail. The fire pushed her to the edge of mortality and judgment (the number six) and eternity (the number three).

The first three stanzas are Bradstreet's vivid recollection of the fire itself, and represent her later meditations on the terrible event.

> In silent night when rest I took,
> For sorrow neer I did not look,
> I waken'd was with thundring nois
> And Piteous shreiks of dreadfull voice.

---

29. Hutchinson, ed., *Poems of Bradstreet,* 123, ll. 106–110.

That fearfull sound of fire and fire,
Let no man know is my Desire. (ll. 1–6)

Like the thief and the Son of Man who "cometh at an hour when ye think
not" (Lk. 12:39–40), the fire struck "in silent night." The "thundring
nois" of the fire and the "Piteous shreiks" apparently of the maid awak-
ened her, but her lack of mention of her husband suggests that he was away
at the time. Bradstreet faced the fire and escaped from the house as she must
face God after death, as an individual.

I, starting up, the light did spye,
And to my God my heart did cry
To strengthen me in my Distresse
And not to leave me succourlesse.
Then coming out beheld a space,
The flame consume my dwelling place. (ll. 7–12)

Puritan spirituality originated in the events of daily life. Accordingly, Ro-
samund R. Rosenmeier has written, "This is by no means a spiritual, al-
legorical, or symbolic fire."[30] The adjectives "thundring," "Piteous,"
"dreadfull," "fearfull" evoke the night's immediate physical terror. Her
prayer ("to my God my Heart did cry") was no methodical exercise, but
an elemental cry for divine help. Once outside Bradstreet "beheld a
space"—that is, watched for a while—as the fire "consume[d] my dwell-
ing place."

The third stanza concluded Bradstreet's reflections on the night of the
fire.

And, when I could no longer look,
I blest his Name that gave and took,
That layd my goods now in the dust:
Yea so it was, and so 'twas just.
It was his own: it was not mine;
Far be it that I should repine. (ll. 13–18)

Her formulaic blessing of God (from Job 1:21) for such a terrible act was
more a ritual act of resignation than spiritual resolution, as her unrequited
sorrow in later return visits demonstrated. The theological affirmation, "so

---

30. Rosamund R. Rosenmeier, " 'Divine Translation': A Contribution to the Study of
Anne Bradstreet's Method in the Marriage Poems," *Early American Literature* (Fall 1977),
131.

it was, and so 'twas just,'' was the best she could muster that night. Sig-
nificantly, however, it was less the house's structure than her ''goods'' con-
tained therein for which she grieved. What were these ''goods''? Scholars
comment on Anne Bradstreet's love for her ''domestic comforts,'' her
''treasured possessions . . . her last link with her happy life in the Old
World.''[31] Her son, the Rev. Simon Bradstreet, however, lamented other
losses. He recorded in his diary: ''Whilst I was at N. London my fathers
house at Andover was burnt, where I lost my books. . . . Tho' my own
losse of books (and papers espec.) was great and my fathers far more being
about 800, yet ye Lord was pleased gratiously many wayes to make up the
same to us.''[32] Far more valuable than a housewife's furniture and even an
intellectual's books, however, are the unpublished papers of an author. For
Anne Bradstreet only her manuscripts were irreplaceable. In fact, she re-
ported the loss of her work on ''The Roman Monarchy'' for a revised edi-
tion of *The Tenth Muse.*

> To finish what's begun, was my intent
> . . . .
> But 'fore I could accomplish my desire,
> My papers fell a prey to th' raging fire.
> And thus my pains (with better things) I lost,
> Which none had cause to wail, nor I to boast.
> (''An Apology,'' ll. 1, 13–16)

Closer to her heart than the formal, public poetry of ''The Four Monar-
chies'' was the private poetry she wrote for God and to her husband and
children. Her ''better things'' were unknown to the public, and so ''none
had cause to wail.'' She did not ''boast'' about its literary quality, but it
expressed the relationships and experiences that mattered most to her.

Bradstreet in several places referred to her poetic work as ''my goods''
or home-made clothing. In her preface to *The Tenth Muse* she defended
herself against anticipated criticism because of Du Bartas' influence. ''I
honour him, but dare not wear his wealth; / My goods are true (though
poor), I love no stealth.'' (''To her most Honoured Father Thomas Dudley
Esq.,'' ll. 35–36). And in ''The Author to her Book'' she modestly apol-
ogized for failing to improve her poems for the revised edition. ''In better
dress to trim thee was my mind, / But nought save home-spun Cloth, i'th'
house I find'' (ll. 17–18). Bradstreet attributed the inspiration of her private
poetry, more than with her public works, to God. Her meditative poems,

---

31. Martin, *An American Triptych,* 75. Piercy, *Anne Bradstreet,* 82.
32. Quoted in Piercy, *Anne Bradstreet,* 24.

which issued from her devotional exercises, were the means by which she communed with God and anticipated heaven. After "Deliverance from another sore Fitt," for example, she prayed:

> Thy Name and praise to celebrate,
> O Lord! for aye is my request.
> O graunt I doe it in this state,
> And then with thee which is the Best. (ll. 25–28)

Her poems therefore belonged to God and not to her. Anne Bradstreet could more truly say this of her private poetry than of any piece of furniture, "It was his own: it was not mine."

The second part of the poem is set in the days after the fire and reflects her solemn meditation on the ashes. She addressed the house itself, which no longer existed physically. But in memory and imagination, God "sufficient for us left." As in classic composition of place a scriptural scene became real in the meditator's mind, the house was again real for Bradstreet.

> He might of All justly bereft,
> But yet sufficient for us left.
> When by the Ruines oft I past,
> My sorrowing eyes aside did cast,
> And here and there the places spye
> Where oft I sate, and long did lye.
>
> Here stood that Trunk, and there that chest;
> There lay that store I counted best:
> My pleasant things in ashes lye,
> And them behold no more shall I.
> Under thy roof no guest shall sitt,
> Nor at thy Table eat a bitt.
>
> No pleasant tale shall 'ere be told,
> Nor things recounted done of old.
> No Candle 'ere shall shine in Thee,
> Nor bridegroom's voice ere heard shall bee.
> In silence ever shalt thou lye;
> Adeiu, Adeiu; All's vanity. (ll. 19–36)

Bradstreet not only recollected the house, but her many occasions of devotional exercise in "the places . . . Where oft I sate, and long did lye."

She recalled times such as those expressed in an earlier poem: "By night
when others soundly slept . . . to lye I found it best. / I sought him whom
my Soul did Love. . . . In vain I did not seek or cry" ("By night when
others soundly slept," ll. 1, 4–5, 8). The chair, the bed, and the table were
not so sacred to her memory as her meditative poems composed in those
places. Of course she thought wistfully of guests and mealtime conversa-
tions. But Bradstreet often used everyday things and relationships as signs
of spiritual realities. Moreover, "things recounted done of old" were the
subject of several of her poems. In "Contemplations" she began her med-
itation on Cain and Abel:

> When present times look back to Ages past,
> And men in being fancy those are dead,
> It makes things gone perpetually to last. (ll. 64–66)

This was the work, and the candle was the symbol, of meditation. Now she
considered that the pieces of paper upon which she had written were less
sacred than the mere fact that she had meditated and written. This knowl-
edge must be "sufficient for us."

Critics point to the trunk and chest as pieces of furniture, and no doubt
Bradstreet loved her things. Yet both of these items are containers. Brad-
street identified the contents, not the containers themselves, as "that store
I counted best." More than the trunk and chest themselves, the "store"
kept therein were her "pleasant things" reduced to ashes. One who defined
her life through her writing could be referring to nothing else than bundles
of notebooks and papers that she could now no longer peruse, revise, med-
itate and pray over. Bradstreet used the word "store" elsewhere in ordinary
references to clothing and material wealth, but also metaphorically in ref-
erence to human emotion and her husband's priceless affection. Most im-
portantly, in her "Elegie upon . . . Sir Philip Sidney" she used the word
to describe the writing of poetry. Bradstreet wrote of the muses that Sid-
ney's first published work did not "exhaust your store", he wrote many
volumes of poetry before his death. She emulated Sidney in her poetry but
confessed her inabilities. Poetic inspiration seemed to have dried up. "The
Muses aid I crav'd . . . they said they gave no more, / Since Sidney had
exhausted all their store. / They took from me the scribling pen I had."[33]
Like Sidney, however, Bradstreet kept writing, and found her own muse.
A woman whose spirituality expressed itself in poetry, one who thought of
herself as a poet and not an amateur versifier, who confessed in several
places that she wrote poetry continually, must have written more than the

---

33. Hutchinson, ed., *Poems of Bradstreet*, 109–111, ll. 18, 71, 73–75.

scant 39 poems and journal entries and the prose "Meditations Divine and Moral" which survived the fire in her published volume and two slender notebooks (only one of which is now extant). Anne Bradstreet's deepest sense of loss as she gazed at the ashes was for her entire oeuvre. This was "that store I counted best." She was forced to say even to her writings: "Adeiu, Adeiu; All's vanity."

The concluding part of the poem expressed Bradstreet's meditation on biblical images of sacrifice and the resolution of her crisis of loss.

> Then streight I gin my heart to chide,
> And did thy wealth on earth abide?
> Didst fix thy hope on mouldring dust,
> The arm of flesh didst make thy trust?
> Raise up thy thoughts above the skye
> That dunghill mists away may flie. (ll. 37–42)

Bradstreet's house, her very life, was a "house of clay, whose foundation is in the dust" (Job 4:19). Beyond the imagery of finitude, however, Bradstreet may also have recalled the story of Elijah when "the fire of the Lord fell, and consumed the burnt sacrifice, and the wood, and the stones, and the dust" and the people "fell on their faces: and they said, The Lord is God" (1 Kings 18:38). She must not think of the work of her own "arm of flesh"—"Ye have kindled a fire in mine anger. . . . Cursed be the man that . . . maketh flesh his arm . . . Blessed is the man that trusteth in the Lord" (Jer. 17:4–7). She must "raise up [her] thoughts" to heaven with the ascent of the smoke. Ezra 6 commanded the people to "offer sacrifices of sweet savours unto the God of heaven," and anyone who refused to contribute animals and produce to the sacrifice would face execution "and let his house be made a dunghill" (6:9–11). Bradstreet's house was reduced to a "dunghill," but in her meditation the "mists" that rose from the house and its contents—and particularly her manuscripts—became a more complete sacrifice or act of worship than they had been in their first composition.

Bradstreet's meditation turned instinctively to one of Puritanism's favorite passages, 2 Corinthians 5:1.

> Thou hast an house on high erect
> Fram'd by that mighty Architect,
> With glory richly furnished,
> Stands permanent tho' this bee fled.
> It's purchased, and paid for too
> By him who hath enough to doe. (ll. 43–48)

If she had offered her sacrifice, it was not to purchase salvation but in full devotion to Christ whose sacrifice alone was ''enough'' to purchase permanent union with God in God's own house. Christ's death on the cross sanctified Bradstreet's experience of mortification as she released her written meditative poems to the God who had first inspired them and whose they truly were. Her aim all along had not been poetic fame but the experience of love, in her family and with God. All sanctified earthly love reached toward heaven. Implicit in her meditation was St. Paul's next verse, ''in this we groan, earnestly desiring to be clothed upon with our house which is from heaven.''

> A Prise so vast as is unknown,
> Yet, by his Gift, is made thine own.
> Ther's wealth enough, I need no more;
> Farewell my Pelf, farewell my Store.
> The world no longer let me Love,
> My hope and Treasure lyes Above. (ll. 49–54)

Quite literally, Bradstreet could say her ''store,'' her ''treasure''—the house, its furnishings, and her lifetime of meditative and private poetry—now ''lyes Above.'' Meditation on Christ's sacrifice and her own, and knowledge that ''where your treasure is, there will your heart be also'' (Lk. 12:34), lifted her soul above this world to God.

3. THE MEDITATIVE POETRY OF EDWARD TAYLOR

The meditative poetry of Edward Taylor, which came to light in 1937 and became available in a complete modern edition only in 1960, changed the way historians think about the Puritans. His vivid and often shocking imagery bespoke a spirituality of passion and an intimacy with Christ previously unsuspected and overlooked. Taylor's descendant, the Hon. Henry W. Taylor, who wrote a biographical sketch in the mid-nineteenth century, had seen the poems but dismissed them without a careful reading. ''Mr. Taylor cannot be said to have possessed a poetic genius of a very high order; but he appears to have had an abiding passion for writing poetry during his whole life.''[34] Only with Thomas H. Johnson's partial edition of *The Po-*

---

34. The Hon. Henry W. Taylor, ''Edward Taylor, 1671–1729,'' in William B. Sprague, ed., *Annals of the American Pulpit* (New York, 1859), vol. I, 177–181. That the judge had not studied the poems is clear from the fact that he reports the existence of only 150 ''Preparatory Meditations,'' while Taylor wrote 217 such poems.

etical Works of Edward Taylor (Princeton, 1943) and Donald E. Stanford's *The Poems of Edward Taylor* (New Haven, 1960) were scholars drawn to re-examine Puritanism from the perspective of a man who for 43 years regularly meditated in a manner traditionally thought of as Catholic in preparation for administering Holy Communion.

Edward Taylor was born in Sketchley, Leicestershire, at the time Civil War broke out in England. Anne Bradstreet, then 30 years old, wrote "A Dialogue between Old England and New" in that year. The issue, as she put it, was that

> . . . there's grown of late
> 'Twixt King and Peers a Question of State,
> Which is the chief, the Law, or else the King. (ll. 156–159)

Bradstreet's voice of "New England" spoke for Puritans on both sides of the Atlantic when she announced:

> Dear Mother cease complaints and wipe your eyes,
> Shake off your dust, chear up, and now arise,
> . . . .
> These are the dayes the Churches foes to crush,
> To root out Popelings head, tail, branch and rush;
> . . . .
> For sure the day of your Redemption's nigh;
> The Scales shall fall from your long blinded eyes,
> And him you shall adore who now despise,
> Then fulness of the Nations in shall flow,
> And Jew and Gentile to one worship go;
> Then follows dayes of happiness and rest. (ll. 204–205, 226–227,
> 277–282)

The Taylor family shared in this Puritan millennial hope, and, according to family tradition, Oliver Cromwell was a lifelong hero of Edward's.[35] It is important to note that, while Puritanism developed its own uniquely American character in New England, it also defined itself throughout the seventeenth century in reaction to political events in England. Anne Bradstreet and her family emigrated during the persecution of Archbishop Laud under Charles I in 1630. New Englanders at first believed the Puritan Revolution of the 1640s was the culmination of a movement toward the new era inaugurated by the establishment of their own holy commonwealth and purely

---

35. Henry W. Taylor, "Edward Taylor," in *Annals*, I, 177.

congregational church order. Edward Taylor was of a different generation. During his childhood the Puritan government in England fell into chaos and the Old Cause virtually disintegrated. Edward Taylor was eighteen at the Restoration of Charles II to the throne. As he came into adulthood, England was merry once more and Puritans struggled to exercise their faith in isolated conventicles.

The Taylor family made its living by farming, but Edward was raised for the ministry. In the "Spiritual Relation" he delivered at the gathering (organization) of his church in Westfield, Massachusetts, he recalled his godly upbringing. An older sister, "when I was but small," spoke of the sin of Adam and Eve. "But oh! this account came in upon me in such a Strang way, that I am not able to express it, but ever since I have had the notion of Sin, and its naughtiness remain, and the wrath of God on the account of the same." Although he was susceptible to "the vanities of youth . . . under the vig[ilant] and watchfull Eye of my Parents who would crop the budding forth of Originall Sin, into any visible Sin with whol[some] reproofs, or the Rod, I was thereby preserved from a Sinful Life." His mother, especially, "was very severe" in her guidance.[36] Edward studied with a local nonconformist schoolmaster, then probably attended one of the dissenting academies that replaced Cambridge University as the seat of Puritan scholarship and training. Like many Puritan ministers-to-be throughout the century, he then kept school for a few years. Chafing at the oppressive Act of Uniformity of 1662, he wrote his first poetry in protest.

An Act there came, from whence I cannot tell,
Some call't an Embryo from th'Pit of [Hell].[37]

When he was banned from teaching under the Act, Taylor turned his thoughts toward the New World. There he would pursue his vocation as a minister of the gospel.

Taylor was in his mid-20s in April 1668. He spent his time on the voyage studying his Greek New Testament and leading worship. The ship arrived on the fourth of July and passengers disembarked the next afternoon, which happened to be the Sabbath. A few weeks later Taylor was admitted as a student at Harvard College. No diary of his has survived except for these months of transition, although he appended a brief narrative of his

---

36. Donald E. Stanford, ed., "Edward Taylor's 'Spiritual Relation,' " *American Literature* 35 (1964), 469–471.

37. "The Lay-mans Lamentation," in Donald E. Stanford, "The Earliest Poems of Edward Taylor," *American Literature* 32 (1960), 138–143. Quoted in Keller, *Example of Edward Taylor*, 25.

college experiences and the events leading to his call to the Westfield pulpit. At Harvard, where he was much older than the other students, Taylor excelled in his studies and as a campus leader. His decision after graduation to go immediately into a distant pastorate rather than staying on as a tutor was made easier by his bitterness at rumors surrounding his innocent but perhaps too-close relationship as spiritual director with Elizabeth Steadman, a married woman. In 1671, 29 and still unordained, Edward Taylor assumed the position of pastor in the town of Westfield in the Connecticut River Valley. His first sermon was from Matthew 3:2, "Repent ye: for the kingdom of heaven is at hand."[38]

Taylor served as unordained town minister for eight years before he could officially form local believers into a church according to the congregational principles of the Cambridge Platform of 1648.[39] Taylor could administer no sacraments during these years. This was a long and frustrating period, fraught with the danger of hostile Indians during King Philip's War and with indecisiveness whether or not to proceed with church organization. Finally, in 1679 the foundation work was laid, neighboring pastors and lay messengers gathered, charter members read their spiritual relations and signed the church covenant, the members called Taylor as pastor of the church (no longer just minister in the town) and ordained him to the Christian ministry. He was 37 years old at his ordination and remained in office until his retirement at age 83 in 1725. Taylor's role as pastor deepened and broadened over the years. In addition to his study, sermon preparation, preaching and worship leadership, and pastoral duties, he acted as the town's physician and lawyer and maintained a farm. Well beloved, as Karl Keller notes, "more than anyone else, he held the town together."[40]

Edward Taylor keenly felt the intellectual isolation of frontier life. Unable to purchase many books, he took to borrowing them from ministerial colleagues and copying them out by hand. He supplied himself in this manner with over a hundred volumes, which he bound himself, on theology, science, and medicine.[41] He carried on an active correspondence with colleagues in Boston, including his Harvard classmate and friend, Samuel Sewall, to keep up with political and ecclesiastical events there. Ironically, he sought to overcome isolation by isolation. The solitary work of writing commanded many hours of his time every day. In addition to his correspondence, book-copying, church and personal records, and voluminous

---

38. "Diary of Edward Taylor," Massachusetts Historical Society *Proceedings,* XVIII (1880), 4–18.

39. See Williston Walker, *The Creeds and Platforms of Congregationalism* (Philadelphia and Boston, 1960; orig. 1893), 194–237.

40. Keller, *Example of Edward Taylor,* 39.

41. Henry W. Taylor, "Edward Taylor," in *Annals,* 179.

poetry, Taylor wrote at least two hour-long sermons a week. The physical labor of writing was closely related to Taylor's spiritual exercises and points to an important fact about Puritan spirituality. While people today tend to avoid solitude, Taylor (and Bradstreet), without neglecting their household and community duties, spent as many hours as possible alone.

The meditative poetry of Edward Taylor was dependent upon the maturation of two elements in his life: a sacramental piety connected with his administration of the Lord's Supper (possible only after his 1679 ordination), and his marriage to Elizabeth Fitch in 1674. The first provided a spiritual focus, the second a model and language of unitive passion. It was a third element, the death of two children in 1677 and 1682, that turned him, at age 40, to the work of meditative poetry.

Apart from his spiritual infatuation with Elizabeth Steadman, Taylor hints nowhere at an interest in women until he courted another Elizabeth, the daughter of the Rev. James Fitch of Norwalk, Connecticut. The prospect of marriage brought out a new side in his character, and a desire to push language to its emotional and rational limits. An elaborately designed acrostic verse and his love letters were filled with the same kind of metaphorical language he would later use in reference to Christ in his meditative poems, images such as the "True-Loves-Knot," sparkling beams of light, "my breast the cabinet of your affections (as I yours mine)," and love as "a Golden Ball of pure Fire rolling up and down my Breast." He rhapsodized, "My cent'red heart doth reek out highest Streams of Love." Taylor even made the connection between sexual love and the spiritual love of Christ explicit in his love letters. "Conjugal love must exceed all other" on earth, yet be "Subordinate to God's Glory." Taylor portrayed this relationship in his acrostic, with extravagant professions of love arranged around a circle ("Loves Ring") within a triangle ("The Trinity"). He convinced himself that his passion for Elizabeth was legitimate because it gave him a new awareness of God's love. The solution was to "offer my heart with you in it as a more rich Sacrifice unto God through Christ."[42] The couple was married on November 5, 1674.

Edward Taylor began at some point in the marriage to experiment with writing poems as part of his meditations. The first of these seem to have been occasional meditations, exercises prompted by some event of the day. When hindered from making a journey because of rain, for example, he chastised himself for his indecision about whether or not to brave the storm. The situation within his soul was equally volatile, Taylor lamented, so he felt like a bottle of ale which "When jog'd, the bung with Violence doth

---

42. The acrostic is reproduced in Keller, *Example of Taylor,* 168; the love letter is quoted 44–45.

burst ([When] Let by Rain, l. 18)''. Similarly, reflecting ''Upon a Spider Catching a Fly,'' his thoughts turned to the awful plot of Satan, ''Hells Spider'' (l. 32), and the deadly effects of sin, from which only God's grace can free us. Taylor's best early effort, however, was born out of his daily life with his family. Perhaps while watching Elizabeth at the wheel or loom, or pondering that scene during his devotions, Taylor spiritualized the tasks of ''Huswifery'' in meditation. While in most of his later meditative poetry Taylor assumed the feminine posture in relation to Christ the Bridegroom, here his wife's household work reminded him of God's work in his soul. He prayed, ''Make me, O Lord, thy Spining Wheele compleate'' (l. 1). He imagined his affections the flyers, his soul the spool, and his conversation (manner of living) the reel. In the second stanza Taylor considered himself as the loom on which God would weave fine cloth, which then was prepared in the ''Fulling Mills'' of the ordinances (sacraments, scriptures, sermons, prayers) of the church. He concluded by asking God to clothe his faculties— ''mine Understanding, Will, / Affections, Judgment, Conscience, Memory / My Words and Actions'' (ll. 13–15)—with this holy garment, in the production of which Taylor himself was instrumental. If he is thus adorned, Taylor comforted himself,

> Then mine apparell shall display before yee
> That I am Cloathd in Holy robes for glory. (ll. 17–18)

The pleasure of family life was soon broken by grief. Elizabeth and Edward Taylor had eight children in fifteen years, but five of them died in infancy. Two boys, Samuel and James, were born in 1675 and 1678, respectively; but the first two daughters, Elizabeth and Abigail, failed to survive. Soon after the death of Abigail on August 22, 1682, Edward Taylor wrote an occasional meditation based on his hours of spiritual wrestling with God over the meaning of life and death. ''Upon Wedlock, and Death of Children'' is filled with tortured ambiguity. Marriage for Taylor was a ''Curious'' (i.e. carefully made) ''True-Love Knot'' (flower garden) created ''in Paradise'' (ll. 1–3), the flowering of which brought nothing but beauty and joy. Why, then, should his flowers (children) sicken and die? One moment he attributed such suffering to ''an Hellish breath'' (l. 8)—an evil wind from Hell. The next, however, asserting the sovereignty of God even in ''that unlookt for, Dolesome, darksome houre'' (l. 22), he saw death as ''a glorious hand from glory'' (l. 19). In either case, he was certain that his child's soul found a home in heaven:

> In Pray're to Christ perfum'de it did ascend,
> And Angells bright did it to heaven tend. (ll. 23–24)

Taylor even took comfort that Christ, "having Choice, chose this my branch forth brought" (l. 27). But then his mind swung again to the misery of his second daughter's death and comfort was gone.

> But oh! the tortures, Vomit, screechings, groans,
> And six weeks Fever would pierce hearts like stones. (ll. 35–36)

Again, like a wave, "Griefe o're doth flow" (l. 37). Taylor struggled to affirm God's goodness in such suffering, weakly contending that if God's sovereign will were not "my Spell Charm, Joy, and Gem," his "nature fault would finde" (ll. 37–38). Holding fast to the faith he had long professed, Taylor released his children to God:

> . . . as I said, I say, take, Lord, they're thine.
> I piecemeale pass to Glory bright in them.
> I joy, may I sweet Flowers for Glory breed,
> Whether thou getst them green, or lets them seed. (ll. 39–42)

The experience of being shaken by grief left Taylor with a more deeply complicated, troubled, and brooding faith. Meditative poetry became for him now an outlet, a way to express repeatedly his yearning for divine and human love that would not die. Meditation One of his first series of "Preparatory Meditations before my Approach to the Lords Supper" is dated July 23, 1682, a month before Abigail died and two weeks after the onset of the "six weeks Fever" that took her life.[43]

The "Preparatory Meditations" are here classified as formal, rather than occasional meditations, but that does not preclude the influence of daily life. Puritan piety was always rooted in the experience of this world; at the very least each meditation was linked with an approaching event, a sermon and a sacrament. The fact that Taylor composed Meditation One as Abigail lay dying, however, sheds fresh light upon its meaning. Taylor employed the extravagant language of his courtship with Elizabeth in praise of God. "What Love is this of thine, that Cannot bee . . . Confinde"? (ll. 1–2). Their conjugal love could not be confined in their hearts, and God's love cannot be confined in his infinity. Edward and Elizabeth consummated their love in marriage, God his in Christ.

---

43. Thomas M. Davis makes a similar connection between this crisis in Taylor's life and his poetic undertaking, but, I believe, wrongly dates "Upon Wedlock" in August 1683 in proximity to "Upon the Sweeping Flood" and the birth of their next child. Thomas M. Davis, "Edward Taylor's 'Occasional Meditations,' " *Early American Literature,* vol. 3 (Winter 1970–1971), 21–23.

What hath thy Godhead, as not satisfide
Marri'de our Manhood, making it its Bride? (ll. 5–6)

God's "Matchless Love" in Christ overflowed heaven and came "all run-
ning o're beside / This World!" (ll. 7–9). Indeed, by quenching the flames
of hell divine love overcame every obstacle to the union of the soul with
Christ. But with the shattering death within his household, Taylor's expe-
rience of this love was at low ebb. He longed for the unfailing intimacy he
had once known. "Oh! that thy Love might overflow my Heart!" (l. 13).
Taylor laid his soul before the Source of love and confessed his condition.
"But oh! my streight'ned Breast! my Lifeless Sparke! / My Fireless Flame!
What Chilly Love, and Cold?" (ll. 15–16). He concluded with an earnest
prayer: "Lord blow the coal: Thy Love enflame in mee" (l. 18).

Taylor's occasional meditations following the spiritual and emotional
crisis of Abigail's death reflect the same inner turmoil. The undated poem,
"The Ebb and Flow," is probably from this period between August 1682
and August 1683 and uses some of the same imagery as in Meditation One.
The meditation takes its title from the rise and fall of the tide, a cyclical
pattern that describes an important characteristic of Puritan piety. Believers
repeatedly undertook exercises to empty their souls in contrition and hu-
miliation before God in order then to be filled again by the inpouring of
God's grace.[44] But particular life experiences could accentuate the cycle.
Taylor was feeling especially empty following his child's death, and no
doubt his wife's new pregnancy filled him with anxiety as much as joy. The
poem does not develop the image of the tide, but, like Meditation One, that
of the fire in Taylor's heart. One may imagine him in his study at night in
secret exercises, warming himself by a tinder box at his feet. Following that
method of occasional meditation of "spiritualizing" a physical object, Tay-
lor considered that when God first "wrought'st thy Sweet Print" his "heart
was made thy tinder box" (ll. 1–2). His reflections focused on those early
days when he first felt the assurance of conversion, but perhaps also on his
first years in Westfield as unordained town preacher and on the early years
of his marriage when he and Elizabeth so joyfully reflected in their union
the divine image of love. In those days his affections or emotions were like
tinder in that box and when the Holy Spirit fell like sparks a "Heavenly Fire
. . . often would out flame" (ll. 5–6) in his soul. Taylor's ordination in
1679 qualified him to administer the sacrament at the church's Communion
Table. In the second stanza, then, he likened his heart not to the purely
functional tinder box but to an ornate censer in which a priest burned in-

---

44. See Hambrick-Stowe, *The Practice of Piety*, passim.

cense at the altar. (The poet here meditated on the Jewish Temple priesthood in the Old Testament, and was not thinking of Catholic liturgical practices which Puritans disdained.) In sad irony, Taylor confessed that now "I finde my tinder scarce thy sparks can feel" (l. 11). During the time of crisis in 1682 Taylor felt "doubts out bud" (l. 13) and even wondered if like "a mocking Ignis Fatuus" (l. 14) his faith was nothing but swamp gas. In his spiritual exercises and in his ministry, however, he could still sense, if faintly, "the bellows of thy Spirit blow / Away mine ashes" (ll. 19–20) now and then. During those days he did not look for a lively fire but simply for moments in prayer when he could say to God, "thy fire doth glow" (l. 20) within the coals of his heart.

Natural disasters were often the occasion for Puritan meditation, as with Anne Bradstreet's on the burning of her house. In Puritan spirituality, no event or detail was without possible meaning. On August 13 and 14, 1683, then, when the Connecticut River and its tributaries overflowed their banks causing substantial property damage, Taylor responded with a meditation "Upon the Sweeping Flood" as an act of God in response to human sinfulness.[45] Even here, one critic has suggested, it is possible that Taylor's personal crisis intruded into his meditations on a public event. The flood occurred almost exactly a year after Abigail's death and halfway into Elizabeth's next pregnancy. Perhaps Taylor experienced remorse for having placed excessive and unrepentant emphasis on his love for his wife apart from his devotion to God. In Meditation 33, composed the day Elizabeth died (July 7, 1689), Taylor confessed that some "strange Charm encrampt my Heart with spite / Making my Love gleame out upon a Toy" (ll. 7–8) to the neglect of God. The wholeness of physical and spiritual life had perhaps eluded Taylor during this year of crisis. "What Violence doth split / True Love, and Life, that they should sunder'd bee?" (ll. 14–15).[46] In his meditation on the flood, therefore, Taylor may have been making a personal as well as a corporate confession.

> Oh! that Id had a tear to've quencht that flame
> > Which did dissolve the Heavens above
> > Into those liquid drops that Came
> > > To drown our Carnall love.
> Our cheeks were dry and eyes refusde to weep.
> Tears bursting out ran down the skies darke Cheeke. (ll. 1–6)

---

45. Keller, *Example of Edward Taylor,* 62.
46. Thomas M. Davis, "Edward Taylor's 'Occasional Meditations,' " *Early American Literature,* vol. 3 (Winter 1970–1971), 23.

Human sinfulness, in which Taylor knew he participated, acted as a purgative to cause the heavens to spew "Excrements upon our lofty heads" (l. 12).

Family life continued to be difficult, as three of the next four children failed to survive. Edward Taylor found strength by periodically focusing his spiritual life through poetry as he prepared to administer Holy Communion. Nor did his confessions to God of his sinfulness diminish his love for Elizabeth or his grief at her death after the birth of their eighth child; repentance was for him a means of spiritual survival. He also wrote a magnificent elegy with the running title, "A Funerall Poem Upon the Death of my ever Endeared, and Tender Wife Mrs. Elizabeth Taylor, Who fell asleep in Christ the 7th day of July at night about two hours after Sun setting 1689 and in the 39 yeare of her Life." The poem, actually a private occasional meditation since it was not a public elegy, is in three parts. Part One is a prayer addressed to God for permission "Not to repine" but to drop "a Teare, or two" upon her grave (ll. 1–3). Taylor states his undying love for his "bosom Friend" (l.17) in moving language.

> Some deem Death doth the True Love Knot unty:
> But I do finde it harder tide [tied] thereby.
> My heart is in't and will be squeez'd therefore
> To pieces if thou draw the Ends much more. (ll. 7–10)

While the death of his five children had been like arrows "into my bowells," with Elizabeth's death they pierced his bosom and "strike and stob me in the very heart" (ll. 14–16). In Part Two, Taylor addresses Elizabeth herself, pouring out his grief. He recalls the verses he wrote during their courtship.

> What shall my Preface to our True Love Knot
> Frisk in Acrostick Rhimes? And may I not
> Now at our parting, with Poetick knocks
> Break a salt teare to pieces as it drops? (ll. 41–44)

And he comforts himself with the romantic thought that "some Angell may my Poem sing / To thee in Glory" (ll. 57–58). The third and longest part is addressed to the angels and saints in heaven, introducing his wife to them. Taylor paints the picture of the perfect Puritan pastor's wife:

Her Husbands Joy, Her Childrens Chiefe Content.
Her Servants Eyes, Her Houses Ornament.
. . . .
She, where he chanc'd to miss, a Cover would lay
Yet would in Secret fore him all Display
. . . .
She laid her neck unto the Yoake he draws:
And was his Faithfull Yoake Mate, in Christ's Cause. (ll. 67–68,
    123–124, 127–128).

Taylor concluded his elegy, interestingly, with the note that "The Dooms-day Verses" of Michael Wigglesworth (*The Day of Doom,* Cambridge, 1662) "perfum'de her Breath" and were "Much in her thoughts, and yet she fear'd not Death" (ll. 151–152).

By November Taylor was able to embrace death positively in his meditations, as the link to heaven. Meditation 34, based on the same text as the one written the day Elizabeth died (1 Cor. 3:22), bears the title, "Death is Yours." After an unusually cursory introductory show of humility ("My tongue Wants Words to tell my thoughts," l. 3), Taylor went on to praise God for his "gracious Chymistry" (l. 19) that transforms death from plague to remedy: "The Golden Dore of Glory is the Grave" (l. 24). Thinking of the classic emblems of death often used in both Catholic and Protestant devotions, he protested:

The Painter lies who pensills death's Face grim
    With White bare butter Teeth, bare staring bones,
With Empty Eyeholes, Ghostly Lookes which fling
    Such Dread to see as raiseth Deadly groans,
    For thou hast farely Washt Deaths grim grim face
    And made his Chilly finger-Ends drop grace. (ll. 25–30)

Taylor concluded with the prayer, "Say I am thine, My Lord" (l. 37), and the promise, "Oh I'le sing / This Triumph o're the Grave! Death where's thy sting?" (ll. 41–42). Decades later, in the 1720s when Taylor faced old age, illness, and his own approaching death, he used the same language and held this same triumphant posture. His meditation in preparation for death, "A Fig for thee Oh! Death," is also reminiscent of Anne Bradstreet's "As weary pilgrim." Taylor looked forward eagerly to the reunion of soul and "Christalized" body (l. 44) in heaven "as two true Lovers" who "Ery night . . . hug and kiss each other" (l. 47–48). But his final word—and gesture, thrusting his thumb between his fingers in fisted position—was one of contempt for the old enemy who had caused him such agony. "Although thy terrours rise to th'highst degree,'' he taunted death, ''I still am where I was, a Fig for thee'' (ll. 55–56).[47]

Three years after Elizabeth's death, Edward Taylor, now 50, married Ruth Wyllys, who was from one of the most prominent and wealthy families in Connecticut. The fact that he wrote no poems about her or the children they had together suggests that Taylor directed his spiritual and artistic energies elsewhere. His love for his second wife, however, influenced his meditative poetry in at least one way. Ruth bore six children, the last when Edward was 66 years old. Taylor's sexuality, which had always manifested itself spiritually and shown itself in his poetry, came increasingly to the fore. During the last decades of his life, the ''Preparatory Meditations'' were almost always centered on texts and imagery from the Song of Solomon, or Canticles as the Puritans called the book, and Taylor became more caught up in the language of eroticism and love. He rejoiced in his relationship with Christ—''Thy Person mine, Mine thine, even weddenwise'' (II:79, l. 30)—and savored the love that would be his in heaven.

> Hence, Oh! my Lord, make thou mee thine that so
> I may be bed wherein thy Love shall ly,
> And be thou mine that thou mayst ever show
> Thyselfe the Bed my Love its lodge may spy.
> Then this shall be the burden of my Song
> My Well belov'de is mine: I'm his become. (ll. 67–72)

Taylor late in life loved to meditate on the ''Dove like Eyes'' (II:119, l. 3), cheeks of ''sweetest Beauty'' (II:120, l. 8), and ''Lilly Lips'' (II:121, l. 9) of the heavenly Christ. In a manner reminiscent of the Spanish mystics, but flowing at least in part from his love for his two wives, Taylor in meditation poured out ''Love to [Christ] in Hottest Streams'' (II:119, l. 28). While these meditations reflect Taylor's preparation for death, his drawing ''away from worldly concerns toward a contemplative foreshadowing of his future state,'' his language of spiritual love was rooted in his experience of the sanctified physical love of marriage.[48]

Before moving to a fuller consideration of the ''Preparatory Meditations,'' mention must be made of another major work in the Taylor corpus.

---

47. See Arthur Forstater and Thomas M. Davis, ''Edward Taylor's 'A Fig for thee Oh! Death,' '' in Calvin Israel, ed., *Discoveries and Considerations: Essays on Early American Literature and Aesthetics Presented to Harold Jantz* (Albany, N.Y., 1976), 67–81; and Jeff Hammond and Thomas M. Davis, ''Edward Taylor: A Note on Visual Imagery, *Early American Literature* (Fall 1973), 126–131.

48. Jeffrey A. Hammond, ''A Puritan *Ars Moriendi:* Edward Taylor's Late Meditations on the Song of Songs,'' *Early American Literature* (Winter 1982–1983), 197.

"Gods Determinations" was probably written in the mid-1680s, just following the turbulent period in Taylor's life associated with the onset of his "Preparatory Meditations" and before the death of his first wife. "Gods Determinations" is a collection of 35 didactic poems that argue for what John Cotton in the first generation had called "the Way of Congregational Churches," popularly termed "the New England way."[49] It was never published, but if it had been it may well have been as popular as Michael Wigglesworth's *The Day of Doom,* for it places New Englanders similarly at the center of salvation history.

Edward Taylor was a quiet crusader for traditional Congregationalism against its enemies. The chief threat in Taylor's day was not Rome or Quakerism, although he excoriated these publicly and privately (e.g. II:81), but the liberalizing ideas of the Rev. Solomon Stoddard (the grandfather of Jonathan Edwards) in nearby Northampton. Most New England ministers in the last decades of the seventeenth century recognized the need for the Halfway Covenant, promulgated at the Synod of 1662, which made partial church membership available to baptized and moral but unconverted persons who intellectually adhered to the tenets of orthodoxy. By the terms of the Synod, their children could be baptized and thus raised within the Christian fellowship.[50] But Stoddard went well beyond these measures when he began to argue in the late 1670s that no profession of faith was necessary for these "half-way" members and that they should receive Holy Communion. In the 1680s he moved toward the position that the Lord's Supper should be open to all who desire it. In 1690 Stoddard declared the Lord's Supper a converting ordinance; that is, the unregenerate should be welcome at the Table since through the sacrament they could receive saving grace. New England orthodoxy held that preaching was the chief converting ordinance, and that the Lord's Supper was reserved for those who, following conversion, were to grow in grace through the process of sanctification. Edward Taylor wrote stern letters to Stoddard, preached against his views in Westfield, and wrote substantial unpublished volumes, including his 1694 *Treatise Concerning the Lord's Supper,* which Stoddard never saw.[51] Taylor stated his position clearly in Meditation II:104:

---

    49. See Larzer Ziff, ed., *John Cotton on the Churches of New England* (Cambridge, Mass., 1968).

    50. Walker, *Creeds and Platforms of Congregationalism,* 238–339.

    51. Norman S. Grabo, ed., *Edward Taylor's Treatise Concerning the Lord's Supper* (Michigan State, 1966). Thomas M. and Virginia Davis, eds., *Edward Taylor vs. Solomon Stoddard: The Nature of the Lord's Supper* (Boston, 1981).

This Bread and Wine begets not Souls; but's set
 'Fore spirituall life to feed upon the Same.
This Feast is no Regenerating fare.
But food for those Regenerate that are. (ll. 57–60)

For Taylor, as for such first generation Puritan pastors as Thomas Hooker, the pastor's task was to prepare souls for church membership within which the Supper was available. Indeed, Puritan piety in general, as Taylor's "Preparatory Meditations" demonstrate, was preparationist in nature. Even the believer could never take salvation for granted, but must always humbly prepare the heart for the dispensation of God's grace. "Gods Determinations" was less a defense than a lyric celebration of the soul's entrance into this church fellowship.

The running title sets out the entire drama: "Gods Determinations touching his Elect: and The Elects Combat in their Conversion, and Coming up to God in Christ together with the Comfortable Effects thereof." New England church membership here was set within a grand drama of Miltonic scope. "The Preface" praises the power of the Creator in language both eloquent (the earth is "Like a Quilt Ball within a Silver Box," l. 12) and quaint ("Who in this Bowling Alley bowld the Sun?" l. 14), and concludes with the tarnishing of created goodness by the Fall. The human condition is summed up in the doctrine, "man did throw down all by Sin" (l. 41). There ensues a dialogue between Justice and Mercy, and poems expressing the perplexity and helplessness of the human soul, the rage of Satan, and the advances of Christ toward the souls of the elect. When the soul "Groan[s] to Christ for Succour" and relief from Satan's assaults, it is a merciful Christ who responds:

Peace, Peace, my Hony, do not Cry,
My Little Darling, wipe thine eye,
 Oh Cheer, cheer up, come see.
Is anything too deare, my Dove,
Is anything too good, my Love
 To get or give for thee? ("Christ's Reply," ll. 1–6)

The climax of the work comes when the soul enters into church fellowship by professing repentance for sins and faith in Christ. Taylor tried valiantly to build suspense as in an epic; desire and fear rage within the embattled soul. The force holding back desire "breaks at last. / Hence on they go, and in they enter . . . They now enCovenant With God: and His" ("The Soul

admiring the Grace of the Church Enters into Church Fellowship,'' ll. 22–
23, 25). The concluding poems celebrate the benefits and promise of mem-
bership:

> In all their Acts, publick, and private, nay
>   And secret too, they praise impart.
> But in their Acts Divine and Worship, they
>   With Hymns do offer up their Heart.
> Thus in Christs Coach they sweetly sing
> As they to Glory ride therein.
>   (''The Joy of Church Fellowship
>   rightly attended,'' ll. 19–24)

''Gods Determinations'' elaborates the same theology as the meditative po-
etry, but in a different tone. In this public poetry, Taylor adopted a voice
similar to that of Anne Bradstreet in her ''Dialogue between Old England
and New'' and ''The Flesh and the Spirit.'' Here, Taylor steps from his
study into the pulpit; a door closes on the humble and searching soul as the
poet becomes apologist for the New England way.[52]

If ''Gods Determinations'' exhibits the public voice of Edward Taylor,
the ''Preparatory Meditations'' reveal his most private devotional hours.
According to family tradition, he instructed his heirs never to publish these
poems, so that as Karl Keller puts it, ''we invade his privacy as we read
him today.''[53] The privacy of the ''Preparatory Meditations'' lies not only
in their composition during what Puritans called ''secret exercises,'' but in
their extremely personal language. Taylor the pastor was all professional
self-confidence; his task was to set forth and embody Calvinist dogma. No
room for doubt or hedging back and forth seemingly existed in the Genevan
doctrines or their English expression, the Westminster Confession. Yet in
the *Institutes of the Christian Religion,* even John Calvin recognized the
continuing spiritual struggle of the saints. ''By regeneration the children of
God are delivered from the bondage of sin, but not as if they had already
obtained full possession of freedom, and no longer felt any annoyance from
the flesh. Materials for an unremitting contest remain, that they may be ex-
ercised, and not only exercised, but may better understand their weak-
ness.''[54] New England Puritans engaged in this ''unremitting contest'' in

---

52. See Agnieszka Salska, ''Puritan Poetry: Its Public and Private Strain,'' *Early Amer-
ican Literature* (Fall 1984), 107–121.

53. Henry W. Taylor, ''Edward Taylor,'' in Sprague, *Annals,* I, 180. Keller, *Example
of Edward Taylor,* 81.

54. John Calvin, *Institutes of the Christian Religion,* Henry Beveridge, trans. (Grand
Rapids, Mich., 1966), I, 516.

their meditations and prayers; in their closet devotions even pastors fought sin, confessed "their weakness," and begged God for fresh effusions of grace. We have already noted that Edward Taylor first began composing his "Preparatory Meditations" during a crisis of finitude and grief. Throughout the meditations, Taylor expressed pained awareness of the awful chasm between this world and heaven. His confessions of sin were so scatologically debased and his yearnings so eschatologically erotic he may well have felt that for other eyes to see his poems would be a major embarrassment. But even if the imagery were more tame, as in Anne Bradstreet, Puritans wrote devotional diaries and meditative poetry for God and for the cure of their souls, not for the scrutiny, admiration, or approval of others.

Before settling into what became his lifelong pattern of composing anticipatory or preparatory meditations, Taylor also experimented briefly with poems stemming from his reflective meditations. Just as in the Ignatian "Examination of Conscience," Puritans were in the habit of regularly scrutinizing their lives and confessing their sinfulness. These exercises in "self-examination" took place in both family prayer and secret devotions every evening, and in periodic days of fasting and humiliation.[55] Preachers and writers of devotional manuals further enjoined the faithful not only to prepare for the coming Sabbath, but to look back on the text, sermon, and overall worship experience in secret exercises for several days afterward. Three of Edward Taylor's meditative poems must be understood in the context of these traditions and practices. Sometime after the service associated with his third preparatory exercise, Taylor composed two such reflective meditations. The first, titled "The Experience," indicates that he had enjoyed a delicious sense of God's presence that Sabbath, especially during his delivery of the eucharistic prayer.

> Oh! that I alwayes breath'd in such an aire,
>> As I suckt in, feeding on sweet Content!
> Disht up unto my Soul ev'n in that pray're
>> Pour'de out to God over last Sacrament.
>> What Beam of Light wrapt up my sight to finde
>> Me neerer God than ere Came in my minde? (ll. 1–6)

He wished that "that Flame" of union with Christ could follow him "ery where," so he could have heaven on earth. Memory, at least, would keep the experience alive. "Oh! Sweet though Short! Ile not forget the same" (ll. 13–17). "The Return" is apparently a later meditation on that same

---

55. See Hambrick-Stowe, *Practice of Piety,* 148–150, 168–175.

administration of the sacrament and other past experiences. Taylor praised God's grace and love in Christ and bemoaned his own sin, ending each stanza until the final two with the lament,

> Oh! that thou wast on Earth below with mee!
> Or that I was in Heaven above with thee.

He recalled that God had in fact been with him.

> But I've thy Pleasant Pleasant Presence had
>   In Word, Pray're, Ordinances, Duties; nay
> And in thy Graces, making me full Glad,
>   In Faith, Hope, Charity, that I do say,
>   That thou hast been on Earth below with mee.
>   And I shall be in Heaven above with thee. (ll. 43–48)

Taylor concluded with the prayer that he be God's "well tun'de Instrument" (l. 50) to praise him while yet on earth.

> Then let thy Spirit keepe my Strings in tune,
> Whilst thou art here on Earth below with mee
> Till I sing Praise in Heaven above with thee. (ll. 52–54)

The third of Taylor's retrospective meditations was "The Reflexion," composed following the fourth meditation. Contemplating the vessels that contained the elements, and identifying himself with them, he chastened himself that while Christ was "at the Table Head above," he had lost the sense of that presence—"not my Trencher, nor my Cup o'reflow" (ll. 1, 4). It had not always been so.

> Once at thy Feast, I saw thee Pearle-like stand
>   'Tween Heaven, and Earth where Heavens Bright glory all
> In streams fell on thee, as a floodgate and,
>   Like Sun Beams through thee on the World to Fall.
>   Oh! sugar sweet then! my Deare sweet Lord, I see
>   Saints Heavens-lost Happiness restor'd by thee. (ll. 25–30)

"So much before, so little now" (l. 35). By remembering these previous experiences of grace, however, Taylor was able to hope that again God's "golden gleams [would] run through this gloom" (l. 39) and finally to pray to Christ for renewed vision.

> Pass o're my Faults: shine forth, bright sun: arise
> Enthrone thy Rosy-selfe within mine Eyes. (ll. 41–42)

Reflection on one's sinfulness and on past "evidences" of divine favor, important elements in their regular spiritual exercises, reminded Puritans that God would be faithful even through their dark times when Christ seemed far away. Taylor never abandoned these exercises of "self-examination," but for reasons we cannot know he apparently stopped writing poems in conjunction with them. He reserved most of his poetic energies for only one type of meditation, his time of preparation before administering Holy Communion.

Edward Taylor composed his "Preparatory Meditations" on a somewhat irregular basis, ranging from six weeks to over 20 weeks between poems, based on the variable period between administrations of the Lord's Supper. While the intervals were irregular, Taylor's overall effort was extraordinarily steady. From July 23, 1682, until his last poetic meditation (II.165, October 1725), no year passed without Taylor having composed at least three and often as many as six meditations (1721, with one poem, being an exception). Moreover, the form of the poems remained unchanged. Innovation was not considered a Puritan virtue. From first to last, Taylor wrote in six-line stanzas of iambic pentameter, although the number of stanzas in the poems varied. The fact that he defined his first 49 Meditations as a group, or series, suggests that, as with Anne Bradstreet in her meditation on the burning of her house, Taylor had numerology in mind. Six was symbolic of the sin and imperfection that Taylor regularly confessed, while the number 49 (seven times seven) bespoke the divine perfection for which he yearned at the conclusion of each exercise.[56] Taylor's themes and imagery underwent little substantial development over the decades. Changes in emphasis had more to do with periodic themes than shifts in dogmatic or spiritual theology. He focused his exercises in blocks of meditations, for example, on typology (II:1–30, 1693–1699), on the person

---

56. See Ursula Brumm, " 'Tuning' the Song of Praise: Observations on the Use of Numbers in Edward Taylor's *Preparatory Meditations, Early American Literature,* 17:2 (Fall 1982), 103–118. It is possible, as Brumm suggests, that Taylor's ten-syllabic lines reminded him of God's Law, although this form was also merely conventional in seventeenth-century poetry. Brumm states that the number six symbolized creation and redemption.

of Christ (II:42–56, 1701–1703, written in conjunction with the *Christo-graphia* sermons[57]), the meaning of the Lord's Supper (II:102–111, 1711–1712), and the Canticles or Song of Solomon (II:115–153, 1713–1719). It is true, however, that as the aging Taylor absorbed himself almost exclusively in the love-imagery of the Canticles he diminished his confession of sin to a mere acknowledgement of finitude ("My Deare-Deare Lord! What shall my speech be dry? / And shall I court thee onely with dull tunes?" II:120, ll. 1–2) or abandoned it altogether in favor of sheer praise (II:119). But the emphasis on Canticles was nothing new for Taylor in the eighteenth century; his first six meditations (1682–1683), as well as his last seven (1722–1725), were on texts from this beloved and mystical book.

The commanding theme of Edward Taylor's "Preparatory Meditations" is the doctrine he termed "Theanthropy," Christ as fully divine and fully human. In meditation Taylor placed himself in paradise where he saw "The Tree of Life whose Bulk's [i.e. trunk is] Theanthropie." The tree's fruit, love, "of th'sap of Godhood-Manhood spring," and, in turn, "sinfull Man [is] the Object of this Love" (II:33, ll. 6–10, 19). By "THEAN-THROPIE," "Two natures distance-standing, infinite, / Are Onifide, in person, and Unite" (II:44, ll. 10–12). Christ's "Nature is Theandricall," he preached to his congregation, "God-Man in Personall Union, forever." Meditation on this central point of Christian theology provided both Taylor's mental focus and the channel for God's grace-filled love. Any language describing the divine-human relationship, he admitted, was bound to be "metaphorical and not proper." But "there may be a nearer likeness in God's filiating Act to the act of Filiation among the Children of men, than to any other act of theirs."[58] By "filiation," the process of producing a son, Taylor meant the sexual union of husband and wife. In the Son, therefore, God has "Marri'de our Manhood, making it its Bride" (I:1, l. 6). As in Christ "Infinity, and Finity Conjoyn'd" (I:1, l. 4), Christ extends this same relationship of love to humanity. Taylor's reaction to this divine courtship and marriage was constant astonishment. Nothing was "more strange" than "to spy

> My Nature with thy Nature all Divine
>> Together joyn'd in Him thats Thou, and I.
>> Flesh of my Flesh, Bone of my Bone. There's run
>> Thy Godhead, and my Manhood in thy Son.
>>> ("The Experience," ll. 8–12)

---

57. Norman S. Grabo, ed., *Edward Taylor's Christographia* (New Haven, 1962).
58. Grabo, ed., *Edward Taylor's Christographia*, 46, 50, 39.

Meditating on two words from Canticles 4:8, "My Spouse," he blurted:

> My Maker, he my Husband? Oh! strange joy!
> . . . .
> I am to Christ more base, than to a King
>   A Mite, Fly, Worm, Ant, Serpent, Divell is,
> Or Can be, being tumbled all in Sin,
>   And shall I be his Spouse? How good is this?
>   It is too good to be declar'de to thee.
>   But not too good to be believ'de by mee.
>   (I:23, ll. 25, 31–36)

Nothing, however, was more real to Taylor than this: "Christ doth Wooe" and "Hee / Appears as Wonders Wonder, wedding mee" (ll. 39, 42).

The doctrine of Theanthropy was tied in Taylor's spirituality to certain biblical texts, notably those passages from Canticles that dominated his meditations, New Testament verses on the role of Christ as mediator, and Old Testament passages on key figures read typologically as pointing to Christ. It was also tied to the administration of the Lord's Supper, which revealed the Christly union of infinite and finite through the physical means of bread and wine. In some poems, Taylor likened the sacramental bread to manna in the wilderness (II:104, l. 24) or showbread in the Temple (I:11, l. 13; II:104, ll. 19–20), but more often the bread was compared to ordinary household bread. Meditating on the text, "I am the Living Bread" (Jn. 6:51), Taylor stood amazed as during vast contemplations and "puzzled thoughts" on "A Golden Path" from the "Throne unto my Threshold," suddenly Christ was personally present. "I finde the Bread of Life in't at my doore" (I:8.ll. 3–6). It is possible that Taylor actually had the elements prepared for the next morning's Communion on the table before him. The loaf represented Christ personally, and not a mere memory or abstract symbol of his attributes. Classical Reformed eucharistic theology held a doctrine of the real spiritual presence of Christ, contrary to popular misconception.[59] Taylor considered how God

> The Purest Wheate in Heaven, his deare-dear Son
>   Grinds, and kneads up into this Bread of Life.
>   Which Bread of Life from Heaven down came and stands
>   Disht on thy Table up by Angells Hands. (ll. 21–24)

---

59. E. Brooks Holifield, *The Covenant Sealed: The Development of Puritan Sacramental Theology in Old and New England, 1570–1720* (New Haven, Conn., 1974), 20–22, 167–168, 220–224.

In his homey way, Taylor termed the sacramental bread "Heavens Sugar Cake" (l. 30) and "My Souls Plumb Cake" (II:81:56). He imagined the work of Christ as "Divine Cookery" that would "knead in / The Pasty Past (his Flesh and Blood) most fine," prepared with "the rowling pin / His Deity did use" (ll. 25–27). In some spiritual sense, God "Did . . . mould up this Bread in Heaven, and bake," send it from his table to Taylor's, and announce, "This Soule Bread take" (I:8, ll. 25–27). As he anticipated taking it in his hands the next morning, the bread itself cried out, "Eate, Eate me, Soul, and thou shalt never dy" (I:8, l. 36). Christ was spiritually present in the physical element of bread, and would unite with Taylor's soul as he took the bread into his body.

The marriage was an accomplished fact; Christ had revealed himself and Taylor had covenanted with him. But the union was not yet constant or complete, for that blissful state awaited the soul in heaven. The chasm that separated his soul (yet on earth) and his spiritual spouse, then, created a perpetual crisis that fueled Taylor's spirituality. The distance between the two was no fault of the bridegroom's, but was entirely Taylor's—outright sinfulness at his worst, and, even at his best, finite inability properly to communicate his love. His confessions were on occasion explosively graphic.

> My Sin! my Sin, My God, these Cursed Dregs,
>> Green, Yellow, Blew streakt Poyson hellish, ranck,
> Bubs hatcht in natures nest on Serpents Eggs,
>> Yelp, Cherp and Cry; they set my Soule a Cramp.
> I frown, Chide, strik and fight them, mourn and Cry
> To Conquour them, but cannot them destroy. (I:39, ll. 1–6)

Compared with his own vileness, meditating on the saints' "White Raiment" in heaven, Taylor expressed embarrassment at wearing such a wedding dress. He would be "A Dirt ball dresst in milk white Lawn" (I:46, l. 7). Taylor began one meditation, "What rocky heart is mine?" and confessed he could "hardly raise a Sigh to blow down Sin" (I:36, ll. 1, 6). Recollecting that "In Him should all Fulness Dwell" (Col. 1:19), Taylor felt "That's Fulness, This it's Emptiness . . . My Damps do out my fire" (I:27, ll. 3, 5). His characteristic expression when he compared his vile unworthiness with Christ's love was "But, oh!" as in Meditation 1: "But oh! my streight'ned Breast! my Lifeless Sparke! (l. 15). The same words could be used as a prayer:

> But oh! thy Wisdom, Lord! thy Grace! thy Praise!
> Open mine Eyes to see the same aright. (I:35, ll. 37–38)

And, "Oh! make it so" (I:44, l. 31). As an expression of praise, such an outburst also emphasized the superiority of Christ to all earthly loves. Considering Christ's "Cheeks . . . as a Bed of Spices" (Cant. 5:13), Taylor denied that "Earthly Dunghills" could "yield more sweet Delight" (II:120, l. 21) than the love of Christ.

> But Oh! my Lord, I do abhorr such notes
> That do besmoot thy Beautious Cheeks like Spice.
> (ll. 37–38)

The chasm between the lovers, therefore, caused Taylor to yearn for Christ the more.

> When I, Lord, eye thy Joy, and my Love, small,
> My heart gives in: what now? Strange! Sure I love thee!
> (I:48, ll. 1–2)

His cry, "Oh! that I ever felt what I profess" (I:35, l. 1), was accompanied by astonishment that the bond yet held firm. "Lord am I thine? art thou, Lord, mine? So rich!" (l. 7). Indeed, the chasm intensified his love for Christ, for the competing loves of this world appeared as "toys," "Puddle Water," and so much urine—"drops dropt in a Closestoole pan" (I:48, ll. 18, 14, 36). With a cry of "Avant adultrous Love" (l. 12), Taylor rededicated himself to singing love songs to his mystic Spouse—

> Thy joyes in mee will make my Pipes to play
> For joy thy Praise while teather'd to my clay. (ll. 41–42)

—and fantasizing love's consummation—

> Make me the Couch on which thy Love doth ly.
> Lord make my heart thy bed, thy heart make mine.
> Thy Love bed in my heart, bed mine in thine. (I:35:46–48)

The chasm separating Taylor from his Lover, together with the preparatory nature of his meditations, evoked within him an eschatological and thoroughly hopeful spirituality. His language only appears conditional and tentative; Taylor was humbly and confidently receptive as he anticipated the sacrament and the heavenly banquet to which it points.

> I fain would love and better love thee should,
> If 'fore me thou thy Loveliness unfold. (I:35, ll. 41–42)

Taylor knew that this was precisely what God would do the next morning
at the Lord's Table. At the conclusion of one meditative poem after another
he used this language of "if . . . then" to express his humble hope and joy.

> If thou Conduct mee in thy Fathers Wayes,
> I'le be the Golden Trumpet of thy Praise. (I:24, ll. 41–42)

> I then shall sweetly tune thy Praise, When hee
> In Whom all Fulness dwells, doth dwell in mee.
> (I:27, ll. 47–48)

> Spring up oh Well. My Cup with Grace make flow.
> Thy Drops will on my Vessell ting thy Praise.
> I'le sing this Song, when I these Drops Embrace.
> My Vessell now's a Vessell of thy Grace.
> (I:28, ll. 27–30)

> Make mee thy Graft, be thou my Golden Stock.
> Thy Glory then I'le make my fruits and Crop.
> (I:29, ll. 41–42)

> Oh! Happy me, if thou wilt Crown me thus.
> Oh! naughty heart! What swell with Sin? fy, fy.
> Oh! Gracious Lord, me pardon: do not Crush
> Me all to mammocks: Crown and not destroy.
> I'le tune thy Prayses while this Crown doth come.
> Thy Glory bring I tuckt up in my Songe. (I:44, ll. 37–42)

> I'le bring thee praise, buskt up in Songs perfum'de
> When thou with grace my Soule hast sweetly tun'de.
> (II:43, ll. 53–54)

Taylor's is the language of promise, that is, of covenant. In one sense, the
promise would be kept perfectly only in heaven, but Taylor's promise also
had immediate bearing upon his life. His vow—

> If I be fed with this rich fare, I will
> Say Grace to thee with Songs of holy Skill. (II:81, ll. 65–66)

—was conditional only upon his faithful presence at the Table the next
morning.

Taylor's promises were predicated on Christ's own unconditional promise to be present in the sacrament. By binding himself so intimately with Christ in the Supper, Taylor vowed that his life would be one of praise and thanksgiving. Although from the literary viewpoint he confessed his "Metaphors are but dull Tacklings tag'd / With ragged Non-Sense" (II:36, ll. 31–32), from the spiritual viewpoint they were something else. As part of his meditative exercises, the poetry became the instrument by which Taylor could "serve [God's] Sacred selfe with Sacred art" (l. 40). He offered his poems to God not for their excellence but as prayerful sacrifice—"my tunes as fume, / From off this Altar rise to thee Most High" (II:18, ll. 61–62)—and asked that Christ "sanctify my gifts" (l. 58). The sacrament and the meditation preparing for its faithful reception were the means of Taylor's sanctification, progressive growth in the "holy Skill" of loving God. The blessings of sanctifying grace operated on Taylor's heart not only to allow him to yearn for heavenly consummation, but to envision God clearly enough to praise him poetically year after year. The same

> Raptures of Love, surprizing Loveliness,
>   That burst through heavens all, in Rapid Flashes
>   (I:14–15, ll. 1–2)

in the person of Christ melted Taylor's soul as he meditated, prayed, and wrote his poems. He rejoiced to feel his affections "break / Out in a rapid Flame of Love to thee" (l. 46).

The poetry of Anne Bradstreet and Edward Taylor suggests how hopeful the prospect is of a comprehensive study of Protestant and Catholic spirituality. The Puritan contemplative meditated and prayed according to classic methodology, employed traditional language, and experienced high spiritual states. English Puritan and Continental Catholic spirituality flowered simultaneously, so the one is not derivative of the other except in the way, for example, St. Francis de Sales' writings derived from centuries of tradition. There is a common, ecumenical history of Christian spirituality. Puritans and Catholics belonged, as Bouyer said, to a "community of religious thought and culture" overarching dogmatic differences.

At the same time, the temptation to collapse the two completely into a single system ignores the real theological differences that separated the great branches of Western Christendom. Protestant anthropology and the Reformed doctrine of sanctification led Puritans to embrace a lay spirituality, based on close study of the Bible, rooted in sanctified love for the people and things of this world, and generated by the crisis of their mortality. Puritanism was a spirituality of the householder, in a family and home blessed by God, yet accepting the inevitable loss of everything in this earthly home. Anne Bradstreet exemplified Puritan spirituality as she watched her house, its furnishings, and "that store [she] counted best," her meditative poetry, rise to the heavens. Edward Taylor adopted a lifelong discipline of writing meditative poetry in response to grief and the crisis of the finitude of human love. The hope of eternal love shone from above, where sanctified believers received the blessings of union with Christ in glorification.

Texts

ANNE BRADSTREET:
OCCASIONAL MEDITATIONS

Occasional meditations were undertaken by Puritans in response to or within the context of specific occurrences in their daily lives (see Introduction, p. 19). Anne Bradstreet habitually composed poems as expressions of these private or "secret" devotions. Often the occasions of her meditations were grief, anxiety, or loneliness, although she also reflected upon her life with thanksgiving to God. The first thirteen poems in this section were published in her posthumous Several Poems *(Boston, 1678). The remaining poems survived in manuscript form in the hand of her son Simon Bradstreet and were finally published in John Harvard Ellis, ed.,* The Works of Anne Bradstreet in Prose and Verse *(Cambridge, Mass., 1867). Included here also, from this same source, are selections from Anne Bradstreet's prose meditations and her spiritual autobiography composed for her family.*

UPON A FIT OF SICKNESS, *ANNO.* 1632
ÆTATIS SUÆ, 19.

Twice ten years old, not fully told
    Since nature gave me breath,
My race is run, my thread is spun,
    lo here is fatal Death.
All men must dye, and so must I   5
    this cannot be revok'd
For Adams sake, this word God spake
    when he so high provok'd.
Yet live I shall, this life's but small,
    in place of highest bliss,   10

Where I shall have all I can crave,
  no life is like to this.
For what's this life, but care and strife?
  since first we came from womb,
Our strength doth waste, our time doth haste,   *15*
  and then we go to th' Tomb.
O Bubble blast, how long can'st last?
  that alwayes art a breaking,
No sooner blown, but dead and gone,
  ev'n as a word that's speaking.   *20*
O whil'st I live, this grace me give,
  I doing good may be,
Then deaths arrest, I shall count best,
  because it's thy decree;
Bestow much cost there's nothing lost,   *25*
  to make Salvation sure,
O great's the gain, though got with pain,
  comes by profession pure.
The race is run, the field is won,
  the victory's mine I see,   *30*
For ever know, thou envious foe,
  the foyle belongs to thee.

TEXT NOTES:
Line 32: *Foyle* (foil), defeat.

UPON SOME DISTEMPER OF BODY.

In anguish of my heart repleat with woes,
And wasting pains, which best my body knows,
In tossing slumbers on my wakeful bed,
Bedrencht with tears that flow'd from mournful head.
Till nature had exhausted all her store,   *5*
Then eyes lay dry, disabled to weep more;
And looking up unto his Throne on high,
Who sendeth help to those in misery;
He chac'd away those clouds, and let me see
My Anchor cast i'th' vale with safety.   *10*
He eas'd my Soul of woe, my flesh of pain,
And brought me to the shore from troubled Main.

BEFORE THE BIRTH OF ONE OF HER CHILDREN.

All things within this fading world hath end,
Adversity doth still our joyes attend;
No tyes so strong, no friends so dear and sweet,
But with deaths parting blow is sure to meet.
The sentence past is most irrevocable,   *5*
A common thing, yet oh inevitable;
How soon, my Dear, death may my steps attend,
How soon't may be thy Lot to lose thy friend,
We both are ignorant, yet love bids me
These farewell lines to recommend to thee,   *10*
That when that knot's unty'd that made us one,
I may seem thine, who in effect am none.
And if I see not half my dayes that's due,
What nature would, God grant to yours and you;
The many faults that well you know I have,   *15*
Let be interr'd in my oblivious grave;
If any worth or virtue were in me,
Let that live freshly in thy memory.
And when thou feel'st no grief, as I no harms,
Yet love thy dead, who long lay in thine arms: *20*
And when thy loss shall be repaid with gains
Look to my little babes my dear remains.
And if thou love thy self, or loved'st me
These O protect from step Dames injury.
And if chance to thine eyes shall bring this verse,   *25*
With some sad sighs honour my absent Herse;
And kiss this paper for thy loves dear sake,
Who with salt tears this last Farewel did take.

TO MY DEAR AND LOVING HUSBAND.

If ever two were one, then surely we.
If ever man were lov'd by wife, then thee;
If ever wife was happy in a man,
Compare with me ye women if you can.
I prize thy love more then whole Mines of gold,   *5*
Or all the riches that the East doth hold.
My love is such that Rivers cannot quench,
Nor ought but love from thee, give recompence.

Thy love is such I can no way repay,
The heavens reward thee manifold I pray.   *10*
Then while we live, in love lets so persever,
That when we live no more, we may live ever.

TEXT NOTES:
Line 4: Read, "Compare with me the women if you can"; not "Compare with me,
ye [i.e. 'you'] women, if you can," as in Hensley, ed., *The Works of Anne
Bradstreet*, p. 225.

A LETTER TO HER HUSBAND, ABSENT UPON PUBLICK EMPLOYMENT.

My head, my heart, mine Eyes, my life, nay more,
My joy, my Magazine of earthly store,
If two be one, as surely thou and I,
How stayest thou there, whilst I at *Ipswich* lye?
So many steps, head from the heart to sever   *5*
If but a neck, soon should we be together:
I like the earth this season, mourn in black,
My Sun is gone so far in's Zodiack,
Whom whilst I 'joy'd, nor storms, nor frosts I felt,
His warmth such frigid colds did cause to melt.   *10*
My chilled limbs now nummed lye forlorn;
Return, return sweet *Sol* from *Capricorn;*
In this dead time, alas, what can I more
Then view those fruits which through thy heat I bore?
Which sweet contentment yield me for a space,   *15*
True living Pictures of their Fathers face.
O strange effect! now thou art *Southward* gone,
I weary grow, the tedious day so long;
But when thou *Northward* to me shalt return,
I wish my Sun may never set, but burn   *20*
Within the Cancer of my glowing breast,
The welcome house of him my dearest guest.
Where ever, ever stay, and go not thence,
Till natures sad decree shall call thee hence;
Flesh of thy flesh, bone of thy bone,   *25*
I here, thou there, yet both but one.

TEXT NOTES:
Line 8: *My Sun,* i.e. her husband.
Line 9: *joy'd* enjoyed

ANOTHER ("PHOEBUS MAKE HASTE").

Phoebus make haste, the day's too long, be gone,
The silent night's the fittest time for moan;
But stay this once, unto my suit give ear,
And tell my griefs in either Hemisphere:
(And if the whirling of thy wheels don't drown'd)   *5*
The woful accents of my doleful sound,
If in thy swift Carrier thou canst make stay,
I crave this boon, this Errand by the way,
Commend me to the man more lov'd than life,
Shew him the sorrows of his widdowed wife;   *10*
My dumpish thoughts, my groans, my brakish tears
My sobs, my longing hopes, my doubting fears,
And if he love, how can he there abide?
My Interest's more than all the world beside.
He that can tell the stars or Ocean sand,   *15*
Or all the grass that in the Meads do stand,
The leaves in th' woods, the hail or drops of rain,
Or in a corn-field number every grain,
Or every mote that in the sun-shine hops,
May count my sighs, and number all my drops: *20*
Tell him, the countless steps that thou dost trace,
That once a day, thy Spouse thou mayst embrace;
And when thou canst not treat by loving mouth,
Thy rayes afar, salute her from the south.
But for one moneth I see no day (poor soul)   *25*
Like those far scituate under the pole,
Which day by day long wait for thy arise,
O how they joy when thou dost light the skyes.
O *Phoebus,* hadst thou but thus long from thine
Restrain'd the beams of thy beloved shine,   *30*
At thy return, if so thou could'st or durst
Behold a Chaos blacker then the first.
Tell him here's worse then a confused matter,
His little world's a fathom under water,
Nought but the fervor of his ardent beams   *35*
Hath power to dry the torrent of these streams.
Tell him I would say more, but cannot well,
Oppressed minds, abruptest tales do tell.
Now post with double speed, mark what I say,
By all our loves conjure him not to stay.   *40*

TEXT NOTES:
Line 1: *Phoebus,* the sun personified.
Line 7: *Carrier.* (career), course, progress.

ANOTHER ("AS LOVING HIND").

As loving Hind that (Hartless) wants her Deer,
Scuds through the woods and Fern with harkning ear,
Perplext, in every bush and nook doth pry,
Her dearest Deer, might answer ear or eye;
So doth my anxious soul, which now doth miss, 5
A dearer Dear (far dearer Heart) than this.
Still wait with doubts, and hopes, and failing eye,
His voice to hear, or person to discry.
Or as the pensive Dove doth all alone
(On withered bough) most uncouthly bemoan 10
The absence of her Love, and loving Mate,
Whose loss hath made her so unfortunate:
Ev'n thus doe I, with many a deep sad groan
Bewail my turtle true, who now is gone,
His presence and his safe return, still wooes, 15
With thousand dolefull sighs and mournfull Cooes.
Or as the loving Mullet, that true Fish,
Her fellow lost, nor joy nor life do wish,
But lanches on that shore, there for to dye,
Where she her captive husband doth espy. 20
Mine being gone, I lead a joyless life,
I have a loving phere, yet seem no wife:
But worst of all, to him can't steer my course,
I here, he there, alas, both kept by force:
Return my Dear, my joy, my only Love, 25
Unto thy Hinde, thy Mullet and thy Dove,
Who neither joyes in pasture, house nor streams.
The substance gone, O me, these are but dreams.
Together at one Tree, oh let us brouze,
And like two Turtles roost within one house, 30
And like the Mullets in one River glide,
Let's still remain but one, till death divide.

{ *Thy loving Love and Dearest Dear,*
  At home, abroad, and every where.

TEXT NOTES:
Line 2: *Scuds,* runs, darts.
Line 14: *Turtle,* turtle-dove.
Line 22: *Phere,* companion.

TO HER FATHER WITH SOME VERSES.

Most truly honoured, and as truly dear,
If worth in me, or ought I do appear,
Who can of right better demand the same?
Then may your worthy self from whom it came.
The principle might yield a greater sum,   5
Yet handled ill, amounts but to this crum;
My stock's so small, I know not how to pay,
My Bond remains in force unto this day;
Yet for part payment take this simple mite,
Where nothing's to be had Kings loose their right   10
Such is my debt, I may not say forgive,
But as I can, I'le pay it while I live:
Such is my bond, none can discharge but I,
Yet paying is not payd until I dye.

IN REFERENCE TO HER CHILDREN, 23. JUNE, 1659.

I had eight birds hatcht in one nest,
Four Cocks there were, and Hens the rest,
I nurst them up with pain and care,
Nor cost, nor labour did I spare,
Till at the last they felt their wing.   5
Mounted the Trees, and learn'd to sing;
Chief of the Brood then took his flight,
To Regions far, and left me quite:
My mournful chirps I after send,
Till he return, or I do end,   10
Leave not thy nest, thy Dam and Sire,
Fly back and sing amidst this Quire.
My second bird did take her flight,
And with her mate flew out of sight;
Southward they both their course did bend,   15
And Seasons twain they there did spend:

Till after blown by *Southern* gales,
They *Norward* steer'd with filled sayles.
A prettier bird was no where seen,
Along the Beach among the treen.   20
I have a third of colour white,
On whom I plac'd no small delight;
Coupled with mate loving and true,
Hath also bid her Dam adieu:
And where *Aurora* first appears,   25
She now hath percht, to spend her years;
One to the Academy flew
To chat among that learned crew:
Ambition moves still in his breast
That he might chant above the rest,   30
Striving for more than to do well,
That nightingales he might excell.
My fifth, whose down is yet scarce gone
Is 'mongst the shrubs and bushes flown,
And as his wings increase in strength,   35
On higher boughs he'l pearch at length.
My other three, still with me nest,
Untill they'r grown, then as the rest,
Or here or there, they'l take their flight,
As is ordain'd, so shall they light.   40
If birds could weep, then would my tears
Let others know what are my fears
Lest this my brood some harm should catch,
And be surpriz'd for want of watch,
Whilst pecking corn, and void of care   45
They fall un'wares in Fowlers snare:
Or whilst on trees they sit and sing,
Some untoward boy at them do fling:
Or whilst allur'd with bell and glass,
The net be spread, and caught, alas.   50
Or least by Lime-twigs they be foyl'd,
Or by some greedy hawks be spoyl'd.
O would my young, ye saw my breast,
And knew what thoughts there sadly rest,
Great was my pain when I you bred,   55
Great was my care, when I you fed,
Long did I keep you soft and warm,

And with my wings kept off all harm,
My cares are more, and fears than ever,
My throbs such now, as 'fore were never: *60*
Alas my birds, you wisdome want,
Of perils you are ignorant,
Oft times in grass, on trees, in flight,
Sore accidents on you may light.
O to your safety have an eye,   *65*
So happy may you live and die:
Mean while my dayes in tunes I'le spend,
Till my weak layes with me shall end.
In shady woods I'le sit and sing,
And things that past, to mind I'le bring.   *70*
Once young and pleasant, as are you,
But former toyes (no joyes) adieu.
My age I will not once lament,
But sing, my time so near is spent.
And from the top bough take my flight,   *75*
Into a country beyond sight,
Where old ones, instantly grow young,
And there with Seraphims set song:
No seasons cold, nor storms they see;
But spring lasts to eternity,   *80*
When each of you shall in your nest
Among your young ones take your rest,
In chirping language, oft them tell,
You had a Dam that lov'd you well,
That did what could be done for young,   *85*
And nurst you up till you were strong,
And 'fore she once would let you fly,
She shew'd you joy and misery;
Taught what was good, and what was ill,
What would save life, and what would kill?   *90*
Thus gone, amongst you I may live,
And dead, yet speak, and counsel give:
Farewel my birds, farewel adieu,
I happy am, if well with you.

TEXT NOTES:
Title: Ellis gives date as 1656, an error that was corrected in copies he did not have
   at hand. (McElvatz and Roff, *Complete Works*, 247.)

Line 7: *Chief of the Brood,* see her poems, "Upon my Son Samuel his goeing for England, Novem. 6, 1657," and "On my Sons Return out of England, July 17, 1661."

Line 11: *Dam and Sire,* mother and father.

Line 13: *My second bird,* Dorothy, who married the Rev. Seaborn Cotton in 1654 and settled first in Connecticut and then New Hampshire.

Line 20: *Treen,* trees.

Line 21: *A third,* Sarah, married to Richard Hubbard of Ipswich.

Line 27: *One to the Academy,* Simon entered Harvard in June 1656. It was Simon who transcribed many of his mother's poems.

Line 33: *My fifth,* Dudley, according to Ellis actually her seventh, born in 1648 (Ellis, *Works of A.B.,* lxvii–lxviii).

Line 37: *My other three,* Hannah, Mercy, and John (b. 1652).

Line 51: *Least,* lest.

IN MEMORY OF MY DEAR GRAND-CHILD ELIZABETH BRADSTREET,
WHO DECEASED AUGUST, 1665
BEING A YEAR AND HALF OLD.

Farewel dear babe, my hearts too much content,
Farewel sweet babe, the pleasure of mine eye,
Farewel fair flower that for a space was lent,
Then ta'en away unto Eternity.
Blest babe why should I once bewail thy fate,   5
Or sigh thy dayes so soon were terminate;
Sith thou art setled in an Everlasting state.

2.

By nature Trees do rot when they are grown.
And Plumbs and Apples thoroughly ripe do fall,
And Corn and grass are in their season mown,   10
And time brings down what is both strong and tall.
But plants new set to be eradicate,
And buds new blown, to have so short a date,
Is by his hand alone that guides nature and fate.

TEXT NOTES:
Title: *Elizabeth Bradstreet,* first child of Samuel.
Line 7: *Sith,* seeing that.

IN MEMORY OF MY DEAR GRAND-CHILD ANNE BRADSTREET.
WHO DECEASED JUNE 20. 1669
BEING THREE YEARS AND SEVEN MONTHS OLD.

With troubled heart and trembling hand I write,
The Heavens have chang'd to sorrow my delight.
How oft with disappointment have I met,
When I on fading things my hopes have set?
Experience might 'fore this have made me wise,   5
To value things according to their price:
Was ever stable joy yet found below?
Or perfect bliss without mixture of woe.
I knew she was but as a withering flour,
That's here to day, perhaps gone in an hour;   10
Like as a bubble, or the brittle glass,
Or like a shadow turning as it was.

More fool than I to look on that was lent,
As if mine own, when thus impermanent.
Farewel dear child, thou ne're shall come to me,   15
But yet a while, and I shall go to thee;
Mean time my throbbing heart's chear'd up with this
Thou with thy Saviour art in endless bliss.

TEXT NOTES:
Title: *Anne Bradstreet*, second child of Samuel.
Line 9: *Flour*, flower.

ON MY DEAR GRAND-CHILD SIMON BRADSTREET,
WHO DYED ON 16. NOVEMBER 1669. BEING BUT
A MONETH, AND ONE DAY OLD.

No sooner come, but gone, and fal'n asleep,
Acquaintance short, yet parting caus'd us weep,
Three flours, two scarcely blown, the last i'th' bud,
Cropt by th' Almighties hand; yet is he good,
With dreadful awe before him let's be mute,   5
Such was his will, but why, let's not dispute,
With humble hearts and mouths put in the dust,
Let's say he's merciful as well as just.

He will return, and make up all our losses,
And smile again, after our bitter crosses.   *10*
Go pretty babe, go rest with Sisters twain
Among the blest in endless joyes remain.

TEXT NOTES:
Title: *Simon Bradstreet,* Samuel's fourth child.
Line 3: *Flours,* flowers.

TO THE MEMORY OF MY DEAR DAUGHTER IN LAW,
MRS. MERCY BRADSTREET, WHO DECEASED SEPT. 6. 1669
IN THE 28. YEAR OF HER AGE.

And live I still to see Relations gone,
And yet survive to sound this wailing tone;
Ah, woe is me, to write thy Funeral Song,
Who might in reason yet have lived long,
I saw the branches lopt the Tree now fall,   *5*
I stood so nigh, it crusht me down withal;
My bruised heart lies sobbing at the Root,
That thou dear Son hath lost both Tree and fruit:
Thou then on Seas sailing to forreign Coast;
Was ignorant what riches thou hadst lost.   *10*
But ah too soon those heavy tydings fly,
To strike thee with amazing misery;
Oh how I sympathize with thy sad heart,
And in thy griefs still bear a second part:
I lost a daughter dear, but thou a wife,   *15*
Who lov'd thee more (it seem'd) than her own life.
Thou being gone, she longer could not be,
Because her Soul she'd sent along with thee.
One week she only past in pain and woe,
And then her sorrows all at once did go;   *20*
A Babe she left before, she soar'd above,
The fifth and last pledg of her dying love,
E're nature would, it hither did arrive,
No wonder it no longer did survive.
So with her Children four, she's now a rest,   *25*
All freed from grief (I trust) among the blest;
She one hath left, a joy to thee and me,
The Heavens vouchsafe she may so ever be.

Chear up (dear Son), thy fainting bleeding heart,
In him alone, that caused all this smart;   30
What though thy strokes full sad and grievous be,
He knows it is the best for thee and me.

TEXT NOTES:

Title: *Mrs. Mercy Bradstreet,* wife of Samuel. Because the poem refers to the death
of an infant immediately prior to her own death—lines 21–24, a child born
Sept. 3, 1670—Ellis suggests that the date 1669 is a misprint for 1670 (Ellis,
Works of A.B., 407).

TO MY DEAR CHILDREN.

This Book by Any yet unread,
I leave for you when I am dead,
That, being gone, here you may find
What was your liveing mother's mind.
Make use of what I leave in Love   5
And God shall blesse you from above.

TEXT NOTES:

Line 1: *This Book,* a manuscript book of devotional poetry, prose meditations, and
spiritual autobiography, now lost, which survived in Simon Bradstreet's tran-
scription. The poems and meditations are found below.

"BY NIGHT WHEN OTHERS SOUNDLY SLEPT."

I.

By night when others soundly slept,
And had at once both ease and Rest,
My waking eyes were open kept,
And so to lye I found it best.

II.

I sought him whom my Soul did Love,   5
With tears I sought him earnestly;
He bow'd his ear down from Above,
In vain I did not seek or cry.

III.

My hungry Soul he fill'd with Good,
He in his Bottle putt my teares,   *10*
My smarting wounds washt in his blood,
And banisht thence my Doubts and feares.

IV.

What to my Saviour shall I give,
Who freely hath done this for me?
I'le serve him here whilst I shall live,   *15*
And Love him to Eternity.

TEXT NOTES:
Line 10: *Bottle . . . teares,* see Psalm 56:8.

FOR DELIVERANCE FROM A FEAVER.

When Sorrowes had begyrt me round,
   And Paines within and out,
When in my flesh no part was sound,
   Then didst thou rid me out.

My burning flesh in sweat did boyle,   *5*
   My aking head did break;
From side to side for ease I toyle,
   So faint I could not speak.

Beclouded was my Soul with fear
   Of thy Displeasure sore,   *10*
Nor could I read my Evidence
   Which oft I read before.

Hide not thy face from me, I cry'd,
   From Burnings keep my soul;
Thou know'st my heart, and hast me try'd;   *15*
   I on thy Mercyes Rowl.

O, heal my Soul, thou know'st I said,
   Tho' flesh consume to nought;
What tho' in dust it shall bee lay'd,
   To Glory't shall bee brought.   *20*

Thou heardst, thy rod thou didst remove,
   And spar'd my Body frail,
Thou shew'st to me thy tender Love,
   My heart no more might quail.

O, Praises to my mighty God,   *25*
    Praise to my Lord, I say,
Who hath redeem'd my Soul from pitt:
    Praises to him for Aye!

TEXT NOTES:

Line 3: *Sound,* although other editions read this as "found," I believe the first letter
    is a long "s."

Line 4: *Rid,* deliver, rescue.

Line 13: *Hide not thy Face,* see Psalm 30, upon which this meditation seems to be
    based.

Line 16: *Rowle* (roll), trust; see *Bay Psalm Book* translation of Psalm 22:8.

FROM ANOTHER SORE FITT.

In my distresse I sought the Lord,
When nought on Earth could comfort give;
And when my Soul these things abhor'd,
Then, Lord, thou said'st unto me, Live.

Thou knowest the sorrowes that I felt,   *5*
My plaints and Groanes were heard of Thee,
And how in sweat I seem'd to melt;
Thou help'st and thou regardest me.

My wasted flesh thou didst restore,
My feeble loines didst gird with strength;   *10*
Yea, when I was most low and poor,
I said I shall praise thee at lenght.

What shall I render to my God
For all his Bounty shew'd to me,
Even for his mercyes in his rod,   *15*
Where pitty most of all I see?

My heart I wholly give to Thee:
O make it fruitfull, faithfull Lord!
My life shall dedicated bee
To praise in thought, in Deed, in Word.   *20*

Thou know'st no life I did require
Longer then still thy Name to praise,
Nor ought on Earth worthy Desire,
In drawing out these wretched Dayes.

Thy Name and praise to celebrate,   *25*
O Lord! for aye is my request.
O, graunt I doe it in this state,
And then with thee which is the Best.

MEDITATIONS WHEN MY SOUL HATH BEEN REFRESHED WITH THE
CONSOLATIONS WHICH THE WORLD KNOWES NOT.

Lord, why should I doubt any more when thou hast given me such
assured Pledges of thy Love? First, thou art my Creator, I thy creature; thou
my master, I thy servant. But hence arises not my comfort: Thou art my
Father, I thy child. Yee shall [be] my Sons and Daughters, saith the Lord
Almighty. Christ is my Brother; I ascend unto my Father and your Father,
unto my God and your God. But least this should not bee enough, thy maker
is thy husband. Nay, more, I am a member of his Body; he, my head. Such
Priviledges, had not the Word of Truth made them known, who or where
is the man that durst in his heart have presumed to have thought it? So won-
derfull are these thoughts that my spirit failes in me at the consideration
thereof; and I am confounded to think that God, who hath done so much
for me, should have so little from me. But this is my comfort, when I come
into Heaven, I shall understand perfectly what he hath done for me, and
then shall I bee able to praise him as I ought. Lord, haveing this hope, let
me purefie myself as thou art Pure, and let me bee no more affraid of Death,
but even desire to bee dissolved, and bee with thee, which is best of All.

July 8th, 1656.

I had a sore fitt of fainting, which lasted 2 or 3 dayes, but not in that
extremity which at first it took me, and so much the sorer it was to me be-
cause my dear husband was from home (who is my chiefest comforter on
Earth); but my God, who never failed me, was not absent, but helped me,
and gratiously manifested his Love to me, which I dare not passe by without
Remembrance, that it may bee a support to me when I shall have occasion
to read this hereafter, and to others that shall read it when I shall possesse
that I now hope for, that so they may bee encouragd to trust in him who is
the only Portion of his Servants.

O Lord, let me never forgett thy Goodnes, nor question thy faithfullnes
to me, for thou art my God: Thou hast said, and shall not I believe it?

Thou hast given me a pledge of that Inheritance thou hast promised to
bestow upon me. O, never let Satan prevail against me, but strengthen my

faith in Thee, 'till I shall attain the end of my hopes, even the Salvation of my Soul. Come, Lord Jesus; come quickly.

"WHAT GOD IS LIKE TO HIM I SERVE."

What God is like to him I serve,
    What Saviour like to mine?
O, never let me from thee swerve,
    For truly I am thine.

My thankfull mouth shall speak thy praise,   *5*
    My Tongue shall talk of Thee:
On High my heart, O, doe thou raise,
    For what thou'st done for me.

Goe, Worldlings, to your Vanities,
    And heathen to your Gods;   *10*
Let them help in Adversities,
    And sanctefye their rods.

My God he is not like to yours,
    Your selves shall Judges bee;
I find his Love, I know his Pow'r,   *15*
    A Succourer of mee.

He is not man that he should lye,
    Nor son of man to unsay;
His word he plighted hath on high,
    And I shall live for aye.   *20*

And for his sake that faithfull is,
    That dy'd but now doth live,
The first and last, that lives for aye,
    Me lasting life shall give.

TEXT NOTES:
Line 18: *Unsay,* deny; retract.

"MY SOUL, REJOICE THOU IN THY GOD."

My soul, rejoice thou in thy God,
    Boast of him all the Day,
Walk in his Law, and kisse his Rod,
    Cleave close to him alway.

What tho' thy outward Man decay,   *5*
    Thy inward shall waxe strong;
Thy body vile it shall bee chang'd,
    And glorious made ere-long.

With Angels-wings thy Soul shall mount
    To Blisse unseen by Eye,   *10*
And drink at unexhausted fount
    Of Joy unto Eternity.

Thy teares shall All bee dryed up,
    Thy Sorrowes all shall flye;
Thy Sinns shall ne'r bee summon'd up,   *15*
    Nor come in memory.

Then shall I know what thou hast done
    For me, unworthy me,
And praise thee shall ev'n as I ought,
    For wonders that I see.   *20*

Base World, I trample on thy face,
    Thy Glory I despise,
No gain I find in ought below,
    For God hath made me wise.

Come, Jesus, quickly, Blessed Lord,   *25*
    Thy face when shall I see?
O let me count each hour a Day
    'Till I dissolved bee.

August 28, 1656.

After much weaknes and sicknes when my spirits were worn out, and many times my faith weak likewise, the Lord was pleased to uphold my drooping heart, and to manifest his Love to me; and this is that which stayes my Soul that this condition that I am in is the best for me, for God doth not afflict willingly, nor take delight in grieving the children of men: he hath no benefitt by my adversity, nor is he the better for my prosperity; but he doth it for my Advantage, and that I may bee a Gainer by it. And if he knowes that weaknes and a frail body is the best to make me a vessell fitt for his use, why should I not bare it, not only willingly but joyfully? The Lord knowes I dare not desire that health that somtimes I have had, least my heart should bee drawn from him, and sett upon the world.

Now I can wait, looking every day when my Saviour shall call for me. Lord graunt that while I live I may doe that service I am able in this frail

Body, and bee in continuall expectation of my change, and let me never forgett thy great Love to my soul so lately expressed, when I could lye down and bequeath my Soul to thee, and Death seem'd no terrible Thing. O let me ever see Thee that Art invisible, and I shall not bee unwilling to come, tho' by so rough a Messenger.

May 11, 1657.

I had a sore sicknes, and weaknes took hold of me, which hath by fitts lasted all this Spring till this 11 May, yet hath my God given me many a respite, and some ability to perform the Dutyes I owe to him, and the work of my famely.

Many a refreshment have I found in this my weary Pilgrimage, and in this valley of Baca many pools of water. That which now I cheifly labour for is a contented, thankfull heart under my affliction and weaknes, seing it is the will of God it should bee thus. Who am I that I should repine at his pleasure, especially seing it is for my spirituall advantage? for I hope my soul shall flourish while my body decayes, and the weaknes of this outward man shall bee a meanes to strenghten my inner man.

Yet a little while and he that shall come will come, and will not tarry.

"AS SPRING THE WINTER DOTH SUCCEED."

May 13, 1657.

> As spring the winter doth succeed,
> And leaves the naked Trees doe dresse,
> The earth all black is cloth'd in green;
> At sun-shine each their joy expresse.
>
> My Suns returned with healing wings.   5
> My Soul and Body doth rejoice;
> My heart exults, and praises sings
> To him that heard my wailing Voice.
>
> My winters past, my stormes are gone,
> And former clowdes seem now all fled;   10
> But, if they must eclipse again,
> I'le run where I was succoured.
>
> I have a shelter from the storm,
> A shadow from the fainting heat;
> I have accesse unto his Throne,   15
> Who is a God so wondrous great.

O hast thou made my Pilgrimage
Thus pleasant, fair, and good;
Bless'd me in Youth and elder Age,
My Baca made a springing flood?   *20*

I studious am what I shall doe,
To show my Duty with delight;
All I can give is but thine own,
And at the most a simple mite.

TEXT NOTES:

Line 5: *Suns . . . healing wings,* Malachi 4:2.
Line 20: *Baca,* Psalm 84:6.

UPON MY SON SAMUEL HIS GOEING FOR ENGLAND, NOVEMBER 6, 1657.

Thou mighty God of Sea and Land,
I here resigne into thy hand
The Son of Prayers, of vowes, of teares,
The child I stay'd for many yeares.
Thou heard'st me then, and gav'st him me;   *5*
Hear me again, I give him Thee.
He's mine, but more, O Lord, thine own,
For sure thy Grace on him is shown.
No freind I have like Thee to trust,
For mortall helpes are brittle Dust.   *10*
Preserve, O Lord, from stormes and wrack,
Protect him there, and bring him back;
And if thou shalt spare me a space,
That I again may see his face,
Then shall I celebrate thy Praise,   *15*
And Blesse the for't even all my Dayes.
If otherwise I goe to Rest,
Thy Will bee done, for that is best;
Perswade my heart I shall him see
For ever happefy'd with Thee.   *20*

TEXT NOTES:

Line 4: *Stay'd,* waited for. In her autobiographical narrative Bradstreet wrote: "It pleased God to keep me a long time without a child, which was a great grief

to me, and cost mee many prayers and tears before I obtained one'' (Ellis, *Works of A.B.*, 5).
Line 11: *Wrack,* shipwreck.
Line 13: *A space,* a period of time.
Line 16: *The,* thee.

May 11, 1661.

It hath pleased God to give me a long Time of respite for these 4 years that I have had no great fitt of sicknes, but this year, from the middle of January 'till May, I have been by fitts very ill and weak. The first of this month I had a feaver seat'd upon me which, indeed, was the longest and sorest that ever I had, lasting 4 dayes, and the weather being very hott made it the more tedious, but it pleased the Lord to support my heart in his goodnes, and to hear my Prayers, and to deliver me out of adversity. But, alas! I cannot render unto the Lord according to all his loving kindnes, nor take the cup of salvation with Thanksgiving as I ought to doe. Lord, Thou that knowest All things know'st that I desire to testefye my thankfullnes not only in word, but in Deed, that my Conversation may speak that thy vowes are upon me.

"MY THANKFULL HEART WITH GLORYING TONGUE."

My thankfull heart with glorying Tongue
    Shall celebrate thy Name,
Who hath restor'd, redeem'd, recur'd
    From sicknes, death, and Pain.

I cry'd thou seem'st to make some stay,   *5*
    I sought more earnestly;
And in due time thou succour'st me,
    And sent'st me help from High.

Lord, whilst my fleeting time shall last,
    Thy Goodnes let me Tell.   *10*
And new Experience I have gain'd,
    My future Doubts repell.

An humble, faitefull life, O Lord,
    For ever let me walk;
Let my obedience testefye,   *15*
    My Praise lyes not in Talk.

Accept, O Lord, my simple mite,
   For more I cannot give;
What thou bestow'st I shall restore,
   For of thine Almes I live.   *20*

TEXT NOTES:
Line 3: *Recur'd,* cured, healed.
Line 5: *Stay,* delay.
Line 13: *Faitefull,* faithful.
Line 17: *Mite,* see Mark 12:42; Luke 21:2.

FOR THE RESTORATION OF MY DEAR HUSBAND
FROM A BURNING AGUE, JUNE, 1661.

When feares and sorrowes me besett,
   Then did'st thou rid me out;
When heart did faint and spirits quail,
   Thou comforts me about.

Thou rais'st him up I feard to loose,   *5*
   Regav'st me him again:
Distempers thou didst chase away;
   With strength didst him sustain.

My thankfull heart, with Pen record
   The Goodnes of thy God;   *10*
Let thy obedience testefye
   He taught thee by his rod.

And with his staffe did thee support,
   That thou by both may'st learn;
And 'twixt the good and evill way,   *15*
   At last, thou mig'st discern.

Praises to him who hath not left
   My Soul as destitute;
Nor turnd his ear away from me,
   But graunted hath my Suit.   *20*

TEXT NOTES:
Line 2: *Rid me out,* delivered me.
Line 5: *Loose,* lose.
Line 16: *Mig'st,* mightest.

UPON MY DAUGHTER HANNAH WIGGIN
HER RECOVERY FROM A DANGEROUS FEAVER.

Bles't bee thy Name, who did'st restore
   To health my Daughter dear
When death did seem ev'n to approach,
   And life was ended near.

Graunt shee remember what thou'st done,   5
   And celebrate thy Praise;
And let her Conversation say,
   Shee loves thee all thy Dayes.

ON MY SONS RETURN OUT OF ENGLAND,
JULY 17, 1661.

All Praise to him who hath now turn'd
My feares to Joyes, my sighes to song,
My Teares to smiles, my sad to glad:
He's come for whom I waited long.

Thou did'st preserve him as he went;   5
In raging stormes did'st safely keep:
Did'st that ship bring to quiet Port.
The other sank low in the Deep.

From Dangers great thou did'st him free
Of Pyrates who were neer at hand;   10
And order'st so the adverse wind,
That he before them gott to Land.

In country strange thou did'st provide,
And freinds rais'd him in every Place;
And courtesies of sundry sorts   15
From such as 'fore nere saw his face.

In sicknes when he lay full sore,
His help and his Physitian wer't;
When royall ones that Time did dye,
Thou heal'dst his flesh, and cheer'd his heart.   20

From troubles and Incumbers Thou,
Without (all fraud), did'st sett him free,
That, without scandall, he might come
To th' Land of his Nativity.

On Eagles wings him hether brought   *25*
Thro' Want and Dangers manifold;
And thus hath graunted my Request,
That I thy Mercyes might behold.

O help me pay my Vowes, O Lord!
That ever I may thankfull bee,   *30*
And may putt him in mind of what
Tho'st done for him, and so for me.

In both our hearts erect a frame
Of Duty and of Thankfullnes,
That all thy favours great receiv'd,   *35*
Oure upright walking may expresse.

O Lord, graunt that I may never forgett thy Loving kindnes in this Particular, and how gratiously thou hast answered my Desires.

TEXT NOTES:

Line 8: *The other sank,* reference to the sinking of a ship that sailed for England about the same time as the one on which Samuel traveled. Several diary entries of the time mention the tragedy (Ellis, *Works of A.B.,* 29–30).

Line 19: *Royall ones,* reference to the deaths of a brother and a sister of Charles II shortly after his restoration (Ellis, *Works of A.B.,* 30–31).

Line 25: *On Eagles wings,* Exodus 19:4.

UPON MY DEAR AND LOVING HUSBAND

HIS GOEING INTO ENGLAND, JAN. 16, 1661.

O thou most high who rulest All,
    And hear'st the Prayers of Thine;
O hearken, Lord, unto my suit,
    And my Petition signe.

Into thy everlasting Armes   *5*
    Of mercy I commend
Thy servant, Lord. Keep and preserve
    My husband, my dear friend.

At thy command, O Lord, he went,
    Nor nought could keep him back;   *10*
Then let thy promis joy his heart:
    O help, and bee not slack.

Uphold my heart in Thee, O God,
   Thou art my strength and stay;
Thou see'st how weak and frail I am,   *15*
   Hide not thy face Away.

I, in obedience to thy Will,
   Thou knowest, did submitt;
It was my Duty so to doe,
   O Lord, accept of it.   *20*

Unthankfullnes for mercyes Past,
   Impute thou not to me;
O Lord, thou know'st my weak desire
   Was to sing Praise to Thee.

Lord, bee thou Pilott to the ship,   *25*
   And send them prosperous gailes;
In stormes and sicknes, Lord, preserve.
   Thy Goodnes never failes.

Unto thy work he hath in hand,
   Lord, graunt Thou good Successe   *30*
And favour in their eyes, to whom
   He shall make his Addresse.

Remember, Lord, thy folk whom thou
   To wildernesse hast brought;
Let not thine own Inheritance   *35*
   Bee sold away for Nought.

But Tokens of thy favour Give—
   With Joy send back my Dear,
That I, and all thy servants, may
   Rejoice with heavenly chear.   *40*

Lord, let my eyes see once Again
   Him whom thou gavest me,
That wee together may sing Praise
   for ever unto Thee.

And the Remainder of oure Dayes   *45*
   Shall consecrated bee,
With an engaged heart to sing
   All Praises unto Thee.

TEXT NOTES:
Title: *Jan. 16, 1661,* the year is Old Style, 1662 New Style.

IN MY SOLITARY HOURES
IN MY DEAR HUSBAND HIS ABSENCE.

O Lord, thou hear'st my dayly moan,
  And see'st my dropping teares:
My Troubles All are Thee before,
  My Longings and my feares.

Thou hetherto hast been my God;   5
  Thy help my soul hath found:
Tho' losse and sicknes me assail'd,
  Thro' the I've kept my Ground.

And thy Abode tho'st made with me;
  With Thee my Soul can talk   10
In secrett places, Thee I find,
  Where I doe kneel or walk.

Tho' husband dear bee from me gone,
  Whom I doe love so well;
I have a more beloved one   15
  Whose comforts far excell.

O stay my heart on thee, my God,
  Uphold my fainting Soul!
And, when I know not what to doe,
  I'll on thy mercyes roll.   20

My weaknes, thou do'st know full well,
  Of Body and of mind.
I, in this world, no comfort have,
  But what from Thee I find.

Tho' children thou hast given me,   25
  And freinds I have also:
Yet, if I see Thee not thro' them,
  They are no Joy, but woe.

O shine upon me, blessed Lord,
  Ev'n for my Saviour's sake;   30
In Thee Alone is more then All,
  And there content I'll take.

O hear me, Lord, in this Request,
  As thou before ha'st done:
Bring back my husband, I beseech,   35
  As thou didst once my Sonne.

So shall I celebrate thy Praise,
  Ev'n while my Dayes shall last;
And talk to my Beloved one
  Of all thy Goodnes past.   *40*

So both of us thy Kindnes, Lord,
  With Praises shall recount,
And serve Thee better then before,
  Whose Blessings thus surmount.

But give me, Lord, a better heart,   *45*
  Then better shall I bee,
To pay the vowes which I doe owe
  For ever unto Thee.

Unlesse thou help, what can I doe
  But still my frailty show?   *50*
If thou assist me, Lord, I shall
  Return Thee what I owe.

TEXT NOTES:
Line 8: *Thro' the,* through thee.
Line 20: *Roll,* trust.

IN THANKFULL ACKNOWLEDGMENT FOR THE LETTERS I RECEIVED
FROM MY HUSBAND OUT OF ENGLAND.

O Thou that hear'st the Prayers of Thine,
And 'mongst them hast regarded Mine,
Hast heard my cry's, and seen my Teares;
Hast known my doubts and All my Feares.

Thou hast releiv'd my fainting heart,   *5*
Nor payd me after my desert;
Thou hast to shore him safely brought
For whom I thee so oft besought.

Thou was the Pilott to the ship,
And rais'd him up when he was sick;   *10*
And hope thou'st given of good successe,
In this his Buisnes and Addresse;

And that thou wilt return him back,
Whose presence I so much doe lack.
For All these mercyes I thee Praise,   *15*
And so desire ev'n all my Dayes.

IN THANKFULL REMEMBRANCE FOR MY DEAR HUSBANDS
SAFE ARRIVALL SEPT. 3, 1662.

What shall I render to thy Name,
  Or how thy Praises speak;
My thankes how shall I testefye?
  O Lord, thou know'st I'm weak.

I ow so much, so little can   *5*
  Return unto thy Name,
Confusion seases on my Soul,
  And I am fill'd with shame.

O thou that hearest Prayers, Lord,
  To Thee shall come all Flesh;   *10*
Thou hast me heard and answered,
  My 'Plaints have had accesse.

What did I ask for but thou gav'st?
  What could I more desire?
But Thankfullnes, even all my dayes,   *15*
  I humbly this Require.

Thy mercyes, Lord, have been so great,
  In number numberles,
Impossible for to recount
  Or any way expresse.   *20*

O help thy Saints that sought thy Face,
  T' Return unto thee Praise,
And walk before thee as they ought,
  In strict and upright wayes.

TEXT NOTES:
Line 7: *Seases on,* seizes on, takes possession of.

*Here followes some verses upon the burning of our house, July 10th,
1666. Copyed out of a loose Paper.*

In silent night when rest I took,
For sorrow neer I did not look,
I waken'd was with thundring nois
And Piteous shreiks of dreadfull voice.
That fearfull sound of fire and fire,   *5*
Let no man know is my Desire.

I, starting up, the light did spye,
And to my God my heart did cry
To strengthen me in my Distresse
And not to leave me succourlesse.   *10*
Then coming out beheld a space,
The flame consume my dwelling place.

And, when I could no longer look,
I blest his Name that gave and took,
That layd my goods now in the dust: *15*
Yea so it was, and so 'twas just.
It was his own: it was not mine;
Far be it that I should repine.

He might of All justly bereft,
But yet sufficient for us left.   *20*
When by the Ruines oft I past,
My sorrowing eyes aside did cast,
And here and there the places spye
Where oft I sate, and long did lye.

Here stood that Trunk, and there that chest;   *25*
There lay that store I counted best:
My pleasant things in ashes lye,
And them behold no more shall I.
Under thy roof no guest shall sitt,
Nor at thy Table eat a bitt.   *30*

No pleasant tale shall 'ere be told,
Nor things recounted done of old.
No Candle 'ere shall shine in Thee,
Nor bridegroom's voice ere heard shall bee.
In silence ever shalt thou lye;   *35*
Adeiu, Adeiu; All's vanity.

Then streight I gin my heart to chide,
And didst thy wealth on earth abide?
Didst fix thy hope on mouldring dust,
The arm of flesh didst make thy trust?   *40*
Raise up thy thoughts above the skye
That dunghill mists away may flie.

Thou hast an house on high erect
Fram'd by that mighty Architect,
With glory richly furnished,   *45*
Stands permanent tho' this bee fled.

It's purchased, and paid for too
By him who hath enough to doe.

A Prise so vast as is unknown,
Yet, by his Gift, is made thine own.   *50*
Ther's wealth enough, I need no more;
Farewell my Pelf, farewell my Store.
The world no longer let me Love,
My hope and Treasure lyes Above.

TEXT NOTES:
Line 5: *fire and fire,* Fire! and Fire!
Line 11: *beheld a space,* watched for a time.
Line 14: *I blest his Name that gave and took,* see Job 1:21.
Line 24: *Sate,* sat.
Line 40: *Arm of flesh,* see 2 Chronicles 32:8; Isaiah 9:18–20; Jeremiah 17:4–7.
Line 42: *Dunghill mists,* see Ezra 6:9–12.
Line 43: *House on high erect,* see 2 Corinthians 5:1; Hebrews 11:10.
Line 48: *Enough to doe,* i.e. enough to do it.
Line 52: *Pelf,* property, possessions.
Line 54: *Treasure lyes Above,* see Luke 12:34.

ANNE BRADSTREET:
FORMAL MEDITATIONS

Formal meditations were systematic, planned spiritual exercises based upon an object or theme external to the life of the believer. This could be a biblical text, physical object, scene in nature, or a religious doctrine or image (see Introduction, p. 19). Not that formal meditations were impersonal, for they could be motivated by some crisis or other life event, and contemplation was not mere rational thought. Anne Bradstreet's most moving poetic formal meditation, "As weary pilgrim," dated August 31, 1669, is the only poem to survive in the author's own hand. It appeared in print for the first time in the Ellis edition of The Works of Anne Bradstreet *(Cambridge, Mass., 1867). "David's Lamentation for Saul and Jonathan" and "The Vanity of all worldly things" were included in* The Tenth Muse *(London, 1650). "The Flesh and the Spirit" and the poem considered to be her best by many critics, "Contemplations," are from* Several Poems *(Boston, 1678).*

"AS WEARY PILGRIM, NOW AT REST."

As weary pilgrim, now at rest,
  Hugs with delight his silent nest
His wasted limbes, now lye full soft
  That myrie steps, have troden oft
Blesses himself, to think upon   5
  his dangers past, and travailes done
The burning sun no more shall heat
  Nor stormy raines, on him shall beat.

95

The bryars and thornes no more shall scratch
    nor hungry wolves at him shall catch   *10*
He erring pathes no more shall tread
    nor wild fruits eate, in stead of bread,
for waters cold he doth not long
    for thirst no more shall parch his tongue
No rugged stones his feet shall gaule   *15*
    nor stumps nor rocks cause him to fall
All cares and feares, he bids farwell
    and meanes in safity now to dwell.
A pilgrim I, on earth, perplext
    with sinns with cares and sorrows vext   *20*
By age and paines brought to decay
    and my Clay house mouldring away
Oh how I long to be at rest
    and soare on high among the blest.
This body shall in silence sleep   *25*
    Mine eyes no more shall ever weep
No fainting fits shall me assaile
    nor grinding paines my body fraile
With cares and fears ne'r cumbred be
    Nor losses know, nor sorrowes see   *30*
What tho my flesh shall there consume
    it is the bed Christ did perfume
And when a few yeares shall be gone
    this mortall shall be cloth'd upon
A Corrupt Carcasse downe it lyes   *35*
    a glorious body it shall rise
In weaknes and dishonour sowne
    in power 'tis rais'd by Christ alone
Then soule and body shall unite
    and of their maker have the sight   *40*
Such lasting joyes shall there behold
    as eare ne'r heard nor tongue e'er told
Lord make me ready for that day
    then Come deare bridgrome Come away.
                [Aug: 31, 69.]

TEXT NOTES:
Line 1: *Pilgrim,* see Hebrews 11:10–16.
Line 2: *Nest,* see Matthew 8:20 and Psalm 84:3.

Lines 33–40: See 1 Corinthians 15.
Line 44: *Come deare bridgrome,* Matthew 25:6.
Line 44: *Come away,* Song of Solomon (Canticles) 2:10.

DAVIDS LAMENTATION FOR SAUL AND JONATHAN. [2. SAMUEL 1. 19.]

Alas slain is the Head of Israel,
Illustrious *Saul* whose beauty did excell,
Upon thy places mountainous and high,
How did the Mighty fall, and falling dye?
In *Gath* let not this thing be spoken on,   *5*
Nor published in streets of *Askalon,*
Lest daughters of the Philistines rejoyce,
Lest the uncircumcis'd lift up their voice.
O *Gilbo* Mounts, let never pearled dew,
Nor fruitfull showres your barren tops bestrew,   *10*
Nor fields of offrings ever on you grow,
Nor any pleasant thing e're may you show;
For there the Mighty Ones did soon decay,
The shield of *Saul* was vilely cast away,
There had his dignity so sore a foyle,   *15*
As if his head ne're felt the sacred oyle.
Sometimes from crimson, blood of gastly slain,
The bow of *Jonathan* ne're turn'd in vain:
Nor from the fat, and spoils of Mighty men
With bloodless sword did *Saul* turn back agen.   *20*
Pleasant and lovely, were they both in life,
And in their death was found no parting strife.
Swifter then swiftest Eagles so were they,
Stronger then Lions ramping for their prey.
O Israels Dames, o'reflow your beauteous eyes   *25*
For valiant *Saul* who on Mount *Gilbo* lyes,
Who cloathed you in Cloath of richest Dye,
And choice delights, full of variety,
On your array put ornaments of gold,
Which made you yet more beauteous to behold.   *30*
O! how in Battle did the mighty fall
In midst of strength not succoured at all.
O lovely *Jonathan!* how wast thou slain?
In places high, full low thou didst remain.
Distrest for thee I am, dear *Jonathan,*   *35*

Thy love was wonderfull, surpassing man,
Exceeding all the love that's Feminine,
So pleasant hast thou been, dear brother mine,
How are the mighty fall'n into decay?
And warlike weapons perished away?   *40*

TEXT NOTES:
Lines 1–4: Paraphrase of the text, 2 Samuel 1:19: "The beauty of Israel is slain upon
    thy high places: how are the mighty fallen!"
Lines 5–8: Paraphrase of 2 Samuel 1:20.
Lines 9–16: Paraphrase of 2 Samuel 1:21.
Lines 17–20: Paraphrase of 2 Samuel 1:22.
Lines 21–24: Paraphrase of 2 Samuel 1:23.
Lines 25–30: Paraphrase of 2 Samuel 1:24.
Lines 31–34: Paraphrase of 2 Samuel 1:25.
Lines 35–38: Paraphrase of 2 Samuel 1:26.
Lines 39–40: Paraphrase of 2 Samuel 1:27.

THE FLESH AND THE SPIRIT.

In secret place where once I stood
Close by the Banks of Lacrim flood
I heard two sisters reason on
Things that are past, and things to come;
One flesh was call'd, who had her eye   *5*
On worldly wealth and vanity;
The other Spirit, who did rear
Her thoughts unto a higher sphere:
Sister, quoth Flesh, what liv'st thou on
Nothing but Meditation?   *10*
Doth Contemplation feed thee so
Regardlesly to let earth goe?
Can Speculation satisfy
Notion without Reality?
Dost dream of things beyond the Moon   *15*
And dost thou hope to dwell there soon?
Hast treasures there laid up in store
That all in th' world thou count'st but poor?
Art fancy sick, or turn'd a Sot
To catch at shadowes which are not?   *20*
Come, come, Ile shew unto thy sence,
Industry hath its recompence.

What canst desire, but thou maist see
True substance in variety?
Dost honour like? acquire the same,   *25*
As some to their immortal fame:
And trophyes to thy name erect
Which wearing time shall ne're deject.
For riches dost thou long full sore?
Behold enough of precious store.   *30*
Earth hath more silver, pearls and gold,
Than eyes can see, or hands can hold.
Affect's thou pleasure? take thy fill,
Earth hath enough of what you will.
Then let not goe, what thou maist find,   *35*
For things unknown, only in mind.
Spir. Be still thou unregenerate part,
Disturb no more my setled heart,
For I have vow'd, (and so will doe)
Thee as a foe, still to pursue.   *40*
And combate with thee will and must,
Untill I see thee laid in th' dust.
Sisters we are, ye twins we be,
Yet deadly feud 'twixt thee and me;
For from one father are we not,   *45*
Thou by old Adam wast begot,
But my arise is from above,
Whence my dear father I do love.
Thou speak'st me fair, but hat'st me sore,
Thy flatt'ring shews Ile trust no more.   *50*
How oft thy slave, hast thou me made,
when I believ'd, what thou hast said,
And never had more cause of woe
Then when I did what thou bad'st doe.
Ile stop mine ears at these thy charms,   *55*
And count them for my deadly harms.
Thy sinfull pleasures I doe hate,
Thy riches are to me no bait,
Thine honours doe, nor will I love;
For my ambition lyes above.   *60*
My greatest honour it shall be
When I am victor over thee,
And triumph shall, with laurel head,
When thou my Captive shalt be led,

How I do live, thou need'st not scoff,   *65*
For I have meat thou know'st not off;
The hidden Manna I doe eat,
The word of life it is my meat.
My thoughts do yield me more content
Then can thy hours in pleasure spent.   *70*
Nor are they shadows which I catch,
Nor fancies vain at which I snatch,
But reach at things that are so high,
Beyond thy dull Capacity;
Eternal substance I do see,   *75*
With which inriched I would be:
Mine Eye doth pierce the heavens, and see
What is Invisible to thee.
My garments are not silk nor gold,
Nor such like trash which Earth doth hold,   *80*
But Royal Robes I shall have on,
More glorious then the glistring Sun;
My Crown not Diamonds, Pearls, and gold,
But such as Angels heads infold.
The City where I hope to dwell,   *85*
There's none on Earth can parallel;
The stately Walls both high and strong,
Are made of pretious *Jasper* stone;
The Gates of Pearl, both rich and clear,
And Angels are for Porters there;   *90*
The Streets thereof transparent gold,
Such as no Eye did e're behold,
A Chrystal River there doth run,
Which doth proceed from the Lambs Throne:
Of Life, there are the waters sure,   *95*
Which shall remain for ever pure,
Nor Sun, nor Moon, they have no need,
For glory doth from God proceed:
No Candle there, nor yet Torch light,
For there shall be no darksome night.   *100*
From sickness and infirmity,
For evermore they shall be free,
Nor withering age shall e're come there,
But beauty shall be bright and clear;
This City pure is not for thee,   *105*
For things unclean there shall not be:

If I of Heaven may have my fill,
Take thou the world, and all that will.

TEXT NOTES:
Title: *The Flesh and the Spirit,* see Galatians 5:16–17.
Line 2: *Lacrim flood,* river of tears (lachrym).
Line 17: *Treasures there laid up,* Matthew 6:21; Luke 12:34.
Line 43: *Ye,* yea, yes.
Line 66: *Off,* of.
Line 82: *Glistring,* brilliant.
Line 85: *The City,* Revelation 21:10–27.
Line 93: *A Chrystal River,* Revelation 22:1–5.

THE VANITY OF ALL WORLDLY THINGS.

As he said vanity, so vain say I,
Oh! vanity, O vain all under Sky;
Where is the man can say, lo I have found
On brittle Earth a Consolation sound?
What is't in honour to be set on high?   5
No, they like Beasts and Sons of men shall dye:
And whil'st they live, how oft doth turn their fate,
He's now a captive, that was King of late.
What is't in wealth, great Treasures to obtain?
No, that's but labour, anxious care and pain,   10
He heaps up riches, and he heaps up sorrow,
It's his to day, but who's his heir to morrow?
What then? Content in pleasures canst thou find,
More vain than all, that's but to grasp the wind.
The sensual senses for a time they please,   15
Mean while the conscience rage, who shall appease?
What is't in beauty? No that's but a snare,
They're foul enough to day, that once were fair.
What is't in flowring youth, or manly age?
The first is prone to vice, the last to rage.   20
Where is it then, in wisdom, learning arts?
Sure if on earth, it must be in those parts:
Yet these the wisest man of men did find
But vanity, vexation of mind.
And he that knowes the most, doth still bemoan   25
He knows not all that here is to be known.

What is it then, to doe as *Stoicks* tell,
Nor laugh, nor weep, let things go ill or well.
Such *Stoicks* are but Stocks such teaching vain,
While man is man, he shall have ease or pain.   *30*
If not in honour, beauty, age nor treasure,
Nor yet in learning, wisdome, youth nor pleasure,
Where shall I climb, sound, seek search, or find
That *Summum Bonum* which may stay my mind?
There is a path, no vultures eye hath seen,   *35*
Where Lion fierce, nor lions whelps have been,
Which leads unto that living Chrystal Fount,
Who drinks thereof, the world doth nought account
The depth and sea have said tis not in me,
With pearl and gold, it shall not valued be.   *40*
For Saphire, Onix, Topaz who would change:
Its hid from eyes of men, they count it strange.
Death and destruction the same hath heard,
But where and what it is, from heaven's declar'd,
It brings to honour, which shall ne're decay,   *45*
It stores with wealth which time can't wear away.
It yieldeth pleasures far beyond conceit,
And truly beautifies without deceit,
Nor strength, nor wisdome nor fresh youth shall fade
Nor death shall see, but are immortal made.   *50*
This pearl of price, this tree of life, this spring
Who is possessed of, shall reign a King.
Nor change of state, nor cares shall ever see,
But wear his crown unto eternity:
This satiates the Soul, this stayes the mind,   *55*
And all the rest, but Vanity we find.

TEXT NOTES:
Line 1: *As he said vanity,* see Ecclesiastes 1:2.
Line 29: *Stocks,* stupid persons.

CONTEMPLATIONS.

1

Some time now past in the Autumnal Tide,
When *Phoebus* wanted but one hour to bed,
The trees all richly clad, yet void of pride,
Where gilded o're by his rich golden head.

Their leaves and fruits seem'd painted, but was true   *5*
Of green, of red, of yellow, mixed hew,
Rapt were my sences at this delectable view.

2

I wist not what to wish, yet sure thought I,
If so much excellence abide below;
How excellent is he that dwells on high?   *10*
Whose power and beauty by his works we know.
Sure he is goodness, wisdome, glory, light,
That hath this under world so richly dight:
More Heaven than Earth was here no winter and no night.

3

Then on a stately Oak I cast mine Eye,   *15*
Whose ruffling top the Clouds seem'd to aspire;
How long since thou wast in thine Infancy?
Thy strength, and stature, more thy years admire,
Hath hundred winters past since thou wast born?
Or thousand since thou brakest thy shell of horn,   *20*
If so, all these as nought, Eternity doth scorn.

4

Then higher on the glistering Sun I gaz'd,
Whose beams was shaded by the leavie Tree,
The more I look'd, the more I grew amaz'd,
And softly said, what glory's like to thee?   *25*
Soul of this world, this Universes Eye,
No wonder, some made thee a Deity:
Had I not better known, (alas) the same had I.

5

Thou as a Bridegroom from thy Chamber rushes,
And as a strong man, joyes to run a race,   *30*
The morn doth usher thee, with smiles and blushes,
The Earth reflects her glances in thy face.
Birds, insects, Animals with Vegative,
Thy heat from death and dulness doth revive:
And in the darksome womb of fruitful nature dive.   *35*

6

Thy swift Annual, and diurnal Course,
Thy daily streight, and yearly oblique path,
Thy pleasing fervor, and thy scorching force,

All mortals here the feeling knowledg hath.
Thy presence makes it day, thy absence night,   *40*
Quaternal Seasons caused by thy might:
Hail Creature, full of sweetness, beauty and delight.

7

Art thou so full of glory, that no Eye
Hath strength, thy shining Rayes once to behold?
And is thy splendid Throne erect so high?   *45*
As to approach it, can no earthly mould.
How full of glory then must thy Creator be?
Who gave this bright light luster unto thee:
Admir'd, ador'd for ever, be that Majesty.

8

Silent alone, where none or saw, or heard,   *50*
In pathless paths I lead my wandring feet,
My humble Eyes to lofty Skyes I rear'd
To sing some Song, my mazed Muse thought meet.
My great Creator I would magnifie,
That nature had, thus decked liberally: *55*
But Ah, and Ah, again, my imbecility!

9

I heard the merry grashopper then sing,
The black clad Cricket, bear a second part,
They kept one tune, and plaid on the same string,
Seeming to glory in their little Art.   *60*
Shall Creatures abject, thus their voices raise?
And in their kind resound their makers praise:
Whilst I as mute, can warble forth no higher layes.

10

When present times look back to Ages past,
And men in being fancy those are dead,   *65*
It makes things gone perpetually to last,
And calls back moneths and years that long since fled
It makes a man more aged in conceit,
Than was *Methuselah*, or's grand-sire great:
While of their persons and their acts his mind doth treat.   *70*

11

Sometimes in *Eden* fair, he seems to be,
Sees glorious *Adam* there made Lord of all,

Fancyes the Apple, dangle on the Tree,
That turn'd his Sovereign to a naked thral.
Who like a miscreant's driven from that place,   *75*
To get his bread with pain, and sweat of face:
A penalty impos'd on his backsliding Race.

12

Here sits our Grandame in retired place,
And in her lap, her bloody *Cain* new born,
The weeping Imp oft looks her in the face,   *80*
Bewails his unknown hap, and fate forlorn;
His Mother sighs, to think of Paradise,
And how she lost her bliss, to be more wise,
Believing him that was, and is, Father of lyes.

13

Here *Cain* and *Abel* come to sacrifice,   *85*
Fruits of the Earth, and Fatlings each do bring,
On *Abels* gift the fire descends from Skies,
But no such sign on false *Cain's* offering;
With sullen hateful looks he goes his wayes.
Hath thousand thoughts to end his brothers dayes,   *90*
Upon whose blood his future good he hopes to raise

14

There *Abel* keeps his sheep, no ill he thinks,
His brother comes, then acts his fratricide,
The Virgin Earth, of blood her first draught drinks
But since that time she often hath been cloy'd;   *95*
The wretch with gastly face and dreadful mind,
Thinks each he sees will serve him in his kind,
Though none on Earth but kindred near then could he find.

15

Who fancyes not his looks now at the Barr,
His face like death, his heart with horror fraught,   *100*
Nor Male-factor ever felt like warr,
When deep dispair, with wish of life hath sought,
Branded with guilt, and crusht with treble woes,
A Vagabond to Land of *Nod* he goes.
A City builds, that wals might him secure from foes.   *105*

16

Who thinks not oft upon the Fathers ages.
Their long descent, how nephews sons they saw,
The starry observations of those Sages,
And how their precepts to their sons were law,
How Adam sigh'd to see his Progeny,   *110*
Cloath'd all in his black sinfull Livery,
Who neither guilt, nor yet the punishment could fly.

17

Our Life compare we with their length of dayes
Who to the tenth of theirs doth now arrive?
And though thus short, we shorten many wayes,   *115*
Living so little while we are alive;
In eating, drinking, sleeping, vain delight
So unawares comes on perpetual night,
And puts all pleasures vain unto eternal flight.

18

When I behold the heavens as in their prime,   *120*
And then the earth (though old) stil clad in green,
The stones and trees, insensible of time,
Nor age nor wrinkle on their front are seen;
If winter come, and greeness then do fade,
A Spring returns, and they more youthfull made;   *125*
But Man grows old, lies down, remains where once he's laid.

20 [19]

By birth more noble than those creatures all,
Yet seems by nature and by custome curs'd,
No sooner born, but grief and care makes fall
That state obliterate he had at first: *130*
Nor youth, nor strength, nor wisdom spring again
Nor habitations long their names retain,
But in oblivion to the final day remain.

20

Shall I then praise the heavens, the trees, the earth
Because their beauty and their strength last longer   *135*
Shall I wish there, or never to had birth,
Because they're bigger, and their bodyes stronger?
Nay, they shall darken, perish, fade and dye,

And when unmade, so ever shall they lye,
But man was made for endless immortality.   *140*

21

Under the cooling shadow of a stately Elm
Close sate I by a goodly Rivers side,
Where gliding streams the Rocks did overwhelm;
A lonely place, with pleasures dignifi'd.
I once that lov'd the shady woods so well,   *145*
Now thought the rivers did the trees excel,
And if the sun would ever shine, there would I dwell.

22

While on the stealing stream I fixt mine eye,
Which to the long'd for Ocean held its course,
I markt, nor crooks, nor rubs that there did lye   *150*
Could hinder ought, but still augment its force:
O happy Flood, quoth I, that holds thy race
Till thou arrive at thy beloved place,
Nor is it rocks or shoals that can obstruct thy pace.

23

Nor is't enough, that thou alone may'st slide,   *155*
But hundred brooks in thy cleer waves do meet,
So hand in hand along with thee they glide
To *Thetis* house, where all imbrace and greet:
Thou Emblem true, of what I count the best,
O could I lead my Rivolets to rest,   *160*
So may we press to that vast mansion, ever blest.

24

Ye Fish which in this liquid Region 'bide,
That for each season, have your habitation,
Now salt, now fresh where you think best to glide
To unknown coasts to give a visitation,   *165*
In Lakes and ponds, you leave your numerous fry,
So nature taught, and yet you know not why,
You watry folk that know not your felicity.

25

Look how the wantons frisk to tast the air,
Then to the colder bottome streight they dive,   *170*
Eftsoon to *Neptun*'s glassie Hall repair

To see what trade they great ones there do drive,
Who forrage o're the spacious sea-green field,
And take the trembling prey before it yield,
Whose armour is their scales, their spreading fins their   *175*
    shield.

26

While musing thus with contemplation fed,
And thousand fancies buzzing in my brain,
The sweet-tongu'd Philomel percht ore my head,
And chanted forth a most melodious strain
Which rapt me so with wonder and delight,   *180*
I judg'd my hearing better then my sight,
And wisht me wings with her a while to take my flight.

27

O merry Bird (said I) that fears no snares,
That neither toyles nor hoards up in thy barn,
Feels no sad thoughts, nor cruciating cares   *185*
To gain more good, or shun what might thee harm
Thy cloaths ne're wear, thy meat is every where,
Thy bed a bough, thy drink the water cleer,
Reminds not what is past, nor whats to come dost fear.

28

The dawning morn with songs thou dost prevent,   *190*
Sets hundred notes unto thy feathered crew,
So each one tunes his pretty instrument,
And warbling out the old, begin anew,
And thus they pass their youth in summer season,
Then follow thee into a better Region,   *195*
where winter's never felt by that sweet airy legion.

29

Man at the best a creature frail and vain,
In knowledg ignorant, in strength but weak,
Subject to sorrows, losses, sickness, pain,
Each storm his state, his mind, his body break,   *200*
From some of these he never finds cessation,
But day or night, within, without, vexation,
Troubles from foes, from friends, from dearest, near'st Relation.

30

And yet this sinfull creature, frail and vain,
This lump of wretchedness, of sin and sorrow, 205
This weather-beaten vessel wrackt with pain,
Joyes not in hope of an eternal morrow;
Nor all his losses, crosses and vexation,
In weight, in frequency and long duration
Can make him deeply groan for that divine Translation. 210

31

The Mariner that on smooth waves doth glide,
Sings merrily, and steers his Barque with ease,
As if he had command of wind and tide,
And now become great Master of the seas;
But suddenly a storm spoiles all the sport, 215
And makes him long for a more quiet port,
Which 'gainst all adverse winds may serve for fort.

32

So he that saileth in this world of pleasure,
Feeding on sweets, that never bit of th' sowre,
That's full of friends, of honour and of treasure, 220
Fond fool, he takes this earth ev'n for heav'ns bower.
But sad affliction comes and makes him see
Here's neither honour, wealth, nor safety;
Only above is found all with security.

33

O Time the fatal wrack of mortal things, 225
That draws oblivions curtains over kings,
Their sumptuous monuments, men know them not,
Their names without a Record are forgot,
Their parts, their ports, their pomp's all laid in th' dust
Nor wit nor gold, nor buildings scape times rust; 230
But he whose name is grav'd in the white stone
Shall last and shine when all of these are gone.

TEXT NOTES:
Line 2: *Phoebus,* the sun personified.
Line 13: *Dight,* ordered; arrayed.
Line 46: *Mould,* clods of earth; mortal (as mortal man).
Line 69: *Methuselah,* see Genesis 5:21.

Line 69: *Grand-sire great,* Mahalaleel, who lived 895 years, Genesis 5:17.
Line 78: *Our Grandame,* Eve.
Line 85: *Cain and Abel,* Genesis 4.
Line 99: *Barr,* court.
Line 104: *Land of Nod,* land east of Eden to which Cain was banished.
Line 142: *Sate,* sat.
Line 148: *Stealing,* gently flowing.
Line 158: *Thetis,* the sea personified.
Line 171: *Eftsoon,* again.
Line 178: *Philomel,* nightingale.
Line 185: *Cruciating,* agonizing.
Line 190: *Prevent,* anticipate, hasten.
Line 219: *Sowre,* sour.
Line 225: *Wrack,* wreck.
Line 231: *The white stone,* see Revelation 2:17.

ANNE BRADSTREET:
SELECTED OTHER POEMS
FROM *THE TENTH MUSE*
AND SEVERAL POEMS

The poems in this section belong to the category of Bradstreet's public poetry (see Introduction p. 24). These works are public in that they address current events and conventional literary themes and, though not originally intended for publication, were modeled on the style of major English and European poets. Further, the author attempted to revise these poems for future editions. The poems "To her most Honoured Father," "The Prologue," "An Apology," and "A Dialogue between Old England and New" all appeared in The Tenth Muse *(London, 1650). The memorial poems for her father and mother and "The Author to her Book" were published in her posthumous* Several Poems *(Boston, 1678). The elegies are included here as public poetry because, unlike her poems of grief for other family losses, these are testimonials to her parents such as could be read at a neighborhood meeting or, according to the custom of the time, nailed to the hearse at the funeral.*

TO HER MOST HONOURED FATHER
THOMAS DUDLEY ESQ.; THESE HUMBLY PRESENTED.

Dear Sir of late delighted with
   the sight
Of your four Sisters cloth'd in black
   and white,

T.D. *On
the four
parts of
the world.*

Of fairer Dames the Sun, ne'r saw the face;
Though made a pedestal for *Adams* Race;
Their worth so shines in these rich lines you show   5
Their paralels to finde I scarcely know
To climbe their Climes, I have nor strength nor skill
To mount so high requires an Eagles quill;
Yet view thereof did cause my thoughts to soar;
My lowly pen might wait upon these four   10
I bring my four times four, now meanly clad
To do their homage, unto yours, full glad:
Who for their Age, their worth and quality
Might seem of yours to claim precedency:
But by my humble hand, thus rudely pen'd   15
They are, your bounden handmaids to attend
These same are they, from whom we being have
These are of all, the Life, the Nurse, the Grave,
These are the hot, the cold, the moist, the dry,
That sink, that swim, that fill, that upwards fly,   20
Of these consists our bodies, Cloathes and Food,
The World, the useful, hurtful, and the good,
Sweet harmony they keep, yet jar oft times
Their discord doth appear, by these harsh rimes
Yours did contest for wealth, for Arts, for Age,   25
My first do shew their good, and then their rage.
My other foures do intermixed tell
Each others faults, and where themselves excell;
How hot and dry contend with moist and cold,
How Air and Earth no correspondence hold,   30
And yet in equal tempers, how they 'gree
How divers natures make one Unity
Something of all (though mean) I did intend
But fear'd you'ld judge *Du Bartas* was my friend
I honour him, but dare not wear his wealth   35
My goods are true (though poor) I love no stealth

But if I did I durst not send them you
Who must reward a Thief, but with his due.
I shall not need, mine innocence to clear
These ragged lines, will do't, when they appear: 40
On what they are, your mild aspect I crave
Accept my best, my worst vouchsafe a Grave.

From her that to your self, more duty owes
Then water in the boundless Ocean flows.

[March 20. 1642.]

TEXT NOTES:

Line 2: *Your four Sisters,* Thomas Dudley's poem, "On the four parts of the world," which is not extant.

Line 7: *Climes,* regions; or read "climbs," place one must climb.

Line 11: *My four times four,* my quaternions, of which this poem is the dedicatory: "The Four Elements"; "Of the four Humours in Mans Constitution"; "Of the four Ages of Man"; "The four Seasons of the Year"; to which is added "The four Monarchyes."

Line 12: *Full glad,* full of brightness and beauty.

Line 34: *Du Bartas,* a French poet (1544–1590) made popular in England through Joshua Sylvester's translation. Bradstreet acknowledged her admiration in a poem, "In honour of Du Bartas, 1641," included in *The Tenth Muse* (Ellis, *Works of A.B.,* 353–356). In his commendatory verses Nathaniel Ward called Bradstreet "a right Du Bartas Girle" (Ellis, *Works of A.B.,* 85).

THE PROLOGUE.

1.

To sing of Wars, of Captains, and of Kings,
Of Cities founded, Common-wealths begun,
For my mean pen are too superiour things:
Or how they all, or each their dates have run
Let Poets and Historians set these forth,   5
My obscure Lines shall not so dim their worth.

2.

But when my wondring eyes and envious heart
Great *Bartas* sugar'd lines, do but read o're
Fool I do grudg the Muses did not part
'Twixt him and me that overfluent store;   10
A *Bartas* can, do what a *Bartas* will
But simple I according to my skill.

3.

From school-boyes tongue no rhet'rick we expect
Nor yet a sweet Consort from broken strings,

Nor perfect beauty, where's a main defect: 15
My foolish, broken, blemish'd Muse so sings
And this to mend, alas, no Art is able,
'Cause nature, made it so irreparable.

4.

Nor can I, like that fluent sweet tongu'd Greek,
Who lisp'd at first, in future times speak plain   20
By Art he gladly found what he did seek
A full requital of his striving pain
Art can do much, but this maxime's most sure
A weak or wounded brain admits no cure.

5.

I am obnoxious to each carping tongue   25
Who says my hand a needle better fits,
A Poets pen all scorn I should thus wrong,
For such despite they cast on Female wits:
If what I do prove well, it won't advance,
They'l say it's stoln, or else it was by chance.   30

6.

But sure the Antique Greeks were far more mild
Else of our Sexe, why feigned they those Nine
And poesy made, *Calliope*'s own Child;
So 'mongst the rest they placed the Arts Divine,
But this weak knot, they will full soon untie,   35
The Greeks did nought, but play the fools and lye.

7.

Let Greeks be Greeks, and women what they are
Men have precedency and still excell,
It is but vain unjustly to wage warre;
Men can do best, and women know it well   40
Preheminence in all and each is yours;
Yet grant some small acknowledgement of ours.

8.

And oh ye high flown quills that soar the Skies,
And ever with your prey still catch your praise,
If e're you daigne these lowly lines your eyes   45
Give Thyme or Parsley wreath, I ask no bayes,
This mean and unrefined ure of mine
Will make you glistring gold, but more to shine.

TEXT NOTES:
Line 8: *Bartas,* Guillaume du Bartas.
Line 19: *Sweet tongu'd Greek,* Demosthenes, 4th C. B.C. orator.
Line 32: *Feigned,* imagined; contrived.
Line 32: *Those Nine,* the nine Muses, goddesses of the arts.
Line 33: *Calliope,* the ninth Muse, goddess of eloquence and heroic poetry.
Line 46: *Bayes,* laurels, emblem of poetic fame.
Line 47: *Ure,* ore.
Line 48: *Glistring,* brilliant.

AN APOLOGY.

To finish what's begun, was my intent,
My thoughts and my endeavours thereto bent;
Essays I many made but still gave out,
The more I mus'd, the more I was in doubt:
The subject large my mind and body weak,   *5*
With many moe discouragements did speak.
All thoughts of further progress laid aside,
Though oft perswaded, I as oft deny'd,
At length resolv'd, when many years had past,
To prosecute my story to the last;   *10*
And for the same, I hours not few did spend,
And weary lines (though lanke) I many pen'd:
But 'fore I could accomplish my desire,
My papers fell a prey to th' raging fire.
And thus my pains (with better things) I lost,   *15*
Which none had cause to wail, nor I to boast.
No more I'le do sith I have suffer'd wrack,
Although my Monarchies their legs do lack:
Nor matter is't this last, the world now sees,
Hath many Ages been upon his knees.   *20*

TEXT NOTES:
Line 1: *To finish what's begun,* i.e. her work on "The four Monarchyes," especially
    the final part, "The Romane Monarchy."
Line 14: *Th' raging fire,* see her poem, "Upon the burning of our house, July 10,
    1666."
Line 17: *Sith,* subsequently; seeing that; since.
Line 17: *Wrack,* wreck; shattered condition.

A DIALOGUE BETWEEN OLD *ENGLAND* AND NEW;
CONCERNING THEIR PRESENT TROUBLES, *ANNO,* 1642.

New-England.

Alas dear Mother, fairest Queen and best,
With honour, wealth, and peace, happy and blest;
What ails thee hang thy head, and cross thine arms?
And sit i'th' dust, to sigh these sad alarms?
What deluge of new woes thus over-whelme   5
The glories of thy ever famous Realme?
What means this wailing tone, this mournful guise?
Ah, tell thy daughter, she may sympathize.

Old England.

Art ignorant indeed of these my woes?
Or must my forced tongue these griefs disclose?   10
And must myself dissect my tatter'd state,
Which 'mazed Christendome stands wondring at?
And thou a Child, a Limbe, and dost not feel
My fainting weakned body now to reel?
This Physick purging potion, I have taken,   15
Will bring consumption, or an Ague quaking,
Unless some Cordial, thou fetch from high,
Which present help may ease my malady.
If I decease, dost think thou shalt survive?
Or by my wasting state dost think to thrive?   20
Then weigh our case, if't be not justly sad;
Let me lament alone, while thou art glad.

New-England.

And thus (alas) your state you much deplore
In general terms, but will not say wherefore:
What medicine shall I seek to cure this woe,   25
If th' wound so dangerous I may not know.
But you perhaps, would have me ghess it out:
What hath some *Hengist* like that *Saxon* stout
By fraud or force usurp'd thy flowring crown,
Or by tempestuous warrs thy fields trod down?   30
Or hath *Canutus,* that brave valiant *Dane*
The Regal peacefull Scepter from thee tane?
Or is't a *Norman,* whose victorious hand
With English blood bedews thy conquered land?

Or is't Intestine warrs that thus offend?   *35*
Do *Maud* and *Stephen* for the crown contend?
Do Barons rise and side against their King,
And call in foraign aid to help the thing?
Must *Edward* be depos'd? or is't the hour
That second *Richard* must be clapt i'th tower?   *40*
Or is't the fatal jarre, again begun
That from the red white pricking roses sprung?
Must *Richmonds* aid, the Nobles now implore?
To come and break the Tushes of the Boar,
If none of these dear Mother, what's your woe?   *45*
Pray do you fear *Spains* bragging *Armado?*
Doth your Allye, fair *France,* conspire your wrack,
Or do the *Scots* play false, behind your back?
Doth *Holland* quit you ill for all your love?
Whence is the storm from Earth or Heaven above?   *50*
Is't drought, is't famine, or is't pestilence?
Dost feel the smart, or fear the Consequence?
Your humble Child intreats you, shew your grief,
Though Arms, nor Purse she hath for your relief,
Such is her poverty: yet shall be found   *55*
A Suppliant for your help, as she is bound.

Old England.

I must confess some of those sores you name,
My beauteous body at this present maime;
But forreign foe, nor feigned friend I fear,
For they have work enough (thou knowst) elsewhere   *60*
Nor is it *Alcies* Son, nor *Henryes* daughter;
Whose proud contention cause this slaughter,
Nor Nobles siding, to make *John* no King,
French Lewis unjustly to the Crown to bring;
No *Edward, Richard,* to lose rule and life,   *65*
Nor no *Lancastrians* to renew old strife:
No Duke of *York,* nor Earl of *March* to soyle
Their hands in kindreds blood whom they did foil
No crafty Tyrant now usurps the Seat,
Who Nephews slew that so he might be great;   *70*
No need of *Tudor,* Roses to unite,
None knows which is the red, or which the white;
Spains braving Fleet, a second time is sunk,
France knows how oft my fury she hath drunk:

By *Edward* third, and *Henry* fifth of fame,   *75*
Her Lillies in mine Arms avouch the same.
My Sister *Scotland* hurts me now no more,
Though she hath been injurious heretofore;
What *Holland* is I am in some suspence?
But trust not much unto his excellence.   *80*
For wants, sure some I feel, but more I fear,
And for the Pestilence, who knows how near;
Famine and Plague, two Sisters of the Sword,
Destruction to a Land, doth soon afford:
They're for my punishment ordain'd on high,   *85*
Unless our tears prevent it speedily.
But yet I Answer not what you demand,
To shew the grievance of my troubled Land?
Before I tell th' Effect, I'le shew the Cause
Which are my sins the breach of sacred Laws,   *90*
Idolatry supplanter of a Nation,
With foolish Superstitious Adoration,
Are lik'd and countenanc'd by men of might,
The Gospel troden down and hath no right:
Church Offices were sold and bought for gain,   *95*
That Pope had hope to find, *Rome* here again,
For Oaths and Blasphemies, did ever Ear,
From *Belzebub* himself such language hear;
What scorning of the Saints of the most high?
What injuries did daily on them lye?   *100*
What false reports, what nick-names did they take
Not for their own, but for their Masters sake?
And thou poor soul, wert jeer'd among the rest,
Thy flying for the truth was made a jest.
For Sabbath-breaking, and for drunkenness,   *105*
Did ever land profaness more express?
From crying blood yet cleansed am not I,
Martyres and others, dying causelessly.
How many princely heads on blocks laid down
For nought but title to a fading crown?   *110*
'Mongst all the crueltyes by great ones done
Of *Edwards* youths, and *Clarence* hapless son,
O *Jane* why didst thou dye in flowring prime?
Because of royal stem, that was thy crime.
For bribery Adultery and lyes,   *115*
Where is the nation, I can't parallize.

With usury, extortion and oppression,
These be the *Hydraes* of my stout transgression.
These be the bitter fountains, heads and roots,
Whence flow'd the source, the sprigs, the boughs and fruits   *120*
Of more than thou canst hear or I relate,
That with high hand I still did perpetrate:
For these were threatned the wofull day,
I mockt the Preachers, put it far away;
The Sermons yet upon Record do stand   *125*
That cri'd destruction to my wicked land:
I then believ'd not, now I feel and see,
The plague of stubborn incredulity.
Some lost their livings, some in prison pent,
Some fin'd, from house and friends to exile went.   *130*
Their silent tongues to heaven did vengeance cry,
Who saw their wrongs, and hath judg'd righteously
And will repay it seven-fold in my lap:
This is fore-runner of my Afterclap.
Nor took I warning by my neighbours falls,   *135*
I saw sad *Germanyes* dismantled walls,
I saw her people famish'd, Nobles slain,
Her fruitfull land, a barren Heath remain.
I saw unmov'd, her Armyes foil'd and fled,
Wives forc'd, babes toss'd, her houses calcined.   *140*
I saw strong *Rochel* yielded to her Foe,
Thousands of starved Christians there also.
I saw poor *Ireland* bleeding out her last,
Such crueltyes as all reports have past;
Mine heart obdurate stood not yet agast.   *145*
Now sip I of that cup, and just't may be
The bottome dreggs reserved are for me.

New-England.

To all you've said, sad Mother I assent,
Your fearfull sins great cause there's to lament,
My guilty hands in part, hold up with you,   *150*
A Sharer in your punishment's my due.
But all you say amounts to this effect,
Not what you feel, but what you do expect,
Pray in plain terms, what is your present grief?
Then let's joyn heads and hearts for your relief.   *155*

Old England.

Well to the matter then, there's grown of late
'Twixt King and Peers a Question of State,
Which is the chief, the Law, or else the King.
One said, it's he, the other no such thing.
'Tis said, my beter part in Parliament   *160*
To ease my groaning Land, shew'd their intent,
To crush the proud, and right to each man deal,
To help the Church, and stay the Common-weal.
So many Obstacles came in their way,
As puts me to a stand what I should say;   *165*
Old customes, new Prerogatives stood on,
Had they not held Law fast, all had been gone:
Which by their prudence stood them in such stead
They took high *Strafford* lower by the head.
And to their *Laud* be't spoke, they held i'th tower   *170*
All *Englands* Metropolitane that hour;
This done, an act they would have passed fain,
No Prelate should his Bishoprick retain;
Here tugg'd they hard (indeed,) for all men saw
This must be done by Gospel, not by Law.   *175*
Next the Militia they urged sore,
This was deny'd (I need not say wherefore),
The King displeas'd at *York,* himself absents,
They humbly beg return, shew their intents;
The writing, printing, posting too and fro,   *180*
Shews all was done, I'le therefore let it go.
But now I come to speak of my disaster,
Contention grown, 'twixt Subjects and their Master;
They worded it so long, they fell to blows,
That thousands lay on heaps, here bleeds my woes,   *185*
I that no wars so many years have known,
Am now destroy'd and slaught'red by mine own;
But could the Field alone this strife decide,
One Battel two or three I might abide:
But these may be beginnings of more woe   *190*
Who knows, but this may be my overthrow.
Oh pity me in this sad perturbation,
My plundred Towns, my houses devastation,
My weeping Virgins and my young men slain;
My wealthy trading fall'n, my dearth of grain,   *195*

The seed-times come, but ploughman hath no hope
Because he knows not who shall inn his Crop:
The poor they want their pay, their children bread,
Their woful Mothers tears unpittied,
If any pity in thy heart remain,   *200*
Or any child-like love thou dost retain,
For my relief, do what there lyes in thee,
And recompence that good I've done to thee.

New England.

Dear Mother cease complaints and wipe your eyes,
Shake off your dust, chear up, and now arise,   *205*
You are my Mother Nurse, and I your flesh,
Your sunken bowels gladly would refresh,
Your griefs I pity, but soon hope to see,
Out of your troubles much good fruit to be;
To see those latter dayes of hop'd for good,   *210*
Though now beclouded all with tears and blood:
After dark Popery the day did clear,
But now the Sun in's brightness shall appear.
Blest be the Nobles of thy noble Land,
With ventur'd lives for Truths defence that stand.   *215*
Blest be thy Commons, who for common good,
And thy infringed Laws have boldly stood.
Blest be thy Counties, who did aid thee still,
With hearts and States to testifie their will.
Blest be thy Preachers, who do chear thee on,   *220*
O cry the Sword of God, and *Gideon;*
And shall I not on them wish *Mero*'s curse,
That help thee not with prayers, Arms and purse?
And for my self let miseries abound,
If mindless of thy State I e're be found.   *225*
These are the dayes the Churches foes to crush,
To root out Popelings head, tail, branch and rush;
Let's bring *Baals* vestments forth to make a fire,
Their Mytires, Surplices, and all their Tire,
Copes, Rotchets, Crossiers, and such empty trash;   *230*
And let their Names consume, but let the flash
Light Christendome, and all the world to see
We hate *Romes* whore, with all her trumpery.
Go on brave *Essex* with a Loyal heart,
Not false to King, nor to the better part;   *235*

But those that hurt his people and his Crown,
As duty binds, expel and tread them down.
And ye brave Nobles chase away all fear,
And to this hopeful Cause closely adhere;
O Mother can you weep, and have such Peers,   *240*
When they are gone, then drown your self in tears
If now you weep so much, that then no more
The briny Ocean will o'reflow your shore.
These, these are they I trust, with *Charles* our King,
Out of all mists such glorious dayes shall bring;   *245*
That dazled eyes beholding much shall wonder
At that thy setled peace, thy wealth and splendor.
Thy Church and weal establish'd in such manner,
That all shall joy, that thou display'dst thy Banner;
And discipline erected so I trust,   *250*
That nursing Kings shall come and lick thy dust:
Then Justice shall in all thy Courts take place,
Without respect of person, or of case;
Then Bribes shall cease, and Suits shall not stick long
Patience and purse of Clients oft to wrong: *255*
Then high Commissions shall fall to decay,
And Pursivants, and Catchpoles want their pay.
So shall thy happy Nation ever flourish,
When truth and righteousnes they thus shall nourish
When thus in peace, thine Armies brave send out,   *260*
To sack proud *Rome,* and all her Vassals rout;
There let thy Name, thy fame, and glory shine,
As did thine Ancestors in *Palestine:*
And let her spoyls full pay, with Interest be,
Of what unjustly once she poll'd from thee.   *265*
Of all the woes thou canst, let her be sped,
And on her pour the vengeance threatned;
Bring forth the Beast that rul'd the World with's beck,
And tear his flesh, and set your feet on's neck;
And make his filthy Den so desolate,   *270*
To th' stonishment of all that knew his state:
This done with brandish'd Swords to *Turky* goe,
For then what is't, but English blades dare do,
And lay her waste for so's the sacred Doom,
And do to *Gog* as thou hast done to *Rome.*   *275*
Oh *Abraham*'s seed lift up your heads on high,
For sure the day of your Redemption's nigh;

The Scales shall fall from your long blinded eyes,
And him you shall adore who now despise,
Then fulness of the Nations in shall flow,   *280*
And Jew and Gentile to one worship go;
Then follows dayes of happiness and rest;
Whose lot doth fall, to live therein is blest:
No Canaanite shall then be found i'th' Land,
And holiness on horses bells shall stand.   *285*
If this make way thereto, then sigh no more,
But if at all, thou didst not see't before;
Farewel dear Mother, rightest cause prevail,
And in a while, you'le tell another tale.

TEXT NOTES:

Title: *Their present Troubles, Anno, 1642,* the beginning of the Civil War.

Line 27: *Ghess,* guess.

Line 28: *Hengist* (Hengest), legendary founder of the Saxon kingdom in Kent.

Line 31: *Canutus* (Cnut), Danish King of England, 1016–1035.

Line 32: *Tane,* taken.

Line 33: *A Norman,* the Norman invasion under William, 1066.

Lines 35–36: *Intestine warrs . . . Maud and Stephen,* the feudal anarchy or civil war under King Stephen (1135–1154) during which Matilda, daughter of Henry I, contended for the throne.

Line 37: *Barons rise,* in 1311 barons forced from Edward II ordinances for the reform of his realm.

Line 39: *Edward be depos'd,* Edward II was forced to abdicate in 1326 when his queen Isabella joined forces with Roger Mortimer in France to invade England and put young Edward III on the throne.

Line 40: *Second Richard,* Richard II died in prison in 1399 after Henry Bolingbroke invaded and seized the throne.

Line 42: *Red white pricking roses,* the War of the Roses, civil wars between the Houses of Lancaster and York, 1455–1471.

Line 43: *Richmonds aid,* in 1483 and 1485 the Duke of Buckingham led revolts against the brief reign of Richard III in favor of Henry Tudor, Earl of Richmond, as Henry VII.

Line 44: *Tushes of the Boar,* tusks of the boar; Richard III is referred to as the "Boar" in Shakespeare's play.

Line 46: *Armado,* the Spanish Armada, 1588.

Line 61: *Alcies Son . . . Henryes daughter,* Stephen and Matilda (above, line 36); Alcies is a contraction of Alice (Adela), Stephen's mother.

Line 63: *John,* barons required King John to sign the Magna Carta in 1215.

Line 64: *French Lewis,* barons invited Louis, son of Philip Augustus, to become king after John denounced the Magna Carta.

Line 65: *Edward, Richard,* above lines 39–40.

Lines 66–67: *Lancastrians . . . Duke of York . . . Earl of March,* participants in the War of the Roses.

Lines 69–70: *No crafty Tyrant . . . great,* in the first edition these lines read: "No Crook-backt Tyrant, now usurps the Seat, / Whose tearing tusks did wound, and kill, and threat."

Line 70: *Nephews slew,* Richard III had the two sons of Edward IV murdered in the Tower.

Line 75: *Edward third,* reigned 1327–1377.

Line 75: *Henry fifth,* reigned 1413–1422, invaded France in 1415 and 1417 and ruled northern France until his death.

Line 82: *The Pestilence,* Plague; the final and worst outbreak of bubonic plague swept London in 1665; in 1666 the city was destroyed by fire.

Line 86: *Our tears,* repentance.

Line 101: *What nick-names,* e.g. "Puritan."

Line 118: *Hydra,* mythical many-headed snake, whose heads grew again as they were cut off; something like the hydra in its evil nature and difficulty of elimination.

Line 134: *Afterclap,* unexpected blow after one has ceased to be on guard.

Line 136: *Germanyes dismantled walls,* reference to the Thirty Years' War (1618–1648).

Line 140: *Calcined,* burned to ashes.

Line 141: *Rochel* (La Rochelle), Huguenot stronghold from 1627 until the Protestant defeat in 1629.

Line 143: *Poor Ireland bleeding,* reference to the Irish Insurrection of 1641.

Line 144: *Past,* surpassed.

Line 169: *Strafford,* Thomas Wentworth, Earl of Strafford, minister of Charles I impeached and imprisoned by Commons and tried unsuccessfully for treason in 1641, finally executed in 1645.

Line 170: *Laud,* William Laud, Archbishop of Canterbury, imprisoned 1641, executed 1645.

Line 221: *The Sword of God, and Gideon,* the cry of the army of Israel when it defeated Midian; Judges 7:18, 20.

Line 222: *Mero's curse,* curse upon those who "came not to the help of the Lord against the mighty"; Judges 5:23.

Line 228: *Baals vestments,* trappings of pagan religion, here seen as the high church party of the Church of England.

Line 229: *Tire,* attire.

Line 233: *Romes whore,* the Pope, with reference to Revelation 17.

Line 234: *Essex,* Robert Devereux, Third Earl of Essex, parliamentary general.

Line 257: *Pursivants (pursuivants), and Catchpoles,* low-ranking court officers.

Line 261: *Sack proud Rome,* the Puritan goal after gaining control of England was to destroy the papacy.

Line 263: *Ancestors in Palestine,* the cause was seen as a crusade.

Line 268: *Beast that rul'd the World,* see Revelation 13.

Line 272–275: *Turky . . . Gog,* the Islamic world, identified with the apocalyptic enemy of God (Ezekiel 38; Revelation 20:8), would fall to the forces of God after Rome.

Lines 276–277: *Abraham's seed . . . your Redemption's nigh,* the conversion of the Jews would be accomplished in these latter days as God establishes his Kingdom.

Line 280: *Then fulness of the Nations in shall flow,* the gathering of the nations into the Kingdom of God, as in Isaiah 2:2, Jeremiah 3:17, Revelation 22:2, and other references.

Line 284: *No Canaanite shall then be found,* i.e. all God's enemies will be defeated and only saints remain in God's Kingdom on earth.

Lines 284–285: *No Canaanite . . . holiness on horses bells shall stand,* reference to Zechariah 14:20–21.

TO THE MEMORY OF MY DEAR AND EVER
HONOURED FATHER THOMAS DUDLEY ESQ.;
WHO DECEASED, JULY 31. 1653. AND OF HIS AGE, 77.

By duty bound, and not by custome led
To celebrate the praises of the dead,
My mournfull mind, sore prest, in trembling verse
Presents my Lamentations at his Herse,
Who was my Father, Guide, Instructer too,   *5*
To whom I ought whatever I could doe:
Nor is't Relation near my hand shall tye;
For who more cause to boast his worth then I?
Who heard or saw, observ'd or knew him better?
Or who alive than I, a greater debtor?   *10*
Let malice bite, and envy knaw its fill,
He was my Father, and I'le praise him still.
Nor was his name, or life lead so obscure
That pitty might some Trumpeters procure.
Who after death might make him falsly seem   *15*
Such as in life, no man could justly deem.
Well known and lov'd, where ere he liv'd, by most
Both in his native, and in foreign coast,
These to the world his merits could make known,
So needs no Testimonial from his own;   *20*
But now or never I must pay my Sum;
While others tell his worth, I'le not be dumb:

One of thy Founders, him *New-England* know,
Who staid thy feeble sides when thou wast low,
Who spent his state, his strength, and years with care   *25*
That After-comers in them might have share.
True Patriot of this little Commonweal,
Who is't can tax thee ought, but for thy zeal?
Truths friend thou wert, to errors still a foe,
Which caus'd Apostates to maligne so.   *30*
Thy love to true Religion e're shall shine,
My Fathers God, be God of me and mine.
Upon the earth he did not build his nest,
But as a Pilgrim, what he had, possest.
High thoughts he gave no harbour in his heart,   *35*
Nor honours pufft him up, when he had part:
Those titles loath'd, which some too much do love
For truly his ambition lay above.
His humble mind so lov'd humility,
He left it to his race for Legacy: *40*
And oft and oft, with speeches mild and wise,
Gave his in charge, that Jewel rich to prize.
No ostentation seen in all his wayes,
As in the mean ones, of our foolish dayes,
Which all they have, and more still set to view,   *45*
Their greatness may be judg'd by what they shew.
His thoughts were more sublime, his actions wise,
Such vanityes he justly did despise.
Nor wonder 'twas, low things ne'r much did move
For he a Mansion had, prepar'd above,   *50*
For which he sigh'd and pray'd and long'd full sore
He might be cloath'd upon, for evermore.
Oft spake of death, and with a smiling chear,
He did exult his end was drawing near,
Now fully ripe, as shock of wheat that's grown,   *55*
Death as a Sickle hath him timely mown,
And in celestial Barn hath hous'd him high,
Where storms, nor showrs, nor ought can damnifie.
His Generation serv'd, his labours cease;
And to his Fathers gathered is in peace.   *60*
Ah happy Soul, 'mongst Saints and Angels blest,
Who after all his toyle, is now at rest:
His hoary head in righteousness was found:
As joy in heaven on earth let praise resound.

Forgotten never be his memory,   65
His blessing rest on his posterity:
His pious Footsteps followed by his race,
At last will bring us to that happy place
Where we with joy each others face shall see,
And parted more by death shall never be.   70

HIS EPITAPH.

Within this Tomb a Patriot lyes
That was both pious, just and wise,
To Truth a shield, to right a Wall,
To Sectaryes a whip and Maul,
A Magazine of History,   75
A Prizer of good Company
In manners pleasant and severe
The Good him lov'd, the bad did fear,
And when his time with years was spent
If some rejoyc'd, more did lament.   80

TEXT NOTES:
Line 77: *Severe*, plain, austere; morally strict.

AN EPITAPH
ON MY DEAR AND EVER HONOURED MOTHER
MRS. DOROTHY DUDLEY,
WHO DECEASED DECEMBER 27. 1643. AND OF HER AGE, 61:

           Here lyes,
A Worthy Matron of unspotted life,
A loving Mother and obedient wife,
A friendly Neighbor, pitiful to poor,
Whom oft she fed, and clothed with her store;
To Servants wisely aweful, but yet kind,   5
And as they did, so they reward did find:
A true Instructer of her Family,
The which she ordered with dexterity.
The publick meetings ever did frequent,
And in her Closet constant hours she spent;   10

Religious in all her words and wayes,
Preparing still for death, till end of dayes:
Of all her Children, Children, liv'd to see,
Then dying, left a blessed memory.

TEXT NOTES:
Line 3: *Pitiful,* full of pity and compassion.
Line 5: *Aweful,* commanding profound respect.
Line 10: *In her Closet,* in secret prayer and meditation.

THE AUTHOR TO HER BOOK.

Thou ill-form'd offspring of my feeble brain,
Who after birth did'st by my side remain,
Till snatcht from thence by friends, less wise then true
Who thee abroad, expos'd to publick view,
Made thee in raggs, halting to th' press to trudg,   5
Where errors were not lessened (all may judg)
At thy return my blushing was not small,
My rambling brat (in print) should mother call,
I cast thee by as one unfit for light,
Thy Visage was so irksome in my sight;   10
Yet being mine own, at length affection would
Thy blemishes amend, if so I could:
I wash'd thy face, but more defects I saw,
And rubbing off a spot, still made a flaw.
I stretcht thy joynts to make thee even feet,   15
Yet still thou run'st more hobling than is meet;
In better dress to trim thee was my mind,
But nought save home-spun Cloth, i'th' house I find
In this array, 'mongst Vulgars mayst thou roam
In Criticks hands, beware thou dost not come;   20
And take thy way where yet thou art not known,
If for thy Father askt, say, thou hadst none:
And for thy Mother, she alas is poor,
Which caus'd her thus to send thee out of door.

EDWARD TAYLOR:
OCCASIONAL MEDITATIONS

Only a few occasional meditations are extant among the poetic works of Edward Taylor. Daily occurrences, the postponement of a trip due to severe rain, observance of insect behavior, or the scene of his wife at work became the occasion for meditation on deeper religious issues. The first three poems are impossible to date but were definitely written after Taylor's 1674 marriage, and perhaps not until the 1680s (see Introduction, p. 42). The method, often termed "spiritualizing the creatures," was popularized by widely read English Puritan devotional writer John Flavel in such books as Husbandry Spiritualized *(1669) and* Navigation Spiritualized *(1682). Extraordinary occasions from 1682 to 1689, the death of children and of wife Elizabeth, and a devastating flood sparked serious meditation on life, loss, grace, and hope (see Introduction, pp. 43–48). The poetry of Edward Taylor remained virtually unknown until the twentieth century. Thomas H. Johnson edited and published selections from his work in the late 1930s; Donald E. Stanford's edition of* The Poems of Edward Taylor *appeared in 1960.*

[WHEN] LET BY RAIN.

Ye Flippering Soule,
   Why dost between the Nippers dwell?
Not stay, nor goe. Not yea, nor yet Controle.
   Doth this doe well?
      Rise journy'ng when the skies fall weeping Showers.   5
      Not o're nor under th'Clouds and Cloudy Powers.

Not yea, nor noe:
   On tiptoes thus? Why sit on thorns?

129

Resolve the matter: Stay thyselfe or goe.
  Be n't both wayes born.   *10*
    Wager thyselfe against thy surplice, see,
    And win thy Coate: or let thy Coate Win thee.

Is this th'Effect,
  To leaven thus my Spirits all?
To make my heart a Crabtree Cask direct?   *15*
  A Verjuicte Hall?
    As Bottle Ale, whose Spirits prisond nurst
    When jog'd, the bung with Violence doth burst?

Shall I be made
  A sparkling Wildfire Shop   *20*
Where my dull Spirits at the Fireball trade
  Do frisk and hop?
    And while the Hammer doth the Anvill pay,
    The fireball matter sparkles ery way.

One sorry fret,   *25*
  An anvill Sparke, rose higher
And in thy Temple falling almost set
  The house on fire.
    Such fireballs droping in the Temple Flame
    Burns up the building: Lord forbid the same.   *30*

TEXT NOTES:
Title: *Let*, hindered.
Line 1: *Flippering*, flip-flopping.
Line 2: *Nippers*, windstorms causing delay of a ship.
Line 11: *Surplice*, overcoat.
Line 15: *Crabtree*, wild apple tree.
Line 16: *Verjuicte*, filled with verjuice, acid juice of crab apple for making into
    liquor.
Line 17: *Nurst*, tended, fostered.
Line 20: *Wildfire Shop*, blacksmith shop.
Line 25: *Fret*, gust of wind.

UPON A SPIDER CATCHING A FLY.

Thou sorrow, venom Elfe.
  Is this thy play,
To spin a web out of thyselfe
  To Catch a Fly?
    For Why?   *5*

I saw a pettish wasp
   Fall foule therein.
Whom yet thy Whorle pins did not clasp
   Lest he should fling
      His sting.   *10*

But as affraid, remote
   Didst stand hereat
And with thy little fingers stroke
   And gently tap
      His back.   *15*

Thus gently him didst treate
   Lest he should pet,
And in a froppish, waspish heate
   Should greatly fret
      Thy net.   *20*

Whereas the silly Fly,
   Caught by its leg
Thou by the throate tookst hastily
   And 'hinde the head
      Bite Dead.   *25*

This goes to pot, that not
   Nature doth call.
Strive not above what strength hath got
   Lest in the brawle
      Thou fall.   *30*

This Frey seems thus to us.
   Hells Spider gets
His intrails spun to whip Cords thus
   And wove to nets
      And sets.   *35*

To tangle Adams race
   In's stratigems
To their Destructions, spoil'd, made base
   By venom things
      Damn'd Sins.   *40*

But mighty, Gracious Lord
   Communicate
Thy Grace to breake the Cord, afford
   Us Glorys Gate
      And State.   *45*

We'l Nightingaile sing like
  When pearcht on high
In Glories Cage, thy glory, bright,
  And thankfully,
    For joy.   *50*

TEXT NOTES:
Line 6: *Pettish,* ill-humored.
Line 8: *Whorle,* part of a spinning wheel.
Line 17: *Pet,* take offense, react negatively.
Line 18: *Froppish,* fretful.
Line 19: *Fret,* destroy.
Line 26: *Pot,* put up, preserve.
Line 31: *Frey* (fray), alarm, terror; assault.
Line 33: *Whip Cords,* thin, tough hempen cord.

HUSWIFERY.

Make me, O Lord, thy Spining Wheele compleate.
  Thy Holy Worde my Distaff make for mee.
Make mine Affections thy Swift Flyers neate
  And make my Soule thy holy Spoole to bee.
  My Conversation make to be thy Reele   *5*
  And reele the yarn thereon spun of thy Wheele.

Make me thy Loome then, knit therein this Twine:
  And make thy Holy Spirit, Lord, winde quills:
Then weave the Web thyselfe. The yarn is fine.
  Thine Ordinances make my Fulling Mills.   *10*
  Then dy the same in Heavenly Colours Choice,
  All pinkt with Varnisht Flowers of Paradise.

Then cloath therewith mine Understanding, Will,
  Affections, Judgment, Conscience, Memory
My Words, and Actions, that their shine may fill   *15*
  My wayes with glory and thee glorify.
  Then mine apparell shall display before yee
  That I am Cloathd in Holy robes for glory.

TEXT NOTES:
Line 1: *Compleate,* fully equipped; without defect.
Line 8: *Winde quills,* fill spools with thread or yarn.
Line 9: *Web,* cloth.

Line 10: *Fulling Mills,* mills where cloth is beaten and cleaned.
Line 12: *Pinkt,* adorned, shining.

UPON WEDLOCK, AND DEATH OF CHILDREN.

A Curious Knot God made in Paradise,
  And drew it out inamled neatly Fresh.
It was the True-Love Knot, more sweet than spice
  And set with all the flowres of Graces dress.
  Its Weddens Knot, that ne're can be unti'de.   *5*
  No Alexanders Sword can it divide.

The slips here planted, gay and glorious grow:
  Unless an Hellish breath do sindge their Plumes.
Here Primrose, Cowslips, Roses, Lilies blow
  With Violets and Pinkes that voide perfumes.   *10*
  Whose beautious leaves ore laid with Hony Dew.
  And Chanting birds Cherp out sweet Musick true.

When in this Knot I planted was, my Stock
  Soon knotted, and a manly flower out brake.
And after it my branch again did knot   *15*
  Brought out another Flowre its sweet breathd mate.
  One knot gave one tother the tothers place.
  Whence Checkling smiles fought in each others face.

But oh! a glorious hand from glory came
  Guarded with Angells, soon did Crop this flowre   *20*
Which almost tore the root up of the same
  At that unlookt for, Dolesome, darksome houre.
  In Pray're to Christ perfum'de it did ascend,
  And Angells bright did it to heaven tend.

But pausing on't, this sweet perfum'd my thought,   *25*
  Christ would in Glory have a Flowre, Choice, Prime,
And having Choice, chose this my branch forth brought.
  Lord take't. I thanke thee, thou takst ought of mine,
  It is my pledg in glory, part of mee
  Is now in it, Lord, glorifi'de with thee.   *30*

But praying ore my branch, my branch did sprout
  And bore another manly flower, and gay
And after that another, sweet brake out,
  The which the former hand soon got away.

But oh! the tortures, Vomit, screechings, groans,   *35*
And six weeks Fever would pierce hearts like stones.

Griefe o're doth flow: and nature fault would finde
  Were not thy Will, my Spell Charm, Joy, and Gem:
That as I said, I say, take, Lord, they're thine.
  I piecemeale pass to Glory bright in them.   *40*
  I joy, may I sweet Flowers for Glory breed,
  Whether thou getst them green, or lets them seed.

TEXT NOTES:

Line 1: *Curious,* clever, fastidious, carefully made.
Line 1: *Knot,* flower bed.
Line 2: *Inamled neatly Fresh,* nicely finished.
Line 3: *True-Love Knot,* marriage bond.
Line 4: *Dress,* array, adornment.
Line 8: *Hellish breath,* bad wind.
Line 10: *Voide,* deprive of efficacy or value; exude.
Line 11: *Hony Dew,* sweet, sticky substance found on leaves, excreted by aphides.
Line 13: *Stock,* garden, marriage.
Line 14: *Knotted,* budded, began to bear fruit.
Line 14: *A manly flower,* Samuel, b. Aug. 27, 1675.
Line 16: *Another Flowre,* Elizabeth, b. Dec. 27, 1676, d. Dec. 25, 1677.
Line 17: *Tothers,* the other's.
Line 18: *Checkling,* chuckling.
Line 32: *Another manly flower,* James, b. Oct. 12, 1678.
Line 33: *Another,* Abigail, b. Aug. 6, 1681, d. Aug. 22, 1682.
Line 38: *Spell Charm,* protection.

THE EBB AND FLOW.

When first thou on me Lord wrought'st thy Sweet Print,
  My heart was made thy tinder box.
  My 'ffections were thy tinder in't.
    Where fell thy Sparkes by drops.
Those holy Sparks of Heavenly Fire that came   *5*
Did ever catch and often out would flame.

But now my Heart is made thy Censar trim,
  Full of thy golden Altars fire,
  To offer up Sweet Incense in
    Unto thyselfe intire: *10*
I finde my tinder scarce thy sparks can feel
That drop out from thy Holy flint and Steel.

Hence doubts out bud for feare thy fire in mee
  'S a mocking Ignis Fatuus
  Or lest thine Altars fire out bee,   *15*
    Its hid in ashes thus.
Yet when the bellows of thy Spirit blow
Away mine ashes, then thy fire doth glow.

TEXT NOTES:

Line 1: *Print,* image.

Line 7: *Trim,* excellent, beautiful, ornate.

Line 14: *Ignis Fatuus,* light that appears over marshy ground, caused by combustion of marsh gas, which disappears upon approaching it; thus, a misleading principle.

UPON THE SWEEPING FLOOD AUG: 13.14. 1683.

Oh! that Id had a tear to've quencht that flame
  Which did dissolve the Heavens above
  Into those liquid drops that Came
    To drown our Carnall love.
Our cheeks were dry and eyes refusde to weep.   *5*
Tears bursting out ran down the skies darke Cheek.

Were th'Heavens sick? must wee their Doctors bee
  And physick them with pills, our sin?
  To make them purg and Vomit, see,
    And Excrements out fling?   *10*
We've griev'd them by such Physick that they shed
Their Excrements upon our lofty heads.

A FUNERALL POEM UPON THE DEATH
OF MY EVER ENDEARED, AND TENDER WIFE MRS. ELIZABETH TAYLOR,
WHO FELL ASLEEP IN CHRIST THE 7TH DAY OF JULY AT NIGHT
ABOUT TWO HOURS AFTER SUN SETTING 1689
AND IN THE 39 YEARE OF HER LIFE.

Part. 1.

My Gracious Lord, I Licence of thee Crave,
Not to repine but drop upon the Grave
Of my Deare Wife a Teare, or two: or wash

Thy Milk White hand in tears that downward pass.
Thou summond hast her Noble part away: *5*
And in Salt Tears I would Embalm her Clay.
Some deem Death doth the True Love Knot unty:
But I do finde it harder tide thereby.
My heart is in't and will be squeez'd therefore
To pieces if thou draw the Ends much more.   *10*
Oh strange Untying! it ti'th harder: What?
Can anything unty a True Love Knot?
Five Babes thou tookst from me before this Stroake.
Thine arrows then into my bowells broake,
But now they pierce into my bosom smart,   *15*
Do strike and stob me in the very heart.
I'de then my bosom Friend a Comfort, and
To Comfort: Yet my Lord, I kiss thy hand.
I Her resign'd, thou tookst her into thine,
Out of my bosom, yet she dwells in mine: *20*
And though her Precious Soule now swims in bliss,
Yet while grim Death, that Dismall Sergeant is,
Between the Parts Essentiall now remote,
And hath this stately Tabernacle broke
My Harp is turnd to mourning: Organ sweet   *25*
Is turn'de into the Voice of them that weep.
Griefe swelling girds the Heart Strings where its purst,
Unless it Vent the Vessell sure will burst.
    My Gracious Lord, grant that my bitter Griefe
    Breath through this little Vent hole for reliefe.   *30*

Part. 2.

    My Dear, Deare Love, reflect thou no such thing,
    Will Griefe permit you at my Grave to sing?
    Oh! Black Black Theme! The Girths of Griefe alone
    Do gird my heart till Gust of Sorrows groan
    And dash a mournfull Song to pieces on   *35*
    The Dolefull Face of thy Sepulcher Stone.
    My Onely DOVE, though Harp and Harrow, loe,
    Better agree than Songs and Sorrows doe,
    Yet spare me thus to drop a blubber'd Verse
    Out of my Weeping Eyes Upon thy Herse.   *40*
    What shall my Preface to our True Love Knot
    Frisk in Acrostick Rhimes? And may I not

Now at our parting, with Poetick knocks
Break a salt teare to pieces as it drops?
Did Davids bitter Sorrow at the Dusts   45
Of Jonathan raise such Poetick gusts?
Do Emperours interr'd in Verses lie?
And mayn't such Feet run from my Weeping Eye?
Nay, Dutie lies upon mee much; and shall
I in thy Coffin naile thy Vertues all?   50
How shall thy Babes, and theirs, thy Vertuous shine
Know, or Persue unless I them define?
Thy Grace will Grace unto a Poem bee
Although a Poem be no grace to thee.
Impute it not a Crime then if I weep   55
A Weeping Poem on thy Winding Sheet.
Maybe some Angell may my Poem sing
To thee in Glory, or relate the thing,
    Which if he do, my mournfull Poem may
    Advance thy Joy, and my Deep Sorrow lay.   60

Part. 3.

    Your Ears, Bright Saints, and Angells: them I Choose
To stough her Praises in: I'le not abuse.
Her Modesty would blush should you profess,
I in Hyperboles her praises dress.
Wherefore as Cramping Griefe permitts to stut   65
Them forth accept of such as here I put.
    Her Husbands Joy, Her Childrens Chiefe Content.
Her Servants Eyes, Her Houses Ornament.
Her Shine as Child, as Neighbour, flies abroad
As Mistress, Mother, Wife, her Walke With God.   70
As Child she was a Tender, Pious Bud
Of Pious Parents, sprang of Pious Blood
Two Grandsires, Gran'ams: one or two, she had
A Father too and Mother, that englad
The Gracious heart to thinke upon, they were   75
Bright Pillars in Gods Temple shining cleare.
Her Father, and her Mothers Father fix
As shining Stars in Golden Candlesticks.
She did Obedient, Tender, Meek Child prove
The Object of her Fathers Eye, and Love.   80
Her Mother being Dead, her heart would melt

When she her Fathers looks not pleasant felt.
His smile Would her enliven, Frown, down pull
Hence she became his Child most Dutifull.
    As Neighbour, she was full of Neighbourhood   *85*
Not Proud, or Strang; Grave, Courteous, ever good.
Compassionate: but unto none was Soure.
Her Fingers dropt with Myrrh, oft, to her power.
    As Mistress she order'd her Family
With all Discretion, and most prudently   *90*
In all things prompt: Dutie in this respect
Would to the meanest in it not neglect.
Ripe at her Fingers Ends, Would nothing flinch.
She was a neate good Huswife every inch.
Although her weakenesse made her let alone   *95*
Things so to go, as made her fetch a groan.
Remiss was not, nor yet severe unto
Her Servants: but i'th' golden mean did goe.
    As Mother, Oh! What tender Mother She?
Her bowells Boiled ore to them that bee   *100*
Bits of her tender Bowells. She a share
Of her affections ever made them ware.
Yet never chose to trick them, nor herselfe
In antick garbs; or Lavishness of Wealth.
But was a Lover much of Comeliness: *105*
And with her Needle work would make their Dress.
The Law of Life within her Lips she would
Be dropping forth upon them as shee should.
Foolishly fond she was not but would give
Correction wisely, that their Soules might Live.   *110*
    As Wife, a Tender, Tender, Loving, Meet,
Meeke, Patient, Humble, Modest, Faithfull, Sweet
Endearing Help she was: Whose Chiefest Treasure
Of Earthly things she held her Husbands pleasure.
But if she spi'de displeasure in his face,   *115*
Sorrow would spoile her own, and marr its grace.
Dear Heart! She would his Joy, Peace, Honour, Name,
Even as her very Life, seeke to mentain.
And if an hasty word by chance dropt in:
She would in secret sigh it or'e with him.   *120*
She was not wedded unto him alone
But had his joy, and sorrow as her own.
She, where he chanc'd to miss, a Cover would lay

Yet would in Secret fore him all Display
In meekness of sweet wisdom, and by Art, 125
As Certainly would winde into the heart.
She laid her neck unto the Yoake he draws:
And was his Faithfull Yoake Mate, in Christ's Cause.
  As to her walk with God, she did inherit
The very Spirits of her Parents Spirit. 130
She was no gaudy Christian, or gilt Weed:
But was a Reall, Israelite indeed.
When in her Fathers house God toucht her Heart,
That Trembling Frame of Spirit, and that Smart,
She then was under very, few did know: 135
Whereof she somewhat to the Church did show.
Repentance now's her Work: Sin poyson is:
Faith, carries her to Christ as one of his.
Fear Temples in her heart; Love flowers apace
To God, Christ, Grace Saints, and the Means of Grace. 140
She's much in Reading, Pray're, Selfe-Application
Holds humbly up, a pious Conversation
In which she makes profession * * * * * * * *
Which unto Westfield Church she did disclose.
Holy in Health; Patient in Sickness long. 145
And very great. Yet gracious Speech doth throng:
She oft had up, An Alwise God Doth this.
And in a filiall way the Rod would kiss.
When Pains were Sore, Justice can do no wrong,
Nor Mercy Cruell be; became her Song. 150
The Doomsday Verses much perfum'de her Breath,
Much in her thoughts, and yet she fear'd not Death.

TEXT NOTES:
Line 8: *Tide,* tied.
Line 33: *Girths,* belts, bands.
Line 34: *Gust,* blast of wind, a burst.
Line 37: *Harrow,* farm tool for breaking clods in soil.
Line 42: *Acrostick Rhimes,* such as Taylor composed during their courtship.
Line 60: *Lay,* allay.
Line 62: *Stough,* stow; stuff.
Line 65: *Stut,* stutter.
Line 86: *Strang* (strange), unfriendly, distant.
Line 93: *Ripe at,* mature to.
Line 93: *Flinch,* draw back from.
Line 94: *Neate,* complete.

Line 103: *Trick,* dress, adorn.
Line 104: *Antick garbs,* antique (thus, aristocratic) clothing.
Line 131: *Gilt Weed,* brightly colored weed, i.e. a hypocrite.
Line 132: *Israelite indeed,* see John 1:47.
Line 134: *Smart,* pain.
Line 136: *To the Church did show,* i.e. in her public confession of faith and relation of her conversion upon joining the Church covenant.
Line 151: *Doomsday Verses,* Michael Wigglesworth's *Day of Doom* (1662).

A FIG FOR THEE OH! DEATH.

Thou King of Terrours with thy Gastly Eyes
With Butter teeth, bare bones Grim looks likewise.
And Grizzly Hide, and clawing Tallons, fell,
Opning to Sinners Vile, Trap Door of Hell,
That on in Sin impenitently trip   5
The Downfall art of the infernall Pit,
Thou struckst thy teeth deep in my Lord's blest Side:
Who dasht it out, and all its venom 'stroyde
That now thy Poundrill shall onely dash
My Flesh and bones to bits, and Cask shall clash.   10
Thou'rt not so frightfull now to me, thy knocks
Do crack my shell. Its Heavenly kernells box
Abides most safe. Thy blows do break its shell,
Thy Teeth its Nut. Cracks are that on it fell.
Thence out its kirnell fair and nut, by worms   15
Once Viciated out, new formd forth turns
And on the wings of some bright Angell flies
Out to bright glory of Gods blissfull joyes.
Hence thou to mee with all thy Gastly face
Art not so dreadfull unto mee through Grace.   20
I am resolvde to fight thee, and ne'er yield,
Blood up to th'Ears; and in the battle field
Chasing thee hence: But not for this my flesh,
My Body, my vile harlot, its thy Mess,
Labouring to drown me into Sin, disguise   25
By Eating and by drinking such evill joyes
Though Grace preserv'd mee that I nere have
Surprised been nor tumbled in such grave.
Hence for my strumpet I'le ne'er draw my Sword

Nor thee restrain at all by Iron Curb 30
Nor for her safty will I 'gainst thee strive
But let thy frozen gripes take her Captive
And her imprison in thy dungeon Cave
And grinde to powder in thy Mill the grave,
Which powder in thy Van thou'st safely keep 35
Till she hath slept out quite her fatall Sleep.
When the last Cock shall Crow the last day in
And the Arch Angells Trumpets sound shall ring
Then th'Eye Omniscient seek shall all there round
Each dust death's mill had very finely ground, 40
Which in death's smoky furnace well refinde
And Each to'ts fellow hath exactly joyn't,
Is raised up anew and made all bright
And Christalized; all top full of delight.
And entertains its Soule again in bliss 45
And Holy Angells waiting all on this,
The Soule and Body now, as two true Lovers
Ery night how do they hug and kiss each other.
And going hand in hand thus through the skies

Up to Eternall glory glorious rise. 50
Is this the Worst thy terrours then canst, why
Then should this grimace at me terrify?
Why camst thou then so slowly? Mend thy pace.
Thy Slowness me detains from Christ's bright face.
Although thy terrours rise to th'highest degree, 55
I still am where I was, a Fig for thee.

TEXT NOTES:

Title: *Fig,* poisoned fig; contemptuous gesture made by thrusting thumb between
    two closed fingers.
Line 1: *King of Terrours,* see Job 18:14, death personified.
Line 2: *Butter teeth,* buck teeth.
Line 3: *Grizzly,* horrible to behold, engendering feelings of the macabre.
Line 3: *Hide,* human skin.
Line 3: *Clawing Tallons,* grasping fingers.
Line 3: *Fell,* human flesh.
Line 9: *Poundrill* (poundrel), head, i.e. death's-head.
Line 10: *Cask,* casket.
Line 10: *Clash,* bang shut.
Line 15: *Nut,* brown.

Line 24: *Mess,* food.
Line 27: *Nere,* never.
Line 28: *Tumbled,* stumbled.
Line 29: *Strumpet,* physical body (cf. line 24).
Line 35: *Van,* winnowing basket.
Line 38: *Trumpets sound,* see 1 Corinthians 15:51–52.

EDWARD TAYLOR:
FROM *GODS DETERMINATIONS*

Taylor's epic poem on the Puritan themes of salvation and church membership carries the full title, Gods Determinations touching his Elect: and The Elects Combat in their Conversion, and Coming up to God in Christ together with the Comfortable Effects thereof. *It is actually a collection of 35 poems, of which eight are included here as representative. These didactic verses reveal Taylor more as preacher and theologian than as Puritan contemplative. The poems nevertheless are a form of devotional literature, for sermons and similar poetic works, such as Michael Wigglesworth's* Day of Doom *(1662), influenced the family and secret devotions of the laity. Moreover, Taylor did not write this or any poem for publication but as part of his own spiritual exercises. Taylor probably composed* Gods Determinations *in the mid-1680s (see Introduction, pp. 50–52).*

THE PREFACE.

Infinity, when all things it beheld
In Nothing, and of Nothing all did build,
Upon what Base was fixt the Lath, wherein
He turn'd this Globe, and riggalld it so trim?
Who blew the Bellows of his Furnace Vast?   5
Or held the Mould wherein the world was Cast?
Who laid its Corner Stone? Or whose Command?
Where stand the Pillars upon which it stands?
Who Lac'de and Fillitted the earth so fine,
With Rivers like green Ribbons Smaragdine?   10

Who made the Sea's its Selvedge, and it locks
Like a Quilt Ball within a Silver Box?
Who Spread its Canopy? Or Curtains Spun?
Who in this Bowling Alley bowld the Sun?
Who made it always when it rises set   15
To go at once both down, and up to get?
Who th'Curtain rods made for this Tapistry?
Who hung the twinckling Lanthorns in the Sky?
Who? who did this? or who is he? Why, know
Its Onely Might Almighty this did doe.   20
His hand hath made this noble worke which Stands
His Glorious Handywork not made by hands.
Who spake all things from nothing; and with ease
Can speake all things to nothing, if he please.
Whose Little finger at his pleasure Can   25
Out mete ten thousand worlds with halfe a Span:
Whose Might Almighty can by half a looks
Root up the rocks and rock the hills by th'roots.
Can take this mighty World up in his hande,
And shake it like a Squitchen or a Wand.   30
Whose single Frown will make the Heavens shake
Like as an aspen leafe the Winde makes quake.
Oh! what a might is this Whose single frown
Doth shake the world as it would shake it down?
Which All from Nothing fet, from Nothing, All: 35
Hath All on Nothing set, lets Nothing fall.
Gave All to nothing Man indeed, whereby
Through nothing man all might him Glorify.
In Nothing then imbosst the brightest Gem
More pretious than all pretiousness in them.   40
But Nothing man did throw down all by Sin:
And darkened that lightsom Gem in him.
    That now his Brightest Diamond is grown
    Darker by far than any Coalpit Stone.

TEXT NOTES:
Line 4: *Riggalld,* grooved.
Line 4: *Trim,* handsome.
Line 9: *Lac'de,* trimmed with lace.
Line 9: *Fillitted,* tied up with ornamental bands.
Line 10: *Smaragdine,* emerald.

Line 11: *Sea's,* sea as.
Line 11: *Selvedge,* ornamental border, edging.
Line 26: *Mete,* measure out.
Line 26: *Span,* handspan.
Line 30: *Squitchen,* switch, whip.
Line 35: *Fet,* fetched.

THE SOULS GROAN TO CHRIST FOR SUCCOUR.

Good Lord, behold this Dreadfull Enemy
   Who makes me tremble with his fierce assaults,
I dare not trust, yet feare to give the ly,
   For in my soul, my soul finds many faults.
   And though I justify myselfe to's face: *5*
   I do Condemn myselfe before thy Grace.

He strives to mount my sins, and them advance
   Above thy Merits, Pardons, or Good Will
Thy Grace to lessen, and thy Wrath t'inhance
   As if thou couldst not pay the sinners bill.   *10*
   He Chiefly injures thy rich Grace, I finde
   Though I confess my heart to sin inclin'de.

Those Graces which thy Grace enwrought in mee,
   He makes as nothing but a pack of Sins.
He maketh Grace no grace, but Crueltie,   *15*
   Is Graces Honey Comb, a Comb of Stings?
   This makes me ready leave thy Grace and run.
   Which if I do, I finde I am undone.

I know he is thy Cur, therefore I bee
   Perplexed lest I from thy Pasture stray.   *20*
He bayghs, and barks so veh'mently at mee.
   Come rate this Cur, Lord, breake his teeth I pray.
   Remember me I humbly pray thee first.
   Then halter up this Cur that is so Curst.

TEXT NOTES:
Line 1: *Enemy,* Satan.
Line 19: *Cur,* sheep dog.
Line 22: *Rate,* reprove.
Line 22: *Breake,* tame, discipline.

CHRISTS REPLY.

Peace, Peace, my Hony, do not Cry,
My Little Darling, wipe thine eye,
    Oh Cheer, Cheer up, come see.
Is anything too deare, my Dove,
Is anything too good, my Love   *5*
    To get or give for thee?

If in the severall thou art
This Yelper fierce will at thee bark:
    That thou art mine this shows.
As Spot barks back the sheep again   *10*
Before they to the Pound are ta'ne,
    So he and hence 'way goes.

But yet this Cur that bayghs so sore
Is broken tootht, and muzzled sure,
    Fear not, my Pritty Heart.   *15*
His barking is to make thee Cling
Close underneath thy Saviours Wing.
    Why did my sweeten start?

And if he run an inch too far,
I'le Check his Chain, and rate the Cur.   *20*
    My Chick, keep clost to mee.
The Poles shall sooner kiss, and greet
And Paralells shall sooner meet
    Than thou shalt harmed bee.

He seeks to aggrivate thy sin   *25*
And screw them to the highest pin,
    To make thy faith to quaile.
Yet mountain Sins like mites should show
And then these mites for naught should goe
    Could he but once prevaile.   *30*

I smote thy sins upon the Head.
They Dead'ned are, though not quite dead:
    And shall not rise again.
I'l put away the Guilt thereof,
And purge its Filthiness cleare off: *35*
    My Blood doth out the stain.

And though thy judgment was remiss
Thy Headstrong Will too Wilfull is.
   I will Renew the same.
And though thou do too frequently
Offend as heretofore hereby
   I'l not severly blaim.

And though thy senses do inveagle
Thy Noble Soul to tend the Beagle,
   That t'hunt her games forth go.
I'le Lure her back to me, and Change
Those fond Affections that do range
   As yelping beagles doe.

Although thy sins increase their race,
And though when thou hast sought for Grace,
   Thou fallst more than before
If thou by true Repentence Rise,
And Faith makes me thy Sacrifice,
   I'l pardon all, though more.

Though Satan strive to block thy way
By all his Stratagems he may:
   Come, come though through the fire.
For Hell that Gulph of fire for sins,
Is not so hot as t'burn thy Shins.
   Then Credit not the Lyar.

Those Cursed Vermin Sins that Crawle
All ore thy Soul, both Greate, and small
   Are onely Satans own:
Which he in his Malignity
Unto thy Souls true Sanctity
   In at the doors hath thrown.

And though they be Rebellion high,
Ath'ism or Apostacy:
   Though blasphemy it bee:
Unto what Quality, or Sise
Excepting one, so e're it rise.
   Repent, I'le pardon thee.

Although thy Soule was once a Stall
Rich hung with Satans nicknacks all;
   If thou Repent thy Sin,

40
45
50
55
60
65
70
75

A Tabernacle in't I'le place
Fild with Gods Spirit, and his Grace.
    Oh Comfortable thing!

I dare the World therefore to show
A God like me, to anger slow: *80*
    Whose wrath is full of Grace.
Doth hate all Sins both Greate, and small:
Yet when Repented, pardons all.
    Frowns with a Smiling Face.

As for thy outward Postures each,   *85*
Thy Gestures, Actions, and thy Speech,
    I Eye and Eying spare,
If thou repent. My Grace is more
Ten thousand times still tribled ore
    Than thou canst want, or ware.   *90*

As for the Wicked Charge he makes,
That he of Every Dish first takes
    Of all thy holy things.
Its false, deny the same, and say,
That which he had he stool away   *95*
    Out of thy Offerings.

Though to thy Griefe, poor Heart, thou finde
In Pray're too oft a wandring minde,
    In Sermons Spirits dull.
Though faith in firy furnace flags,   *100*
And Zeale in Chilly Seasons lags.
    Temptations powerfull.

These faults are his, and none of thine
So far as thou dost them decline.
    Come then receive my Grace.   *105*
And when he buffits thee therefore
If thou my aid, and Grace implore
    I'le shew a pleasant face.

But still look for Temptations Deep,
Whilst that thy Noble Sparke doth keep   *110*
    Within a Mudwald Cote.
These White Frosts and the Showers that fall
Are but to whiten thee withall.
    Not rot the Web they smote.

If in the fire where Gold is tride   *115*
Thy Soule is put, and purifide
   Wilt thou lament thy loss?
If silver-like this fire refine
Thy Soul and make it brighter shine:
   Wilt thou bewaile the Dross?   *120*

Oh! fight my Field: no Colours fear:
I'l be thy Front, I'l be thy reare.
   Fail not: my Battells fight.
Defy the Tempter, and his Mock.
Anchor thy heart on mee thy Rock.   *125*
   I do in thee Delight.

TEXT NOTES:
Line 7: *The several*, the elect.
Line 20: *Rate the Cur*, reprove the dog.
Line 26: *Pin*, tuning pin or peg on a stringed instrument.
Line 27: *Quaile*, fail, wither.
Line 60: *The Lyar*, Satan; see Matthew 27:63.
Line 70: *Sise*, size.
Line 71: *Excepting one*, blasphemy against the Holy Ghost (Matthew 12:31).
Line 73: *Stall*, quarters.
Line 89: *Tribled ore*, trebled over, increased three times.
Line 90: *Ware*, be aware of.
Line 95: *Stool*, stolen.
Line 111: *Mudwald Cote*, mud-walled cottage.
Line 115: *Tride*, tried, extracted, refined.

AN EXTASY OF JOY LET IN BY THIS REPLY RETURND IN ADMIRATION.

My Sweet Deare Lord, for thee I'le Live, Dy, Fight.
   Gracious indeed! My Front! my Rear!
   Almighty magnify a Mite:
     O! What a Wonder's here?

Had I ten thousand times ten thousand hearts: *5*
   And Every Heart ten thousand Tongues;
   To praise, I should but stut odd parts
     Of what to thee belongs.

If all the world did in Alimbeck ly,
   Bleeding its Spirits out in Sweat;   *10*
   It could not halfe enlife a Fly
     To Hum thy Praises greate.

If all can't halfe enlife a Fly to hum,
    (Which scarce an Animall we call)
    Thy Praises then which from me come,   *15*
        Come next to none at all.

For I have made myselfe ten thousand times
    More naught than nought itselfe, by Sin.
    Yet thou extendst thy Gracious Shines
        For me to bath therein.   *20*

Oh! Stand amaizd yee Angells Bright, come run
    Yee Glorious Heavens and Saints, to sing:
    Place yee your praises in the sun,
        Ore all the world to ring.

Nay stand agast, ye sparkling Spirits bright!   *25*
    Shall little Clods of Dust you peere?
    Shall they toote Praises on your pipe?
        Oh! that we had it here.

What can a Crumb of Dust sally such praise
    Which do from Earth all heaven o're ring   *30*
    Who swaddle up the suns bright rayes
        Can in a Flesh Flie's Wing?

Can any Ant stand on the Earth and spit
    Another out to peer with this?
    Or Drink the Ocean up, and yet   *35*
        Its belly empty is?

Thou may'st this World as easily up hide
    Under the Blackness of thy naile:
    As scape Sins Gulph without a Guide:
        Or Hell without a bale.   *40*

If all the Earthy Mass were rambd in Sacks
    And saddled on an Emmet small,
    Its Load were light unto those packs
        Which Sins do bring on all.

But sure this burden'd Emmet moves no wing.   *45*
    Nay, nay, Compar'd with thee, it flies.
    Yet man is easd his weight of Sin.
        From hell to Heav'n doth rise.

When that the World was new, its Chiefe Delight,
    One Paradise alone Contain'de: *50*
    The Bridle of Mans Appetite
        The Appletree refrain'de.

The which he robbing, eat the fruit as good,
　　Whose Coare hath Chokd him and his race.
　　And juyce hath poyson'd all their blood,   *55*
　　　Hes' in a Dismall Case.

None can this Coare remove, Poyson expell:
　　He, if his Blood ben't Clarifi'de
　　Within Christs veans, must fry in Hell,
　　　Till God be satisfi'de.   *60*

Christ to his Father saith, Incarnate make
　　Mee, Mee thy Son; and I will doe't:
　　I'le purify his Blood, and take
　　　The Coare out of his Throate.

All this he did, and did for us, vile Clay: *65*
　　Oh! let our Praise his Grace assaile.
　　To free us from Sins Gulph each way,
　　　He's both our Bridge, and Raile.

Although we fall and Fall, and Fall and Fall
　　And Satan fall on us as fast.   *70*
　　He purgeth us and doth us call
　　　Our trust on him to Cast.

My Lumpish Soule why art thou hamper'd thus
　　Within a Crumb of Dust? Arise,
　　Trumpet out Praises. Christ for us   *75*
　　　Hath slain our Enemies.

Screw up, Deare Lord, upon the highest pin:
　　My soul thy ample Praise to sound.
　　O tune it right, that every string
　　　May make thy praise rebound.   *80*

But oh! how slack, slow, dull? with what delay,
　　Do I this Musick to, repare,
　　While tabernacled in Clay
　　　My Organs Cottag'de are?

Yet Lord accept this Pittance of thy praise   *85*
　　Which as a Traveller I bring,
　　While travelling along thy wayes
　　　In broken notes I sing.

And at my journies end in endless joyes
　　I'l make amends where Angells meet   *90*
　　And sing their flaming Melodies
　　　In Ravishing tunes most sweet.

TEXT NOTES:

Line 3: *Mite,* insect, small object.

Line 7: *Stut,* stutter.

Line 9: *Alimbeck,* distilling equipment.

Line 10: *Sweat,* life-blood; sweat-like drops.

Line 18: *Naught,* evil.

Line 26: *Peere,* make equal.

Line 29: *Sally,* burst out with; utter; dance; first movement of a bell when "set" for ringing.

Line 34: *Peer with,* equal.

Line 38: *Under the Blackness of thy naile,* under a dirty fingernail.

Line 39: *Gulph,* chasm, abyss.

Line 40: *Bale,* delivery, release (from prison).

Line 41: *Rambd,* packed, stuffed.

Line 42: *Emmet,* ant.

Line 58: *Ben't,* be not.

THE SOUL ADMIRING THE GRACE OF THE CHURCH ENTERS INTO CHURCH FELLOWSHIP.

How is this City, Lord, of thine bespangled
    With Graces shine?
With Ordinances alli'de, and inam'led,
    Which are Divine?
Walld in with Discipline her Gates obtaine   5
Just Centinalls with Love Imbellisht plain.

Hence glorious, and terrible she stands;
    That Converts new
Seing her Centinalls of all demand
    The Word to shew;   10
Stand gazing much between two Passions Crusht
Desire, and Feare at once which both wayes thrust.

Thus are they wrackt. Desire doth forward screw
    To get them in,
But Feare doth backward thrust, that lies purdue,   15
    And slicks that Pin.
You cannot give the word, Quoth she, which though
You stumble on't its more than yet you know.

But yet Desires Screw Pin doth not slack:
    It still holds fast.   20
But Fears Screw Pin turns back or Screw doth Crack
    And breaks at last.

Hence on they go, and in they enter: where
Desire Converts to joy: joy Conquours Fear.

They now enCovenant With God: and His: *25*
   They thus indent.
The Charters Seals belonging unto this
   The Sacrament
So God is theirs avoucht, they his in Christ.
In whom all things they have, with Grace are splic'te.   *30*

Thus in the usuall Coach of Gods Decree
   They bowle and swim
To Glory bright, if no Hypocrisie
   Handed them in.
For such must shake their handmaid off lest they   *35*
Be shakt out of this Coach, or dy in th'way.

TEXT NOTES:

Line 3: *Alli'de,* allied (joined); or aligned.

Line 3: *Inam'led,* enameled.

Line 6: *Centinalls,* sentinels.

Line 6: *Imbellisht plain,* clearly decorated.

Line 11: *Between two Passions Crusht,* as in a vice (see below, image of the screw-pin).

Line 13: *Screw,* press.

Line 15: *Purdue* (perdu), sentinel in advanced, dangerous position.

Line 16: *Slicks that Pin,* lubricates that screwpin (screw of a vice); or perhaps read "slacks," to reduce the force or strength of.

Line 18: *Stumble on't,* discover it.

Line 26: *Indent,* engage, bind oneself.

Line 29: *Avoucht,* certified.

Line 32: *Bowle and swim,* conveyed on wheels (in a carriage) and on water (in a boat).

THE GLORY OF AND GRACE
IN THE CHURCH SET OUT.

   Come now behold
  Within this Knot What Flowers do grow:
    Spanglde like gold:
  Whence Wreaths of all Perfumes do flow.
Most Curious Colours of all sorts you shall   *5*
With all Sweet Spirits sent. Yet thats not all.

Oh! Look, and finde
These Choicest Flowers most richly sweet
  Are Disciplinde
With Artificiall Angells meet.   *10*
An heap of Pearls is precious: but they shall
When set by Art Excell: Yet that's not all.

  Christ's Spirit showers
Down in his Word, and Sacraments
  Upon these Flowers   *15*
The Clouds of Grace Divine Contents.
Such things of Wealthy Blessings on them fall
As make them sweetly thrive: Yet that's not all.

  Yet still behold!
All flourish not at once. We see   *20*
  While some Unfold
Their blushing Leaves, some buds there bee.
Here's Faith, Hope, Charity in flower, which call
On yonders in the Bud. Yet that's not all.

  But as they stand   *25*
Like Beauties reeching in perfume
  A Divine Hand
Doth hand them up to Glories room:
Where Each in sweet'ned Songs all Praises shall
Sing all ore heaven for aye. And that's but all.   *30*

TEXT NOTES:
Line 2: *Knot,* garden.
Line 5: *Curious,* of interest to the connoisseur.
Line 6: *Sent,* scent.
Line 9: *Disciplinde,* arranged.
Line 10: *Artificiall Angells,* statues of angels.
Line 10: *Meet,* of proper dimensions.
Line 26: *Reeching,* reeking, putting forth pleasant smells.

THE SOULS ADMIRATION HEREUPON.

What I such Praises sing! How can it bee?
  Shall I in Heaven sing?
What I, that scarce durst hope to see
  Lord, such a thing?

Though nothing is too hard for thee: *5*
One Hope hereof seems hard to mee.

What, Can I ever tune those Melodies
   Who have no tune at all?
Not knowing where to stop nor Rise,
    Nor when to Fall.   *10*
  To sing thy Praise I am unfit.
  I have not learn'd my Gam-Ut yet.

But should these Praises on string'd Instruments
   Be sweetly tun'de? I finde
I nonplust am: for no Consents   *15*
   I ever minde.
  My Tongue is neither Quill, nor Bow:
  Nor Can my Fingers Quavers show.

But was it otherwise I have no Kit:
   Which though I had, I could   *20*
Not tune the strings, which soon would slip
   Though others should.
  But should they not, I cannot play:
  But for an F should strike an A.

And should thy Praise upon Winde Instruments   *25*
   Sound all o're Heaven Shrill?
My Breath will hardly through such Vents
   A Whistle fill,
  Which though it should, its past my spell
  By Stops, and Falls to sound it Well.   *30*

How should I then, joyn in such Exercise?
   One sight of thee'l intice
Mine Eyes to heft: Whose Extasies
   Will stob my Voice.
  Hereby mine Eyes will bind my Tongue.   *35*
  Unless thou, Lord, do Cut the thong.

What Use of Uselesse mee, then there, poore snake?
   There Saints, and Angels sing,
Thy Praise in full Cariere, which make
   The Heavens to ring.   *40*
  Yet if thou wilt thou Can'st me raise
  With Angels bright to sing thy Praise.

TEXT NOTES:
Line 12: *Gam-Ut,* gamut, musical scale.
Line 15: *Consents,* feelings, opinions, or their expression.
Line 16: *Minde,* remember, think of, contemplate.
Line 17: *Quill,* musical pipe, made from hollow stem.
Line 18: *Quavers,* musical notes, trills.
Line 19: *Kit,* small fiddle.
Line 33: *Heft,* lift up.
Line 34: *Stob,* stop.
Line 39: *In full Cariere* (career), at full speed.

THE JOY OF CHURCH FELLOWSHIP RIGHTLY ATTENDED.

In Heaven soaring up, I dropt an Eare
    On Earth: and oh! sweet Melody:
And listening, found it was the Saints who were
    Encoacht for Heaven that sang for Joy.
    For in Christs Coach they sweetly sing;   5
    As they to Glory ride therein.

Oh! joyous hearts! Enfir'de with holy Flame!
    Is speech thus tassled with praise?
Will not your inward fire of Joy contain;
    That it in open flames doth blaze?   10
    For in Christ's Coach Saints sweetly sing,
    As they to Glory ride therein.

And if a string do slip, by Chance, they soon
    Do screw it up again: whereby
They set it in a more melodious Tune   15
    And a Diviner Harmony.
    For in Christs Coach they sweetly sing
    As they to Glory ride therein.

In all their Acts, publick, and private, nay
    And secret too, they praise impart.   20
But in their Acts Divine and Worship, they
    With Hymns do offer up their Heart.
    Thus in Christs Coach they sweetly sing
    As they to Glory ride therein.

Some few not in; and some whose Time, and Place   25
    Block up this Coaches way do goe

As Travellers afoot, and so do trace
  The Road that gives them right thereto
  While in this Coach these sweetly sing
  As they to Glory ride therein.   *30*

TEXT NOTES:
Line 4: *Encoacht,* on board the coach.
Line 7: *Enfir'de,* on fire.

EDWARD TAYLOR:
PREPARATORY MEDITATIONS BEFORE MY APPROACH TO THE LORDS SUPPER.
FIRST SERIES

Taylor's Preparatory Meditations *epitomize Puritan formal medita-tion. The pastor wrote these poems as expressions of his regular devotions on Saturday night as he readied himself to preach and administer the sac-rament of Holy Communion the next morning, basing his meditations on the sermon text and eucharistic and other spiritual themes (see Introduction, pp. 55–61). He began this sustained, systematic, entirely secret religious work on July 23, 1682, during a period of family crisis and continued it faithfully prior to each celebration of the Lord's Supper until his retirement at age 83 in 1725. Taylor identified the first 49 poems as a set, indicating a sense of completion or divine wholeness (49 is seven times seven). The First Series, therefore, is included here in its entirety. Also among these early preparatory meditations are three reflective meditations that look back on sermon and sacrament of the previous Sabbath (see Introduction, pp. 53–55). Taylor never intended for eyes other than his own and God's to view these products of his secret devotions.*

1. MEDITATION.

Westfield 23.5m [July] 1682.

What Love is this of thine, that Cannot bee
  In thine Infinity, O Lord, Confinde,
Unless it in thy very Person see,

Infinity, and Finity Conjoyn'd?
What hath thy Godhead, as not satisfide   *5*
Marri'de our Manhood, making it its Bride?

Oh, Matchless Love! filling Heaven to the brim!
O're running it: all running o're beside
This World! Nay Overflowing Hell; wherein
    For thine Elect, there rose a mighty Tide!   *10*
    That there our Veans might through thy Person bleed,
    To quench those flames, that else would on us feed.

Oh! that thy Love might overflow my Heart!
    To fire the same with Love: for Love I would.
But oh! my streight'ned Breast! my Lifeless Sparke!   *15*
    My Fireless Flame! What Chilly Love, and Cold?
    In measure small! In Manner Chilly! See.
    Lord blow the Coal: Thy Love Enflame in mee.

2. MEDITATION ON CAN. 1.3.

THY NAME IS AN OINTMENT POURED OUT.

12.9m [Nov.] 1682.

My Dear, Deare, Lord I do thee Saviour Call:
    Thou in my very Soul art, as I Deem,
Soe High, not High enough, Soe Great; too small:
    Soe Deare, not Dear enough in my esteem.
    Soe Noble, yet So Base: too Low; too Tall: *5*
    Thou Full, and Empty art: Nothing, yet ALL.

A Precious Pearle, above all price dost 'bide.
    Rubies no Rubies are at all to thee.
Blushes of burnisht Glory Sparkling Slide
    From every Square in various Colour'd glee   *10*
    Nay Life itselfe in Sparkling Spangles Choice.
    A Precious Pearle thou art above all price.

Oh! that my Soul, Heavens Workmanship (within
    My Wicker'd Cage,) that Bird of Paradise
Inlin'de with Glorious Grace up to the brim   *15*
    Might be thy Cabbinet, oh Pearle of Price.
    Oh! let thy Pearle, Lord, Cabbinet in mee.
    I'st then be rich! nay rich enough for thee.

My Heart, oh Lord, for thy Pomander gain.
  Be thou thyselfe my sweet Perfume therein.   *20*
Make it thy Box, and let thy Pretious Name
  My Pretious Ointment be emboxt therein.
  If I thy box and thou my Ointment bee
  I shall be sweet, nay, sweet enough for thee.

Enough! Enough! oh! let me eat my Word.   *25*
  For if Accounts be ballanc'd any way,
Can my poore Eggeshell ever be an Hoard,
  Of Excellence enough for thee? Nay: nay.
  Yet may I Purse, and thou my Mony bee.
  I have enough. Enough in having thee.   *30*

TEXT NOTES:
Line 10: *Glee,* bright color, beauty.
Line 15: *Inlin'de* (enlimned), painted in bright colors.
Line 19: *Pomander,* perfume box.

3. MEDITATION. CAN. 1.3.

THY GOOD OINTMENT.

11.12m [Feb.] 1682.

How sweet a Lord is mine? If any should
  Guarded, Engarden'd, nay, Imbosomd bee
In reechs of Odours, Gales of Spices, Folds
  Of Aromaticks, Oh! how sweet was hee?
  He would be sweet, and yet his sweetest Wave   *5*
  Compar'de to thee my Lord, no Sweet would have.

A Box of Ointments, broke; sweetness most sweet.
  A surge of spices: Odours Common Wealth,
A Pillar of Perfume: a steaming Reech
  Of Aromatick Clouds: All Saving Health.   *10*
  Sweetness itselfe thou art: And I presume
  In Calling of thee Sweet, who art Perfume.

But Woe is mee! who have so quick a Sent
  To Catch perfumes pufft out from Pincks, and Roses
And other Muscadalls, as they get Vent,   *15*
  Out of their Mothers Wombs to bob our noses.
  And yet thy sweet perfume doth seldom latch
  My Lord, within my Mammulary Catch.

Am I denos'de? or doth the Worlds ill sents
    Engarison my nosthrills narrow bore?   *20*
Or is my smell lost in these Damps it Vents?
    And shall I never finde it any more?
    Or is it like the Hawks, or Hownds whose breed
    Take stincking Carrion for Perfume indeed?

This is my Case. All things smell sweet to mee: *25*
    Except thy sweetness, Lord. Expell these damps.
Breake up this Garison: and let me see
    Thy Aromaticks pitching in these Camps.
    Oh! let the Clouds of thy sweet Vapours rise,
    And both my Mammularies Circumcise.   *30*

Shall Spirits thus my Mammularies suck?
    (As Witches Elves their teats,) and draw from thee
My Dear, Dear Spirit after fumes of muck?
    Be Dunghill Damps more sweet than Graces bee?
    Lord, clear these Caves. These Passes take, and keep.   *35*
    And in these Quarters lodge thy Odours sweet.

Lord, breake thy Box of Ointment on my Head;
    Let thy sweet Powder powder all my hair:
My Spirits let with thy perfumes be fed
    And make thy Odours, Lord, my nosthrills fare.   *40*
    My Soule shall in thy sweets then soar to thee:
    I'le be thy Love, thou my sweet Lord shalt bee.

TEXT NOTES:
Line 2: *Guarded,* ornamented.
Line 2: *Engardened,* enclosed in a garden; possibly "engarlanded," wreathed with.
Line 2: *Embosomd,* embraced, enveloped.
Line 3: *Reechs* (reeks), emission of (usually unpleasant, but here pleasant) smells.
Line 13: *So quick a sent,* so lively a scent.
Line 14: *Pincks,* sweet-smelling flowers.
Line 15: *Muscadalls,* muscatel grapes.
Line 15: *Vent,* discharged, poured out.
Line 16: *Bob,* strike.
Line 17: *Latch,* snare.
Line 18: *Mammulary,* breast; nostrils, compared figuratively with breasts (see Michael Schuldiner, "Edward Taylor's 'Problematic' Imagery," *Early American Literature* [Spring 1978], 92–101).
Line 19: *Denos'de,* de-nosed.
Line 20: *Engarison,* station troops within.
Line 21: *Damps,* noxious vapors.

Line 27: *Garison,* troop of soldiers.
Line 40: *Fare,* travel; assault.

THE EXPERIENCE.

Oh! that I alwayes breath'd in such an aire,
　　As I suckt in, feeding on sweet Content!
Disht up unto my Soul ev'n in that pray're
　　Pour'de out to God over last Sacrament.
　　　What Beam of Light wrapt up my sight to finde   *5*
　　　Me neerer God than ere Came in my minde?

Most strange it was! But yet more strange that shine
　　Which filld my Soul then to the brim to spy
My Nature with thy Nature all Divine
　　Together joyn'd in Him thats Thou, and I.   *10*
　　　Flesh of my Flesh, Bone of my Bone. There's run
　　　Thy Godhead, and my Manhood in thy Son.

Oh! that that Flame which thou didst on me Cast
　　Might me enflame, and Lighten ery where.
Then Heaven to me would be less at last   *15*
　　So much of heaven I should have while here.
　　　Oh! Sweet though Short! Ile not forget the same.
　　　My neerness, Lord, to thee did me Enflame.

I'le Claim my Right: Give place, ye Angells Bright.
　　Ye further from the Godhead stande than I.   *20*
My Nature is your Lord; and doth Unite
　　Better than Yours unto the Deity.
　　　Gods Throne is first and mine is next: to you
　　　Onely the place of Waiting-men is due.

Oh! that my Heart, thy Golden Harp might bee   *25*
　　Well tun'd by Glorious Grace, that e'ry string
Screw'd to the highest pitch, might unto thee
　　All Praises wrapt in sweetest Musick bring.
　　　I praise thee, Lord, and better praise thee would
　　　If what I had, my heart might ever hold.   *30*

TEXT NOTES:
Line 2: *Content,* subject-matter; satisfaction, pleasure.

THE RETURN.

Inamoring Rayes, thy Sparkles, Pearle of Price
  Impearld with Choisest Gems, their beams Display
Impoysoning Sin, Guilding my Soule with Choice
  Rich Grace, thy Image bright, making me pray,
  Oh! that thou Wast on Earth below with mee   *5*
  Or that I was in Heaven above with thee.

Thy Humane Frame, with Beauty Dapled, and
  In Beds of Graces pald with golden layes,
Lockt to thy Holy Essence by thy hand,
  Yields Glances that enflame my Soul, that sayes   *10*
  Oh! that thou wast on Earth below with mee!
  Or that I was in Heaven above with thee.

All Love in God, and's Properties Divine
  Enam'led are in thee: thy Beauties Blaze
Attracts my Souls Choice golden Wyer to twine   *15*
  About thy Rose-sweet selfe. And therefore prayes
  Oh! that thou wast on Earth below with mee!
  Or, that I was in Heaven above with thee.

A Magazeen of Love: Bright Glories blaze:
  Thy Shine fills Heaven with Glory; Smile Convayes   *20*
Heavens Glory in my Soule, which it doth glaze
  All ore with amoring Glory; that she sayes,
  Oh! that thou wast on Earth below with mee!
  Or, that I was in Heaven above with thee!

Heavens Golden Spout thou art where Grace most Choice   *25*
  Comes Spouting down from God to man of Clay.
A Golden Stepping Stone to Paradise
  A Golden Ladder into Heaven! I'l pray
  Oh! that thou wast on Earth below with mee
  Or that I was in Heaven above with thee.   *30*

Thy Service is my Freedom Pleasure, Joy,
  Delight, Bliss, Glory, Heaven on Earth, my Stay,
In Gleams of Glory thee to glorify.
  But oh! my Dross and Lets. Wherefore I say
  Oh! that thou wast on Earth below with mee: *35*
  Or that I was in Heaven above with thee.

If off as Offall I be put, if I
   Out of thy Vineyard Work be put away:
Life would be Death: my Soule would Coffin'd ly,
    Within my Body; and no longer pray   *40*
      Oh! that thou wast on Earth below with mee:
      But that I was in Heaven above with thee.

But I've thy Pleasant Pleasant Presence had
   In Word, Pray're, Ordinances, Duties; nay,
And in thy Graces, making me full Glad,   *45*
    In Faith, Hope, Charity, that I do say,
      That thou hast been on Earth below with mee.
      And I shall be in Heaven above with thee.

Be thou Musician, Lord, Let me be made
   The well tun'de Instrument thou dost assume.   *50*
And let thy Glory be my Musick plaide.
    Then let thy Spirit keepe my Strings in tune,
      Whilst thou art here on Earth below with mee
      Till I sing Praise in Heaven above with thee.

TEXT NOTES:
Line 8: *Pald* (palled), covered.
Line 8: *Layes,* layers.
Line 14: *Enam'led* (enameled), beautifully colored.
Line 19: *Magazeen,* storehouse.
Line 32: *Stay,* support.
Line 34: *Lets,* hinderances.
Line 51: *Plaide,* played.

4. MEDITATION. CANT. 2.1.

I AM THE ROSE OF SHARON.

22.2m [April] 1683.

My Silver Chest a Sparke of Love up locks:
   And out will let it when I can't well Use.
The gawdy World me Courts t'unlock the Box,
    A motion makes, where Love may pick and choose.
      Her Downy Bosom opes, that pedlars Stall,   *5*
      Of Wealth, Sports, Honours, Beauty, slickt up all.

Love pausing on't, these Clayey Faces she
   Disdains to Court; but Pilgrims life designs,

And Walkes in Gilliads Land, and there doth see
  The Rose of Sharon which with Beauty shines.   *10*
Her Chest Unlocks; the Sparke of Love out breaths
  To Court this Rose: and lodgeth in its leaves.

No flower in Garzia Horti shines like this:
  No Beauty sweet in all the World so Choice:
It is the Rose of Sharon sweet, that is   *15*
  The Fairest Rose that Grows in Paradise.
Blushes of Beauty bright, Pure White, and Red
  In Sweats of Glory on Each Leafe doth bed.

Lord lead me into this sweet Rosy Bower:
  Oh! Lodge my Soul in this Sweet Rosy bed: *20*
Array my Soul with this sweet Sharon flower:
  Perfume me with the Odours it doth shed.
Wealth, Pleasure, Beauty Spirituall will line
  My pretious Soul, if Sharons Rose be mine.

The Blood Red Pretious Syrup of this Rose   *25*
  Doth all Catholicons excell what ere.
Ill Humours all that do the Soule inclose
  When rightly usd, it purgeth out most clear.
Lord purge my Soul with this Choice Syrup, and
  Chase all thine Enemies out of my land.   *30*

The Rosy Oyle, from Sharons Rose extract
  Better than Palma Christi far is found.
Its Gilliads Balm for Conscience when she's wrackt
  Unguent Apostolorum for each Wound.
Let me thy Patient, thou my Surgeon bee.   *35*
  Lord, with thy Oyle of Roses Supple mee.

No Flower there is in Paradise that grows
  Whose Virtues Can Consumptive Souls restore
But Shugar of Roses made of Sharons Rose
  When Dayly usd, doth never fail to Cure.   *40*
Lord let my Dwindling Soul be dayly fed
  With Sugar of Sharons Rose, its dayly Bread.

God Chymist is, doth Sharons Rose distill.
  Oh! Choice Rose Water! Swim my Soul herein.
Let Conscience bibble in it with her Bill.   *45*
  Its Cordiall, ease doth Heart burns Causd by Sin.
Oyle, Syrup, Sugar, and Rose Water such.
  Lord, give, give, give; I cannot have too much.

But, oh! alas! that such should be my need
   That this Brave Flower must Pluckt, stampt, squeezed bee,
And boyld up in its Blood, its Spirits sheed,   *51*
   To make a Physick sweet, sure, safe for mee.
But yet this mangled Rose rose up again
And in its pristine glory, doth remain.

All Sweets, and Beauties of all Flowers appeare   *55*
   In Sharons Rose, whose Glorious Leaves out vie
In Vertue, Beauty, Sweetness, Glory Cleare,
   The Spangled Leaves of Heavens cleare Chrystall Sky.
Thou Rose of Heaven, Glory's Blossom Cleare
Open thy Rosie Leaves, and lodge mee there.   *60*

My Dear-Sweet Lord, shall I thy Glory meet
   Lodg'd in a Rose, that out a sweet Breath breaths.
What is my way to Glory made thus sweet,
   Strewd all along with Sharons Rosy Leaves.
I'le walk this Rosy Path: World fawn, or frown   *65*
And Sharons Rose shall be my Rose, and Crown.

TEXT NOTES:
Line 6: *Slickt up,* made elegant.
Line 7: *Clayey,* mortal.
Line 9: *Gilliads Land,* see Canticle of Canticles 4:1.
Line 13: *Garzia Horti,* probably a reference to famous Italian Renaissance gardens, possibly the ones at villa Garzoni in Tuscany begun in 1653. (Christopher Thacker, *The History of Gardens,* Berkeley and Los Angeles, 1979, 109–110. See generally, Terry Comito, *The Idea of the Garden in the Renaissance,* New Brunswick, N.J., 1978; and Ellen C. Eyler, *Early English Gardens and Garden Books,* Ithaca, N.Y., 1963.)
Line 26: *Catholicons,* panaceas.
Line 31: *Rosy,* red.
Line 32: *Palma Christi,* castor oil.
Line 33: *Gilliads Balm,* see Jeremiah 8:22, 46:11.
Line 34: *Unguent Apostolorum,* see James 5:14, Apostles' ointment.
Line 36: *Supple,* anoint.
Line 45: *Bibble,* drink like a duck.

THE REFLEXION.

Lord, art thou at the Table Head above
   Meat, Med'cine, sweetness, sparkling Beautys to

Enamour Souls with Flaming Flakes of Love,
  And not my Trencher, nor my Cup o'reflow?
  Be n't I a bidden Guest? Oh! sweat mine Eye.   5
  Oreflow with Teares: Oh! draw thy fountains dry.

Shall I not smell thy sweet, oh! Sharons Rose?
  Shall not mine Eye salute thy Beauty? Why?
Shall thy sweet leaves their Beautious sweets upclose?
  As halfe ashamde my sight should on them ly?   10
  Woe's me! for this my sighs shall be in grain
  Offer'd on Sorrows Altar for the same.

Had not my Soule's thy Conduit, Pipes stopt bin
  With mud, what Ravishment would'st thou Convay?
Let Graces Golden Spade dig till the Spring   15
  Of tears arise, and cleare this filth away.
  Lord, let thy spirit raise my sighings till
  These Pipes my soule do with thy sweetness fill.

Earth once was Paradise of Heaven below
  Till inkefac'd sin had it with poyson stockt   20
And Chast this Paradise away into
  Heav'ns upmost Loft, and it in Glory Lockt.
  But thou, sweet Lord, hast with thy golden Key
  Unlockt the Doore, and made, a golden day.

Once at thy Feast, I saw thee Pearle-like stand   25
  'Tween Heaven, and Earth where Heavens Bright glory all
In streams fell on thee, as a floodgate and,
  Like Sun Beams through thee on the World to Fall.
  Oh! sugar sweet then! my Deare sweet Lord, I see
  Saints Heavens-lost Happiness restor'd by thee.   30

Shall Heaven, and Earth's bright Glory all up lie
  Like Sun Beams bundled in the sun, in thee?
Dost thou sit Rose at Table Head, where I
  Do sit, and Carv'st no morsell sweet for mee?
  So much before, so little now! Sprindge, Lord,   35
  Thy Rosie Leaves, and me their Glee afford.

Shall not thy Rose my Garden fresh perfume?
  Shall not thy Beauty my dull Heart assaile?
Shall not thy golden gleams run through this gloom?
  Shall my black Velvet Mask thy fair Face Vaile?   40
  Pass o're my Faults: shine forth, bright sun: arise
  Enthrone thy Rosy-selfe within mine Eyes.

TEXT NOTES:
Line 3: *Flakes,* flames, flashes.
Line 11: *In grain,* pure and simple, thoroughly.
Line 13: *Soule's,* soul as.
Line 35: *Sprindge* (sprenge), spread; cleanse by sprinkling.
Line 36: *Glee,* joy; beauty.

5. MEDITATION. CANT. 2.1.

THE LILLY OF THE VALLIES.

2.7m [Sept.] 1683.

My Blessed Lord, art thou a Lilly Flower?
  Oh! that my Soul thy Garden were, that so
Thy bowing Head root in my Heart, and poure
  Might of its Seeds, that they therein might grow.
  Be thou my Lilly, make thou me thy knot: *5*
  Be thou my Flowers, I'le be thy Flower Pot.

My barren heart thy Fruitfull Vally make:
  Be thou my Lilly flouerishing in mee:
Oh Lilly of the Vallies. For thy sake,
  Let me thy Vally, thou my Lilly bee.   *10*
  Then nothing shall me of thyselfe bereave.
  Thou must not me, or must thy Vally leave.

How shall my Vallie's Spangling Glory spred,
  Thou Lilly of the Vallies Spangling
There springing up? Upon thy bowing Head   *15*
  All Heavens bright Glory hangeth dangling.
  My Vally then with Blissfull Beams shall shine,
  Thou Lilly of the Vallys, being mine.

TEXT NOTES:
Line 5: *Knot,* flower-bed, garden.
Line 14: *Spangling,* glistening.

6. ANOTHER MEDITATION AT THE SAME TIME.

Am I thy Gold? Or Purse, Lord, for thy Wealth;
  Whether in mine, or mint refinde for thee?
Ime counted so, but count me o're thyselfe,

Lest gold washt face, and brass in Heart I bee.
    I Feare my Touchstone touches when I try   *5*
    Mee, and my Counted Gold too overly.
Am I new minted by thy Stamp indeed?
    Mine Eyes are dim; I cannot clearly see.
Be thou my Spectacles that I may read
    Thine Image, and Inscription stampt on mee.   *10*
    If thy bright Image do upon me stand
    I am a Golden Angell in thy hand.

Lord, make my Soule thy Plate: thine Image bright
    Within the Circle of the same enfoile.
And on its brims in golden Letters write   *15*
    Thy Superscription in an Holy style.
    Then I shall be thy Money, thou my Hord:
    Let me thy Angell bee, bee thou my Lord.

TEXT NOTES:
Line 5: *Touchstone touches,* the testing of the fineness of gold or silver.
Line 12: *Golden Angell,* old English gold coin.
Line 14: *Enfoile,* cover with thin sheet of metal.
Line 15: *Brims,* borders, edges.
Line 16: *Style,* inscription; manner of expression.
Line 18: *Angell,* coin; messenger.

7. MEDITATION. PS. 45.2.

GRACE IN THY LIPS IS POURED OUT.

10.12m [Feb.] 1683.

Thy Humane Frame, my Glorious Lord, I spy,
    A Golden Still with Heavenly Choice drugs filld;
Thy Holy Love, the Glowing heate whereby,
    The Spirit of Grace is graciously distilld.
    Thy Mouth the Neck through which these spirits still.   *5*
    My Soul thy Violl make, and therewith fill.

Thy Speech the Liquour in thy Vessell stands,
    Well ting'd with Grace a blessed Tincture, Loe,
Thy Words distilld, Grace in thy Lips pourd, and,
    Give Graces Tinctur in them where they go.   *10*
    Thy words in graces tincture stilld, Lord, may
    The Tincture of thy Grace in me Convay.

That Golden Mint of Words, thy Mouth Divine,
  Doth tip these Words, which by my Fall were spoild;
And Dub with Gold dug out of Graces mine   *15*
  That they thine Image might have in them foild.
  Grace in thy Lips pourd out's as Liquid Gold.
  Thy Bottle make my Soule, Lord, it to hold.

TEXT NOTES:
Line 6: *Violl,* vial.
Line 8: *Loe,* Lo!
Line 14: *Tip,* pour out, empty out.
Line 15: *Dub,* smear, clothe, array.
Line 16: *Foild,* covered; defeated.

8. MEDITATION. JOH. 6.51.

I AM THE LIVING BREAD.

8.4m [June] 1684.

I kening through Astronomy Divine
  The Worlds bright Battlement, wherein I spy
A Golden Path my Pensill cannot line,
  From that bright Throne unto my Threshold ly.
  And while my puzzled thoughts about it pore   *5*
  I finde the Bread of Life in't at my doore.

When that this Bird of Paradise put in
  This Wicker Cage (my Corps) to tweedle praise
Had peckt the Fruite forbad: and so did fling
  Away its Food; and lost its golden dayes;   *10*
  It fell into Celestiall Famine sore:
  And never could attain a morsell more.

Alas! alas! Poore Bird, what wilt thou doe?
  The Creatures field no food for Souls e're gave.
And if thou knock at Angells dores they show   *15*
  An Empty Barrell: they no soul bread have.
  Alas! Poore Bird, the Worlds White Loafe is done.
  And cannot yield thee here the smallest Crumb.

In this sad state, Gods Tender Bowells run
  Out streams of Grace: And he to end all strife   *20*

The Purest Wheate in Heaven, his deare-dear Son
    Grinds, and kneads up into this Bread of Life.
    Which Bread of Life from Heaven down came and stands
    Disht on thy Table up by Angells Hands.

Did God mould up this Bread in Heaven, and bake,   *25*
    Which from his Table came, and to thine goeth?
Doth he bespeake thee thus, This Soule Bread take.
    Come Eate thy fill of this thy Gods White Loafe?
    Its Food too fine for Angells, yet come, take
    And Eate thy fill. Its Heavens Sugar Cake.   *30*

What Grace is this knead in this Loafe? This thing
    Souls are but petty things it to admire.
Yee Angells, help: This fill would to the brim
    Heav'ns whelm'd-down Chrystall meele Bowle, yea and higher.
    This Bread of Life dropt in thy mouth, doth Cry.   *35*
    Eate, Eate me, Soul, and thou shalt never dy.

TEXT NOTES:
Line 1: *Kening,* seeing.
Line 8: *Tweedle,* play carelessly on musical instrument; of a bird, whistle with mod-
ulations of tone.
Line 19: *Gods Tender Bowells,* God's compassion.
Line 34: *Whelm'd-down,* overloaded.

9. MEDITATION. JOH. 6.51.
I AM THE LIVING BREAD.

7.7m [Sept.] 1684.

Did Ever Lord such noble house mentain,
    As my Lord doth? Or such a noble Table?
'T would breake the back of kings, nay, Monarchs brain
    To do it. Pish, the Worlds Estate's not able.
    I'le bet a boast with any that this Bread   *5*
    I eate excells what ever Caesar had.

Take earth's Brightst Darlings, in whose mouths all flakes
    Of Lushous Sweets she hath do croude their Head,
Their Spiced Cups, sweet Meats, and Sugar Cakes
    Are but dry Sawdust to this Living Bread.   *10*
    I'le pawn my part in Christ, this Dainti'st Meate,
    Is Gall, and Wormwood unto what I eate.

The Boasting Spagyrist (Insipid Phlegm,
  Whose Words out strut the Sky) vaunts he hath rife
The Water, Tincture, Lozenge, Gold, and Gem,   *15*
  Of Life itselfe. But here's the Bread of Life.
  I'le lay my Life, his Aurum Vitae Red
  Is to my Bread of Life, worse than DEAD HEAD.

The Dainti'st Dish of Earthly Cookery
  Is but to fat the body up in print.   *20*
This Bread of Life doth feed the Soule, whereby
  Its made the Temple of Jehovah in't.
  I'le Venture Heav'n upon't that Low or High
  That eate this Living Bread shall never dy.

This Bread of Life, so excellent, I see   *25*
  The Holy Angells doubtless would, if they
Were prone unto base Envie, Envie't mee.
  But oh! come, tast how sweet it is. I say,
  I'le Wage my Soule and all therein uplaid,
  This is the sweetest Bread that e're God made.   *30*

What wonder's here, that Bread of Life should come
  To feed Dead Dust? Dry Dust eate Living Bread?
Yet Wonder more by far may all, and some
  That my Dull Heart's so dumpish when thus fed.
  Lord Pardon this, and feed mee all my dayes,   *35*
  With Living Bread to thy Eternall Prayse.

TEXT NOTES:
Line 4: *Pish,* an exclamation, expressing impatience or disgust.
Line 8: *Croude,* crowd.
Line 13: *Spagyrist,* alchemist.
Line 14: *Strut,* cause to swell or bulge; flaunt, swagger.
Line 17: *Aurum Vitae Red,* alchemist's concoction.
Line 18: *Dead Head, caput mortuum,* residue after distillation.
Line 34: *Dumpish,* inert, spiritless.

10. MEDITATION. JOH. 6.55.
MY BLOOD IS DRINKE INDEED.

26.8m [Oct.] 1684.

Stupendious Love! All Saints Astonishment!
  Bright Angells are black Motes in this Suns Light.

Heav'ns Canopy the Paintice to Gods tent
  Can't Cover't neither with its breadth, nor height.
  Its Glory doth all Glory else out run,   *5*
  Beams of bright Glory to't are motes i'th'sun.

My Soule had Caught an Ague, and like Hell
  Her thirst did burn: she to each spring did fly,
But this bright blazing Love did spring a Well
    Of Aqua-Vitae in the Deity,   *10*
    Which on the top of Heav'ns high Hill out burst
    And down came running thence t'allay my thirst.

But how it came, amazeth all Communion.
  Gods onely Son doth hug Humanity,
Into his very person. By which Union   *15*
    His Humane Veans its golden gutters ly.
    And rather than my Soule should dy by thirst,
    These Golden Pipes, to give me drink, did burst.

This Liquour brew'd, thy sparkling Art Divine
  Lord, in thy Chrystall Vessells did up tun,   *20*
(Thine Ordinances,) which all Earth o're shine
    Set in thy rich Wine Cellars out to run.
    Lord, make thy Butlar draw, and fill with speed
    My Beaker full: for this is drink indeed.

Whole Buts of this blesst Nectar shining stand   *25*
  Lockt up with Saph'rine Taps, whose splendid Flame
Too bright do shine for brightest Angells hands
    To touch, my Lord. Do thou untap the same.
    Oh! make thy Chrystall Buts of Red Wine bleed
    Into my Chrystall Glass this Drink-Indeed.   *30*

How shall I praise thee then? My blottings Jar
  And wrack my Rhymes to pieces in thy praise.
Thou breath'st thy Vean still in my Pottinger
    To lay my thirst, and fainting spirits raise.
    Thou makest Glory's Chiefest Grape to bleed   *35*
    Into my cup: And this is Drink-Indeed.

Nay, though I make no pay for this Red Wine,
  And scarce do say I thank-ye-for't; strange thing!
Yet were thy silver skies my Beer bowle fine
    I finde my Lord, would fill it to the brim.   *40*
    Then make my life, Lord, to thy praise proceed
    For thy rich blood, which is my Drink-Indeed.

TEXT NOTES:

Line 2: *Motes,* dust particles.
Line 3: *Paintice,* penthouse, sloping roof.
Line 7: *Ague,* fever, chill.
Line 10: *Aqua-Vitae,* water of life; alchemist's term for ardent spirits; see John 4:10.
Line 20: *Up tun,* store up.
Line 25: *Buts,* casks.
Line 26: *Saph'rine Taps,* sapphire-like plugs.
Line 33: *Pottinger,* bowl.

11. MEDITATION. ISAI. 25.6.

A FEAST OF FAT THINGS.

31.3m [Mar.] 1685.

A Deity of Love Incorporate
   My Lord, lies in thy Flesh, in Dishes stable
Ten thousand times more rich than golden Plate
   In golden Services upon thy Table,
      To feast thy People with. What Feast is this!   5
      Where richest Love lies Cookt in e'ry Dish?

A Feast, a Feast, a Feast of Spiced Wine
   Of Wines upon the Lees, refined well
Of Fat things full of Marrow, things Divine
   Of Heavens blest Cookery which doth excell.   10
      The Smell of Lebanon, and Carmell sweet
      Are Earthly damps unto this Heavenly reech.

This Shew-Bread Table all of Gold with white
   Fine Table Linen of Pure Love, 's ore spred
And Courses in Smaragdine Chargers bright   15
   Of Choicest Dainties Paradise e're bred.
      Where in each Grace like Dainty Sippits lie
      Oh! brave Embroderies of sweetest joy!

Oh! what a Feast is here? This Table might
   Make brightest Angells blush to sit before.   20
Then pain my Soule! Why wantst thou appitite?
   Oh! blush to thinke thou hunger dost no more.
      There never was a feast more rich than this:
      The Guests that Come hereto shall swim in bliss.

Hunger, and Thirst my Soule, goe Fasting Pray,   25
   Untill thou hast an Appitite afresh:
And then come here; here is a feast will pay
   Thee for the same with all Deliciousness.
   Untap Loves Golden Cask, Love run apace:
   And o're this Feast Continually say Grace.   30

TEXT NOTES:

Line 8: *Lees,* mountain shelter; see text, Isaiah 25:6.
Line 11: *Lebanon, and Carmell,* biblical places of beauty; see Isaiah 35:2.
Line 12: *Damps,* noxious vapors.
Line 12: *Reech* (reek), smell.
Line 13: *Shew-Bread,* bread offered to God; see Hebrews 9:2 and many Old Testament references.
Line 15: *Smaragdine Chargers,* emerald platter or soup-plate.
Line 17: *Sippits,* bread sops.

12. MEDITATION. ISAI. 63.1.

GLORIOUS IN HIS APPARELL.

19.5m [July] 1685.

This Quest rapt at my Eares broad golden Doores
   Who's this that comes from Edom in this shine
In Died Robes from Bozrah? this more ore
   All Glorious in's Apparrell: all Divine?
   Then through that Wicket rusht this buss there gave,   5
   Its I that right do speake mighty to save.

I threw through Zions Lattice then an Eye
   Which spide one like a lump of Glory pure
Nay, Cloaths of gold button'd with pearls do ly
   Like Rags, or shooclouts unto his he wore.   10
   Heavens Curtains blancht with Sun, and Starrs of Light
   Are black as sackcloath to his Garments bright.

One shining sun guilding the skies with Light
   Benights all Candles with their flaming Blaze
So doth the Glory of this Robe benight   15
   Ten thousand suns at once ten thousand wayes.
   For e'ry thrid therein's dy'de with the shine
   Of All, and Each the Attributes Divine.

The sweetest breath, the sweetest Violet
 Rose, or Carnation ever did gust out   *20*
Is but a Foist to that Perfume beset
 In thy Apparell steaming round about:
 But is this so? My Peuling soul then pine
 In Love untill this Lovely one be thine.

Pluck back the Curtains, back the Window Shutts: *25*
 Through Zions Agate Window take a view;
How Christ in Pinckted Robes from Bozrah puts
 Comes Glorious in's Apparell forth to Wooe.
 Oh! if his Glory ever kiss thine Eye,
 Thy Love will soon Enchanted bee thereby.   *30*

Then Grieve, my Soul, thy vessell is so small
 And holds no more for such a Lovely Hee.
That strength's so little, Love scarce acts at all.
 That sight's so dim, doth scarce him lovely see.
 Grieve, grieve, my Soul, thou shouldst so pimping bee, *35*
 Now such a Price is here presented thee.

All sight's too little sight enough to make
 All strength's too little Love enough to reare
All Vessells are too small to hold or take
 Enough Love up for such a Lovely Deare.   *40*
 How little to this Little's then thy ALL.
 For Him whose Beauty saith all Love's too small?

My Lovely One, I fain would love thee much
 But all my Love is none at all I see,
Oh! let thy Beauty give a glorious tuch   *45*
 Upon my Heart, and melt to Love all mee.
 Lord melt me all up into Love for thee
 Whose Loveliness excells what love can bee.

TEXT NOTES:

Lines 2–6: Taylor meditates on Isaiah 63:1–4: "Who is this that cometh from Edom, with dyed garments from Bozrah? this that is glorious in his apparel, travelling in the greatness of his strength? I that speak in righteousness, mighty to save. Wherefore art thou red in thine apparel, and thy garments like him that treadeth in the winefat? I have trodden the winepress alone; and of the people there was none with me: for I will tread them in mine anger, and trample them in my fury; and their blood shall be sprinkled upon my garments, and I will stain all my raiment. For the day of vengeance is in mine heart, and the year of my redeemed is come." Bozrah was famous for its sheep (Micah 2:12), hence the garment is of wool.

Line 5: *Buss* (busk), attire.
Line 10: *Shooclouts,* cloths for wiping shoes.
Line 17: *Thrid,* thread.
Line 20: *Gust,* burst.
Line 21: *Foist,* musty smell.
Line 22: *Steaming,* emitting.
Line 23: *Peuling* (puling), whining.
Line 25: *Shutts,* shutters.
Line 27: *Pinckted,* dyed pink or red.
Line 35: *Pimping,* pandering (to other loves).

13. MEDITATION. COL. 2.3.
ALL THE TREASURES OF WISDOM.

27.7m [Sept.] 1685.

Thou Glory Darkning Glory, with thy Flame
  Should all Quaint Metaphors teem ev'ry Bud
Of Sparkling Eloquence upon the same
  It would appeare as dawbing pearls with mud.
  Nay Angells Wits are Childish tricks, and like   5
  The Darksom night unto thy Lightsom Light.

Oh! Choicest Cabbinet, more Choice than gold
  Or Wealthist Pearles Wherein all Pearls of Price
All Treasures of Choice Wisdom manifold
  Inthroned reign. Thou Cabinet most Choice   10
  Not scant to hold, not staind with cloudy geere
  The Shining Sun of Wisdom bowling there.

Thou Shining Golden Lanthorn with pain'd Lights
  Of Chrystall cleare, thy golden Candles flame,
Makes such a Shine, as doth the Sun benights.   15
  Its but a Smoaky vapor to the Same. .
  All Wisdom knead into a Chrystall Ball,
  Shines like the Sun in thee, its azure Hall.

Thou rowling Eye of Light, to thee are sent
  All Dazzling Beams of Shine the Heavens distill.   20
All Wisdoms Troops do quarter in thy Tents
  And all her Treasures Cabin in thy tills.
  Be thou, Lord, mine: then I shall Wealthy bee,
  Enricht with Wisdoms Treasures, Stoughd in thee.

That little Grain within my golden Bowle,   *25*
   Should it attempt to poise thy Talent cleare,
It would inoculate into my Soule,
   As illookt Impudence as ever were.
But, loe, it stands amaizd, and doth adore,
Thy Magazeen of Wisdom, and thy Store.   *30*

TEXT NOTES:
Line 2: *Teem,* produce, bring forth.
Line 11: *Geere,* pus, corrupt matter.
Line 18: *Azure Hall,* the vault of heaven.
Line 19: *Rowling,* rolling, revolving.
Line 22: *Tills,* money-boxes.
Line 24: *Stoughd,* stowed.
Line 26: *Poise,* measure, balance.
Line 26: *Talent,* wealth.
Line 27: *Inoculate,* engraft.
Line 28: *Illookt* (ill-looked), evil, ugly.
Line 30: *Magazeen,* storehouse.

14./15. MEDITATIONS. HEB. 4.14.

A GREAT HIGH PRIEST.

14.9m [Nov.] 1685. 10.11m [Jan.] 1685.

Raptures of Love, surprizing Loveliness,
   That burst through Heavens all, in Rapid Flashes,
Glances guilt o're with smiling Comliness!
   (Wonders do palefac'd stand smit by such dashes).
   Glory itselfe Heartsick of Love doth ly   *5*
   Bleeding out Love o're Loveless mee, and dy.

Might I a glance of this bright brightness shew;
   Se it in him who gloriously is dresst:
A Gold Silk Stomacher of Purple, blew
   Blancht o're with Orient Pearles being on his Breast: *10*
   And all his Robes being answerable, but
   This glory seen, to that unseen's a Smut.

Yea, Beauteous Hee, in all his Glory stands,
   Tendring himselfe to God, and Man where hee

Doth Justice thus bespeake, Hold out thy hands: *15*
    Come, take thy Penworths now for mine of mee.
    I'le pay the fine that thou seest meet to set
    Upon their Heads: I'le dy to cleare their debts.

Out Rampant Justice steps in Sparkling White,
    Him rends in twain, who on her Altar lies   *20*
A Lump of Glory flaming in her bright
    Devouring Flames, to be my Sacrifice
    Untill her Fire goes out well Satisfide:
    And then he rose in Glory to abide.

To Heav'n went he, and in his bright Throne sits   *25*
    At Gods right hand pleading poor Sinners Cases.
With Golden Wedges he of Promise, splits
    The Heav'ns ope, to shew what Glory 'braces.
    And in its thickness thus with Arms extended,
    Calls, come, come here, and ever be befriended.   *30*

Frost bitten Love, Frozen Affections! Blush;
    What icy Chrystall mountain lodge you in?
What Wingless Wishes, Hopes pinfeatherd tush!
    Sore Hooft Desires hereof do in you spring?
    Oh hard black Kirnell at the Coare! not pant?   *35*
    Encastled in an heart of Adamant!

What strange Congealed Heart have I when I
    Under such Beauty shining like the Sun
Able to make Frozen Affection fly,
    And Icikles of Frostbitt Love to run.   *40*
    Yea, and Desires lockt in an heart of Steel
    Or Adamant, breake prison, nothing feel.

Lord may thy Priestly Golden Oares but make
    A rowing in my Lumpish Heart, thou'lt see
My Chilly Numbd Affections Charm, and break   *45*
    Out in a rapid Flame of Love to thee.
    Yea, they unto thyselfe will fly in flocks
    When thy Warm Sun my frozen Lake unlocks.

Be thou my High Priest, Lord; and let my name
    Ly in some Grave dug in these Pearly rocks   *50*
Upon thy Ephods Shoulder piece, like flame
    Or graved in thy Breast Plate-Gem: brave Knops.

Thou'lt then me beare before thy Fathers Throne
Rowld up in Folds of Glory of thine own.

One of these Gems I beg, Lord, that so well   *55*
  Begrace thy Breast Plate, and thy Ephod cleaver
To stud my Crown therewith: or let me dwell
  Among their sparkling, glancing Shades for ever.
  I'st then be deckt in glory bright to sing
  With Angells, Hallelujahs to my King.   *60*

TEXT NOTES:

Line 3: *Glances guilt o're,* read either (a) "glances [noun: looks] gilt [gilded] over'';
  or (b) "glances [verb: strikes; shines] guilt over."

Line 4: *Dashes,* gay appearances [as in (a) above]; violent blows [as in (b) above];
  gifts.

Line 8: *Se,* see.

Line 9: *Stomacher,* waistcoat.

Line 9: *Blew,* blue.

Line 10: *Blancht o're,* made white.

Line 16: *Penworths,* pennyworth.

Line 33: *Pinfeatherd,* with undeveloped feathers.

Line 33: *Tush,* exclamation expressing impatient contempt.

Line 36: *Adamant,* supposed to be the hardest of metals.

Line 42: *Breake,* read "bleake"?

Line 51: *Ephod,* upper garment worn by ancient Jewish priests; see Exodus 28:4–
  12 and other Old Testament references.

Line 52: *Brave,* splendid, showy, grand, fine.

Line 52: *Knops,* ornamental studs.

Line 56: *Cleaver,* handsome.

Line 58: *Glancing,* shining.

Line 58: *Shades,* tints of color; shadows.

16. MEDITATION. LU. 7.16.

A GREATE PROPHET IS RISEN UP.

6.1m [Mar.] 1685/6.

Leafe Gold, Lord of thy Golden Wedge o'relaid
  My Soul at first, thy Grace in e'ry part
Whose peart, fierce Eye thou such a Sight hadst made
  Whose brightsom beams could break into thy heart
  Till thy Curst Foe had with my Fist mine Eye   *5*
  Dasht out, and did my Soule Unglorify.

I cannot see, nor Will thy Will aright.
　Nor see to waile my Woe, my loss and hew
Nor all the Shine in all the Sun can light
　　My Candle, nor its Heate my Heart renew.   *10*
　　See, waile, and Will thy Will, I must, or must
　　From Heavens sweet Shine to Hells hot flame be thrust.

Grace then Conceald in God himselfe, did rowle
　Even Snow Ball like into a Sunball Shine
And nestles all its beams buncht in thy Soule   *15*
　　My Lord, that sparkle in Prophetick Lines.
　　Oh! Wonder more than Wonderfull! this Will
　　Lighten the Eye which Sight Divine did spill.

What art thou, Lord, this Ball of Glory bright?
　A Bundle of Celestiall Beams up bound   *20*
In Graces band fixt in Heavens topmost height
　　Pouring thy golden Beams thence, Circling round
　　Which shew thy Glory, and thy glories Way
　　And ery Where will make Celestiall Day.

Lord let thy Golden Beams pierce through mine Eye   *25*
　And leave therein an Heavenly Light to glaze
My Soule with glorious Grace all o're, whereby
　　I may have Sight, and Grace in mee may blaze.
　　Lord ting my Candle at thy Burning Rayes,
　　To give a gracious Glory to thy Prayse.   *30*

Thou Lightning Eye, let some bright Beames of thine
　Stick in my Soul, to light and liven it:
Light, Life, and Glory, things that are Divine;
　　I shall be grac'd withall for glory fit.
　　My Heart then stufft with Grace, Light, Life, and Glee   *35*
　　I'le sacrifice in Flames of Love to thee.

TEXT NOTES:
Line 1: *Wedge,* an ingot of gold.
Line 3: *Peart* (pert), bold.
Line 8: *Waile,* bewail.
Line 13: *Rowle,* roll.
Line 18: *Spill,* destroy, damage.
Line 29: *Ting,* perhaps tinge; impart as with color; or ding, strike, overcome, throw
　　down.

17. MEDITATION. REV. 19.16.
KING OF KINGS.

13.4m [June] 1686.

A King, a King, a King indeed, a King
  Writh up in Glory! Glorie's glorious Throne
Is glorifide by him, presented him.
  And all the Crowns of Glory are his own.
  A King, Wise, Just, Gracious, Magnificent.   *5*
  Kings unto him are Whiffles, Indigent.

What is his Throne all Glory? Crown all Gay?
  Crown all of Brightest Shine of Glory's Wealth?
This is a Lisp of Non-sense. I should say,
  He is the Throne, and Crown of Glory 'tselfe.   *10*
  Should Sun beams come to gilde his glory they
  Would be as 'twere to gild the Sun with Clay.

My Phancys in a Maze, my thoughts agast,
  Words in an Extasy; my Telltale Tongue
Is tonguetide, and my Lips are padlockt fast   *15*
  To see thy Kingly Glory in to throng.
  I can, yet cannot tell this Glory just,
  In Silence bury't, must not, yet I must.

This King of King's Brave Kingdom doth Consist
  Of Glorious Angells, and Blesst Saints alone   *20*
Or Chiefly. Where all Beams of Glory twist,
  Together, beaming from, lead to his throne
  Which Beams his Grace Coiles in a Wreath to Crown
  His, in the End in Endless Bright Renown.

His Two-Edg'd Sword, not murdering Steel so base,   *25*
  Is made of Righteousness, unspotted, bright
Imbellisht o're with overflowing Grace
  Doth killing, Cure the Sinner, kills Sin right.
  Makes milkwhite Righteousness, and Grace to reign,
  And Satan and his Cubs with Sin ly slain.   *30*

Were all Kings deckt with Sparkling Crowns, and arm'd
  With flaming Swords, and firy Courage traind
And led under their King Abaddon, Charmd
  In battell out against their foes disdaind
  One smiling look of this bright Shine would fell   *35*
  Them and their Crowns of Glory all to Hell.

Thou art my king: let me not be thy Shame.
  Thy Law my Rule: my Life thy Life in Mee.
Thy Grace my Badge: my Glory bright thy Name.
  I am resolv'd to live and dy with thee.   *40*
  Keep mee, thou King of Glory on Record.
  Thou art my King of Kings, and Lord of Lords.

TEXT NOTES:
Line 2: *Writh,* wreathed.
Line 6: *Whiffles,* trifles.
Line 33: *King Abaddon,* see Revelation 9:11; "the angel of the bottomless pit,"
Apollyon (Destroyer) in Greek, who leads scorpion-like locusts in battle after
the fifth angel blows his trumpet in conjunction with the opening of the seventh
seal.

18.MEDITATION. ISAI. 52.14. HIS VISSAGE
WAS MARR'D MORE THAN ANY MAN.

29.6m [Aug.] 1686.

Astonisht stand, my Soule; why dost not start
  At this surprizing Sight shewn here below?
Oh! let the twitch made by my bouncing Heart
  Gust from my breast this Enterjection, Oh!
  A Sight so Horrid, sure its Mercies Wonder   *5*
  Rocks rend not at't, nor Heavens split asunder.

Souls Charg'd with Sin, Discharge at God, beside
  Firld up in Guilt, Wrapt in Sins Slough, and Slime,
Wills wed to Wickedness, Hearts Stonifide
  Flinty Affections, Conscience Chalybdine   *10*
  Flooding the World with Horrid Crimes, arise
  Daring Almighty God Contemptuouswise.

Hence Vengeance rose with her fierce Troops in Buff,
  Soul-piercing Plagues, Heart-Aching Griefs, and Groans,
Woes Pickled in Revenges Powdering Trough: *15*
  Pain fetching forth their Proofs out of the boanes.
  Doth all in Flames of Fire surround them so
  Which they can ne're o'recome, nor undergo.

In this sad Plight the richest Beauty Cleare
  That th'bravest Flower, that bud was big with, wore,   *20*

Did glorify those Cheeks, whose Vissage were
  Marr'd more than any mans, and Form spoild more.
Oh! Beauty beautifull, not toucht with vice!
  The fairest Flower in all Gods Paradise!

Stept in, and in its Glory 'Counters all.   *25*
  And in the Belly of this Dismall Cloud,
Of Woes in Pickle is gulpht up, whose Gall
  He dranke up quite. Whose Claws his Face up plow'd.
  Yet in these Furrows sprang the brightest Shine
  That Glory's Sun could make, or Love Enshrine.   *30*

Then Vengeance's Troops are routed, Pickled Woe
  Heart-aching Griefes, Pains plowing to the boanes,
Soul piercing Plagues, all Venom do foregoe.
  The Curse now Cures, though th'Griefe procureth groans.
  As th'Angry Bee doth often lose her Sting,   *35*
  The Law was Cursless made in Cursing him.

And now his shining Love beams out its rayes
  My Soul, upon thy Heart to thaw the same:
To animate th'Affections till they blaze;
  To free from Guilt, and from Sins Slough, and Shame. *40*
  Open thy Casement wide, let Glory in,
  To Guild thy Heart to be an Hall for him.

My Breast, be thou the ringing Virginalls:
  Ye mine Affections, their sweet Golden Strings,
My Panting Heart, be thou for Stops, and Falls: *45*
  Lord, let thy quick'ning Beams dance o're the Pins.
  Then let thy Spirit this sweet note resume,
  ALTASCHATH MICHTAM, in Seraphick Tune.

TEXT NOTES:
Line 8: *Firld*, furled.
Line 10: *Chalybdine*, steely.
Line 13: *Buff*, military coat.
Line 15: *Powdering Trough*, tub in which the flesh of animals is "powdered," or salted and pickled.
Line 16: *Boanes*, bones.
Line 27: *In pickle*, in reserve.
Line 27: *Gulpht*, gulped.
Line 43: *Virginalls*, keyed musical instrument, like a spinet but without legs.
Line 48: *Altaschath Michtam*, words found at the head of Psalms 57, 58, 59, 75, probably designating the tune.

19. MEDITATION. PHIL. 2.9.

GOD HATH HIGHLY EXALTED HIM.

14.9m [Nov.] 1686.

Looke till thy Looks look Wan, my Soule; here's ground.
   The Worlds bright Eye's dash't out: Day-Light so brave
Bemidnighted; the sparkling sun, palde round
    With flouring Rayes lies buri'de in its grave
    The Candle of the World blown out, down fell.   *5*
    Life knockt a head by Death: Heaven by Hell.

Alas! this World all filld up to the brim
   With Sins, Deaths, Divills, Crowding men to Hell.
For whose reliefe Gods milkwhite Lamb stept in
    Whom those Curst Imps did worry, flesh, and fell.   *10*
    Tread under foot, did Clap their Wings and so
    Like Dunghill Cocks over their Conquourd, Crow.

Brave Pious Fraud; as if the Setting Sun:
   Dropt like a Ball of Fire into the Seas,
And so went out. But to the East come, run: *15*
    You'l meet the morn Shrinde with its flouring Rayes.
    This Lamb in laying of these Lyons dead;
    Drank of the brooke: and so lift up his Head.

Oh! sweet, sweet joy! These Rampant Fiends befoold:
   They made their Gall his Winding sheete; although   *20*
They of the Heart-ach dy must, or be Coold
    With Inflamation of the Lungs, they know.
    He's Cancelling the Bond, and making Pay:
    And Ballancing Accounts: its Reckoning day.

See, how he from the Counthouse shining went,   *25*
   In Flashing Folds of Burnisht Glory, and
Dasht out all Curses from the Covenant
    Hath Justices Acquittance in his hand
    Pluckt out Deaths Sting, the Serpents Head did mall
    The Bars and Gates of Hell he brake down all.   *30*

The Curse thus Lodgd within his Flesh, and Cloyde,
   Can't run from him to his, so much he gave.
And like a Gyant he awoke, beside,
    The Sun of Righteousness rose out of's Grave.
    And setting Foot upon its neck I sing   *35*
    Grave, where's thy Victory? Death, Where's thy Sting?

TEXT NOTES:
Line 3: *Palde,* paled, made pale.
Line 4: *Flouring* (flowering), becoming turbid, cloudy.
Line 10: *Flesh, and fell,* flesh and skin, i.e. the whole substance of the body; hence, entirely.
Line 13: *Brave,* showy.
Line 16: *Shrinde* (shrined), proclaimed.
Line 16: *Flouring* (flowering), blooming, rising.
Line 31: *Cloyde* (cloyed), burdened, cumbered.

20. MEDITATION. PHIL. 2.9. GOD HATH
HIGHLY EXALTED HIM.

9.11m [Jan.] 1686.

View all ye eyes above, this sight which flings
  Seraphick Phancies in Chill Raptures high,
A Turffe of Clay, and yet bright Glories King
  From dust to Glory Angell-like to fly.
  A Mortall Clod immortalizde, behold,   *5*
  Flyes through the Skies swifter than Angells could.

Upon the Wings he of the Winde rode in
  His Bright Sedan, through all the Silver Skies
And made the Azure Cloud his Charriot bring
  Him to the Mountain of Celestiall joyes.   *10*
  The Prince o'th'Aire durst not an Arrow spend
  While through his Realm his Charriot did ascend.

He did not in a Fiery Charriot's Shine,
  And Whirlewinde, like Elias upward goe.
But th'golden Ladders Jasper rounds did climbe   *15*
  Unto the Heavens high from Earth below.
  Each step trod on a Golden Stepping Stone
  Of Deity unto his very Throne.

Methinks I see Heavens sparkling Courtiers fly,
  In flakes of Glory down him to attend: *20*
And heare Heart Cramping notes of Melody,
  Surround his Charriot as it did ascend
  Mixing their Musick making e'ry string
  More to inravish as they this tune sing.

God is Gone up with a triumphant Shout   *25*
  The Lord with sounding Trumpets melodies.
Sing Praise, sing Praise, sing Praise, sing Praises out,
  Unto our King sing praise seraphickwise.
  Lift up your Heads ye lasting Doore they sing
  And let the King of Glory Enter in.   *30*

Art thou ascended up on high, my Lord,
  And must I be without thee here below?
Art thou the sweetest Joy the Heavens afford?
  Oh! that I with thee was! what shall I do?
  Should I pluck Feathers from an Angells Wing,   *35*
  They could not waft me up to thee my King.

Lend mee thy Wings, my Lord, I'st fly apace.
  My Soules Arms stud with thy strong Quills, true Faith,
My Quills then Feather with thy Saving Grace,
  My Wings will take the Winde thy Word displai'th.   *40*
  Then I shall fly up to thy glorious Throne
  With my strong Wings whose Feathers are thine own.

TEXT NOTES:
Line 2: *Chill,* quivering.
Line 3: *Turffe,* sod, clump.
Line 11: *Prince o'th'Aire,* Satan; see Ephesians 2:2.
Line 14: *Like Elias,* see 2 Kings 2:11.
Line 15: *Jasper,* stone mentioned in the Bible in connection with the Garden of Eden
    (Ezekiel 28:13) and heaven (Revelation 21:11, 18, 19).
Line 20: *Flakes,* flames.
Line 29: *Lift up your Heads . . . ,* Psalm 24:7.

21. MEDITATION. PHIL. 2.9. GOD HATH
HIGHLY EXALTED HIM.

13.1m [Mar.] 1686/7.

What Glory's this, my Lord? Should one small Point
  Of one small Ray of't touch my Heart 'twould spring
Such joy as would an Adamant unjoynt
  If in't, and tare it, to get out and sing.
  T'run on Heroick golden Feet, and raise   *5*
  Heart Ravishing Tunes, Curld with Celestiall praise.

Oh! Bright! Bright thing! I fain would something say:
  Lest Silence should indict me. Yet I feare
To say a Syllable lest at thy day
  I be presented for my Tattling here.   *10*
  Course Phancy, Ragged Faculties, alas!
  And Blunted Tongue don't Suit: Sighs Soile the Glass.

Yet shall my mouth stand ope, and Lips let run
  Out gliding Eloquence on each light thing?
And shall I gag my mouth, and ty my Tongue,   *15*
  When such bright Glory glorifies within?
  That makes my Heart leape, dancing to thy Lute?
  And shall my tell tale tongue become a Mute?

Lord spare I pray, though my attempts let fall
  A slippery Verse upon thy Royall Glory.   *20*
I'le bring unto thine Altar th'best of all
  My Flock affords. I have no better Story.
  I'le at thy Glory my dark Candle light:
  Not to descry the Sun, but use by night.

A Golden Throne whose Banisters are Pearles,   *25*
  And Pomills Choicest Gems: Carbuncle-Stayes
Studded with Pretious Stones, Carv'd with rich Curles
  Of Polisht Art, sending out flashing Rayes,
  Would him surround with Glory, thron'de therein.
  Yet this is to thy Throne a dirty thing.   *30*

Oh! Glorious Sight! Loe, How Bright Angells stand
  Waiting with Hat in hand on Him alone
That is Enthron'de, indeed at Gods right hand:
  Gods Heart itselfe being his Happy Throne.
  The Glory that doth from this Person fall,   *35*
  Fills Heaven with Glory, else there's none at all.

TEXT NOTES:
Line 3: *Adamant,* supposed to be the hardest of metals.
Line 6: *Curld,* adorned?
Line 10: *Tattling,* idle talk; stammering.
Line 26: *Pomills,* ornamental balls.
Line 26: *Stay,* arm or back of chair.

22. MEDITATION. PHIL. 2.9. GOD HATH
HIGHLY EXALTED HIM.

12.4m [June] 1687.

When thy Bright Beams, my Lord, do strike mine Eye,
    Methinkes I then could truely Chide out right
My Hide bound Soule that stands so niggardly
    That scarce a thought gets glorified by't.
    My Quaintest Metaphors are ragged Stuff,   5
    Making the Sun seem like a Mullipuff.

Its my desire, thou shouldst be glorifi'de:
    But when thy Glory shines before mine eye,
I pardon Crave, lest my desire be Pride.
    Or bed thy Glory in a Cloudy Sky.   10
    The Sun grows wan; and Angells palefac'd shrinke,
    Before thy Shine, which I besmeere with Inke.

But shall the Bird sing forth thy Praise, and shall
    The little Bee present her thankfull Hum?
But I who see thy shining Glory fall   15
    Before mine Eyes, stand Blockish, Dull, and Dumb?
    Whether I speake, or speechless stand, I spy,
    I faile thy Glory: therefore pardon Cry.

But this I finde; My Rhymes do better suite
    Mine own Dispraise than tune forth praise to thee.   20
Yet being Chid, whether Consonant, or Mute,
    I force my Tongue to tattle, as you see.
    That I thy glorious Praise may Trumpet right,
    Be thou my Song, and make Lord, mee thy Pipe.

This shining Sky will fly away apace,   25
    When thy bright Glory splits the same to make
Thy Majesty a Pass, whose Fairest Face
    Too foule a Path is for thy Feet to take.
    What Glory then, shall tend thee through the Sky
    Draining the Heaven much of Angells dry?   30

What Light then flame will in thy Judgment Seate,
    'Fore which all men, and angells shall appeare?
How shall thy Glorious Righteousness them treate,
    Rend'ring to each after his Works done here?

Then Saints With Angells thou wilt glorify: *35*
And burn Lewd Men, and Divells Gloriously.

One glimps, my Lord, of thy bright Judgment day,
    And Glory piercing through, like fiery Darts,
All Divells, doth me make for Grace to pray,
    For filling Grace had I ten thousand Hearts.   *40*
    I'de through ten Hells to see thy Judgment Day
    Wouldst thou but guild my Soule with thy bright Ray.

TEXT NOTES:
Line 6: *Mullipuff,* fuzz-ball, term of contempt.
Line 21: *Chid,* rebuked.
Line 21: *Consonant,* in agreement.
Line 42: *Guild,* gild.

23. MEDITATION. CANT. 4.8. MY SPOUSE.

21.6m [Aug.] 1687.

Would God I in that Golden City were,
    With Jaspers Walld, all garnisht, and made swash,
With Pretious Stones, whose Gates are Pearles most cleare
    And Street Pure Gold, like to transparent Glass.
    That my dull Soule, might be inflamde to see   *5*
    How Saints and Angells ravisht are in Glee.

Were I but there, and could but tell my Story,
    'Twould rub those Walls of Pretious Stones more bright:
And glaze those Gates of Pearle, with brighter Glory;
    And pave the golden Street with greater light.   *10*
    'Twould in fresh Raptures Saints, and Angells fling.
    But I poore Snake Crawl here, scarce mudwalld in.

May my Rough Voice, and my blunt Tongue but spell
    My Tale (for tune they can't) perhaps there may
Some Angell catch an end of't up, and tell   *15*
    In Heaven, when he doth return that way,
    He'l make thy Palace, Lord, all over ring,
    With it in Songs, thy Saint, and Angells sing.

I know not how to speak't, it is so good:
    Shall Mortall, and Immortall marry? nay,   *20*
Man marry God? God be a Match for Mud?
    The King of Glory Wed a Worm? mere Clay?

This is the Case. The Wonder too in Bliss.
Thy Maker is thy Husband. Hearst thou this?
My Maker, he my Husband? Oh! strange joy!   *25*
    If Kings wed Worms, and Monarchs Mites wed should,
Glory spouse Shame, a Prince a Snake or Fly
    An Angell Court an Ant, all Wonder would.
    Let such wed Worms, Snakes, Serpents, Divells, Flyes.
    Less Wonder than the Wedden in our Eyes.   *30*

I am to Christ more base, than to a King
    A Mite, Fly, Worm, Ant, Serpent, Divell is,
Or Can be, being tumbled all in Sin,
    And shall I be his Spouse? How good is this?
    It is too good to be declar'de to thee.   *35*
    But not too good to be believ'de by mee.

Yet to this Wonder, this is found in mee,
    I am not onely base but backward Clay,
When Christ doth Wooe: and till his Spirit bee
    His Spokes man to Compell me I deny.   *40*
    I am so base and Froward to him, Hee
    Appears as Wonders Wonder, wedding mee.

Seing, Dear Lord, its thus, thy Spirit take
    And send thy Spokes man, to my Soul, I pray.
Thy Saving Grace my Wedden Garment make: *45*
    Thy Spouses Frame into my Soul Convay.
    I then shall be thy Bride Espousd by thee
    And thou my Bridesgroom Deare Espousde shalt bee.

TEXT NOTES:
Line 2: *Jaspers,* see Revelation 21:18.
Line 2: *Swash,* showy.
Line 33: *Tumbled,* fallen; rumpled.
Line 41: *Froward,* perverse, contrary.

24. MEDITATION. EPH. 2.18. THROUGH HIM WE HAVE—AN ACCESS—UNTO THE FATHER.

6.9m [Nov.] 1687.

Was there a Palace of Pure Gold, all Ston'de
    And pav'de with Pearles, whose Gates Rich Jaspers were,

And Throne a Carbuncle, whose King Enthronde
  Sat on a Cushion all of Sunshine Cleare;
  Whose Crown a Bunch of Sun Beams was: I should   *5*
  Prize such as in his favour shrine me Would.

Thy Milke white Hand, my Glorious Lord, doth this:
  It opes this Gate, and me Conducts into
This Golden Palace whose rich Pavement is
  Of Pretious Pearles: and to this King also.   *10*
  Thus Thron'de, and Crown'd: whose Words are 'bellisht all
  With brighter Beams, than e're the Sun let fall.

But oh! Poore mee, thy sluggish Servant, I
  More blockish than a block, as blockhead, stand.
Though mine Affections Quick as Lightning fly   *15*
  On toys, they Snaile like move to kiss thy hand.
  My Coal-black doth thy Milke white hand avoide,
  That would above the Milky Way me guide.

What aim'st at, Lord? that I should be so Cross.
  My minde is Leaden in thy Golden Shine.   *20*
Though all o're Spirit, when this dirty Dross
  Doth touch it with its smutting leaden lines.
  What shall an Eagle t'catch a Fly thus run?
  Or Angell Dive after a Mote ith'Sun?

What Folly's this? I fain would take, I thinke,   *25*
  Vengeance upon myselfe: But I Confess,
I can't. Mine Eyes, Lord, shed no Tears but inke.
  My handy Works, are Words, and Wordiness.
  Earth's Toyes ware Knots of my Affections, nay,
  Though from thy Glorious Selfe they're Stoole away.   *30*

Oh! that my heart was made thy Golden Box
  Full of Affections, and of Love Divine
Knit all in Tassles, and in True-Love Knots,
  To garnish o're this Worthy Worke of thine.
  This Box and all therein more rich than Gold,   *35*
  In sacred Flames, I to thee offer would.

With thy rich Tissue my poore Soule array:
  And lead me to thy Fathers House above.
Thy Graces Storehouse make my Soule I pray.
  Thy Praise shall then ware Tassles of my Love.   *40*
  If thou Conduct mee in thy Fathers Wayes,
  I'le be the Golden Trumpet of thy Praise.

TEXT NOTES:

Line 24: *Mote,* dust particle.

Line 29: *Ware,* lay out.

Line 29: *Knots,* tangles, bonds.

Line 30: *Stoole,* stolen.

Line 33: *True-Love Knots,* marriage bonds.

Line 37: *Tissue,* fine cloth, often interwoven with gold or silver.

25. MEDITATION. EPH. 5.27.

A GLORIOUS CHURCH.

22.11m [Jan.] 1687.

Why should my Bells, which Chime thy Praise, when thou
    My Shew-Bread, on thy Table wast, my King,
Their Clappers, or their Bell-ropes want even now?
    Or those that can thy Changes sweetly ring?
    What is a Scar-Fire broken out? No, no.   *5*
    The Bells would backward ring if it was so.

Its true: and I do all things backward run,
    Poor Pillard I have a sad tale to tell:
My soule starke nakt, rowld all in mire, undone.
    Thy Bell may tole my passing Peale to Hell.   *10*
    None in their Winding sheet more naked stay
    Nor Dead than I. Hence oh! the Judgment Day.

When I behold some Curious Piece of Art,
    Or Pritty Bird, Flower, Star, or Shining Sun,
Poure out o'reflowing Glory: oh! my Heart   *15*
    Achs seing how my thoughts in Snick-Snarls run.
    But all this Glory to my Lord's a spot
    While I instead of any, am all blot.

But, my sweet Lord, what glorious robes are those
    That thou hast brought out of thy Grave for thine?   *20*
They do outshine the Sun-Shine, Grace the Rose.
    I leape for joy to thinke, shall these be mine?
    Such are, as waite upon thee in thy Wars,
    Cloathd with the Sun, and Crowned with twelve Stars.

Dost thou adorn some thus, and why not mee?   *25*
    Ile not believe it. Lord, thou art my Chiefe.
Thou me Commandest to believe in thee.

I'l not affront thee thus with Unbeliefe.
Lord, make my Soule Obedient: and when so,
Thou saist Believe, make it reply, I do.   *30*

I fain the Choicest Love my soule Can get,
   Would to thy Gracious selfe a Gift present
But cannot now unscrew Loves Cabbinet.
   Say not this is a Niggards Complement.
   For seing it is thus I choose now rather   *35*
   To send thee th'Cabbinet, and Pearle together.

TEXT NOTES:
Line 2: *Shew-Bread,* offering of bread in Old Testament worship, here suggestive
   of the bread of the Lord's Supper.
Line 3: *Want,* lack.
Line 4: *Changes,* go through all variations in peal of bells.
Line 5: *Scar-Fire* (scarefire), sudden conflagration.
Line 8: *Pillard,* one who is stripped; also, robber.
Line 9: *Rowld,* rolled.
Line 10: *Peale,* summons.
Line 16: *Snick-Snarls,* tangles.
Line 24: *Cloathd with the Sun, and Crowned with twelve Stars,* see Revelation 12:1;
   the woman thus clothed and crowned is the Church.

26. MEDITATION. ACT. 5.31.

TO GIVE—FORGIVENESS OF SINS.

15.1m [Mar.] 1688.

My Noble Lord, thy Nothing Servant I
   Am for thy sake out with my heart, that holds,
So little Love for such a Lord: I Cry

                    . . .

   How should I be but angry thus to see   *5*
   My Heart so hidebound in her Acts to thee?
Thou art a Golden Theame: but I am lean,
   A Leaden Oritor upon the same.
Thy Golden Web excells my Dozie Beam:
   Whose Linsy-Wolsy Loom deserves thy blame.   *10*
   Its all defild, unbiasst too by Sin:
   An hearty Wish for thee's scarce shot therein.

It pitties mee who pitty Cannot show,
   That such a Worthy Theame abusd should bee.

I am undone, unless thy Pardons doe   *15*
   Undoe my Sin I did, undoing mee.
My Sins are greate, and grieveous ones, therefore
Carbuncle Mountains can't wipe out their Score.

But thou, my Lord, dost a Free Pardon bring.
   Thou giv'st Forgiveness: yet my heart through Sin,   *20*
Hath naught but naught to file thy Gift up in.
   An hurden Haump doth Chafe a Silken Skin.
   Although I pardons beg, I scarce can see,
   When thou giv'st pardons, I give praise to thee.

O bad at best! what am I then at worst?   *25*
   I want a Pardon: and when pardon'd, want
A Thankfull Heart: Both which thou dost disburst.
   Giv'st both, or neither: for which Lord I pant.
   Two such good things at once! methinks I could
   Avenge my heart, lest it should neither hold.   *30*

Lord tap mine Eyes, seing such Grace in thee,
   So little doth affect my Graceless Soule.
And take my teares in lue of thanks of mee,
   New make my heart: then take it for thy tole.
   Thy Pardons then will make my heart to sing   *35*
   Its Michtam-David: With sweet joy Within.

TEXT NOTES:
Line 4: This line is missing.
Line 9: *Web,* woven cloth.
Line 9: *Dozie* (dozen), coarse woolen cloth.
Line 9: *Beam,* wooden roller on which cloth is wound as it is woven.
Line 11: *Unbiasst,* made crooked?
Line 22: *Hurden Haump,* coarse smock-frock (see Glossary, Stanford, ed., *Poems of E.T.*).
Line 36: *Michtam-David,* Psalm tune; see heading of Psalms 57, 58, 59.

27. MEDITATION. COL. 1.19. IN HIM
SHOULD ALL FULNESS DWELL.

1.5m [July] 1688.

Oh! Wealthy Theam! Oh! Feeble Phancy: I
   Must needs admire, when I recall to minde,
That's Fulness, This it's Emptiness, though spy
   I have no Flowring Brain thereto inclinde.

My Damps do out my fire. I cannot, though   5
    I would Admire, finde heate enough thereto.

What shall I say? Such rich rich Fullness would
    Make stammering Tongues speake smoothly, and Enshrine
The Dumb mans mouth with Silver Streams like gold
    Of Eloquence making the Aire to Chime.   10
    Yet I am Tonguetide stupid, sensless stand,
    And Drier drain'd than is my pen I hand.

Oh! Wealthy Box: more Golden far than Gold
    A Case more Worth than Wealth: a richer Delph,
Than Rubies; Cabbinet, than Pearles here told   15
    A Purse more glittering than Glory 'tselfe
    A Golden Store House of all Fulness: Shelfe,
    Of Heavenly Plate. All Fulness in thyselfe.

Oh! Godhead Fulness! There doth in thee flow
    All Wisdoms Fulness; Fulness of all Strength: 20
Of Justice, Truth, Love, Holiness also
    And Graces Fulness to its upmost length
    Do dwell in thee. Yea and thy Fathers Pleasure.
    Thou art their Cabbinet, and they thy Treasure.

All Office Fulness with all Office Gifts   25
    Imbossed are in thee, Whereby thy Grace,
Doth treat both God, and Man, bringst up by hifts
    Black Sinner and White Justice to imbrace.
    Making the Glory of Gods Justice shine:
    And making Sinners to Gods glory Climbe.   30

All Graces Fulness dwells in thee, from Whom
    The Golden Pipes of all Convayance ly,
Through which Grace to our Clayie Panchins Come.
    Fullness of Beauty, and Humanity.
    Oh! Glorious Flow're, Glory, and Sweetness splice,   35
    In thee to Grace, and sweeten Paradise!

But, oh! the Fathers Love! herein most vast!
    Angells engrave't in brightest Marble, t'see
This Flower that in his Bosom sticks so fast,
    Stuck in the Bosom of such stuffe as wee   40
    That both his Purse, and all his Treasure thus,
    Should be so full, and freely sent to us.

Were't not more than my heart can hold, or hord,
    Or than my Tongue can tell; I thus would pray,

Let him in Whom all Fulness Dwells, dwell, Lord   *45*
    Within my Heart: this Treasure therein lay.
    I then shall sweetly tune thy Praise, When hee
    In Whom all Fulness dwells, doth dwell in mee.

TEXT NOTES:
Line 14: *Delph,* quarry, mine.
Line 25: *Office,* service, kindness.
Line 27: *Hifts,* lifts.
Line 33: *Panchin* (pancheon), bowl.

28. MEDITATION. JOH. 1.16. OF HIS FULNESS
WEE ALL RECEIVE: AND GRACE—

2.7m [Sept.] 1688.

When I Lord, send some Bits of Glory home,
    (For Lumps I lack) my Messenger, I finde,
Bewildred, lose his Way being alone
    In my befogg'd Dark Phancy, Clouded minde.
    Thy Bits of Glory packt in Shreds of Praise   *5*
    My Messenger doth lose, losing his Wayes.

Lord Cleare the Coast: and let thy sweet sun shine.
    That I may better speed a second time:
Oh! fill my Pipkin with thy Blood red Wine:
    I'l drinke thy Health: To pledge thee is no Crime.   *10*
    Although I but an Earthen Vessell bee
    Convay some of thy Fulness into mee.

Thou, thou my Lord, art full, top full of Grace,
    The Golden Sea of Grace: Whose springs thence come,
And Pretious Drills, boiling in ery place.   *15*
    Untap thy Cask, and let my Cup Catch some.
    Although its in an Earthen Vessells Case,
    Let it no Empty Vessell be of Grace.

Let thy Choice Caske, shed, Lord, into my Cue
    A Drop of Juyce presst from thy Noble Vine.   *20*
My Bowl is but an Acorn Cup, I sue
    But for a Drop: this will not empty thine.
    Although I'me in an Earthen Vessells place,
    My Vessell make a Vessell, Lord, of Grace.

My Earthen Vessell make thy Font also: *25*
  And let thy Sea my Spring of Grace in't raise.
Spring up oh Well. My Cup with Grace make flow.
  Thy Drops will on my Vessell ting thy Praise.
  I'l sing this Song, when I these Drops Embrace.
  My Vessell now's a Vessell of thy Grace.   *30*

TEXT NOTES:
Line 9: *Pipkin,* earthenware pot.
Line 15: *Drills,* rivulet, rill; also, a small draught of liquid.
Line 15: *Boiling,* overflowing.
Line 19: *Cue,* half-pint beer cup (Glossary, Stanford, ed., *Poems of E.T.*).
Line 28: *Ting,* sound of a small bell or glass when struck.

29. MEDITATION. JOH. 20.17. MY FATHER,
AND YOUR FATHER, TO MY GOD, AND YOUR GOD.

11.9m [Nov.] 1688.

My shattred Phancy stole away from mee,
  (Wits run a Wooling over Edens Parke)
And in Gods Garden saw a golden Tree,
  Whose Heart was All Divine, and gold its barke.
  Whose glorious limbs and fruitfull branches strong   *5*
  With Saints, and Angells bright are richly hung.

Thou! thou! my Deare-Deare Lord, art this rich Tree
  The Tree of Life Within Gods Paradise.
I am a Withred Twig, dri'de fit to bee
  A Chat Cast in thy fire, Writh off by Vice.   *10*
  Yet if thy Milke white-Gracious Hand will take mee
  And grafft mee in this golden stock, thou'lt make mee.

Thou'lt make me then its Fruite, and Branch to spring.
  And though a nipping Eastwinde blow, and all
Hells Nymps with spite their Dog's sticks thereat ding   *15*
  To Dash the Grafft off, and it's fruits to fall,
  Yet I shall stand thy Grafft, and Fruits that are
  Fruits of the Tree of Life thy Grafft shall beare.

I being grafft in thee there up do stand
  In us Relations all that mutuall are.   *20*
I am thy Patient, Pupill, Servant, and
  Thy Sister, Mother, Doove, Spouse, Son, and Heire.

Thou art my Priest, Physician, Prophet, King,
  Lord, Brother, Bridegroom, Father, Ev'ry thing.
I being grafft in thee am graffted here   *25*
  Into thy Family, and kindred Claim
To all in Heaven, God, Saints, and Angells there.
  I thy Relations my Relations name.
  Thy Father's mine, thy God my God, and I
  With Saints, and Angells draw Affinity.   *30*

My Lord, what is it that thou dost bestow?
  The Praise on this account fills up, and throngs
Eternity brimfull, doth overflow
  The Heavens vast with rich Angelick Songs.
  How should I blush? how Tremble at this thing,   *35*
  Not having yet my Gam-Ut, learnd to sing.

But, Lord, as burnish't Sun Beams forth out fly
  Let Angell-Shine forth in my Life out flame,
That I may grace thy gracefull Family
  And not to thy Relations be a Shame.   *40*
  Make mee thy Grafft, be thou my Golden Stock.
  Thy Glory then I'le make my fruits and Crop.

TEXT NOTES:
Line 1: *Phancy stole away,* imagination ran away.
Line 2: *Wooling,* woolgathering, aimlessly thinking.
Line 10: *Chat,* twig used for kindling.
Line 10: *Writh,* twisted.
Line 15: *Nymps,* imps.
Line 15: *Dog's sticks,* sticks for beating dogs.
Line 15: *Ding,* hammer, beat.
Line 22: *Doove* (dove), loved one.
Line 36: *Gam-Ut,* musical scale.

30. MEDITATION. 2 COR. 5.17.—

HE IS A NEW CREATURE.

6.11m [Jan.] 1688.

The Daintiest Draught thy Pensill ever Drew:
  The finest vessell, Lord, thy fingers fram'de:
The statelist Palace Angells e're did view,
  Under thy Hatch betwixt Decks here Contain'd

Broke, marred, spoild, undone, Defild doth ly   *5*
In Rubbish ruinde by thine Enemy.

What Pittie's this? Oh Sunshine Art! What Fall?
Thou that more Glorious wast than glories Wealth!
More Golden far than Gold! Lord, on whose Wall
Thy scutchons hung, the Image of thyselfe!   *10*
Its ruinde, and must rue, though Angells should
To hold it up heave while their Heart Strings hold.

But yet thou stem of Davids stock when dry
And shrivled held, although most green was lopt
Whose sap a sovereign Sodder is, whereby   *15*
The breach repared is in which its dropt.
Oh Gracious Twig! thou Cut off? bleed rich juyce
T'Cement the Breach, and Glories shine reduce?

Oh Lovely One! how doth thy Loveliness
Beam through the Chrystall Casements of the Eyes   *20*
Of Saints, and Angells sparkling Flakes of Fresh
Heart Ravishing Beauty, filling up their joyes?
And th'Divells too; if Envies Pupills stood
Not peeping there these sparkling Rayes t'exclude?

Thou Rod of Davids Root, Branch of his Bough   *25*
My Lord, repare thy Palace, Deck thy Place.
I'm but a Flesh and Blood bag: Oh! do thou
Sill, Plate, Ridge, Rib, and Rafter me with Grace.
Renew my Soule, and guild it all within:
And hang thy saving Grace on ery Pin.   *30*

My Soule, Lord, make thy Shining Temple, pave
Its Floore all o're with Orient Grace: thus guild
It o're with Heavens gold: Its Cabbins have
Thy Treasuries with Choicest thoughts up filld.
Pourtray thy Glorious Image round about   *35*
Upon thy Temple Walls within, and Out.

Garnish thy Hall with Gifts, Lord, from above
With that Rich Coate of Male thy Righteousness,
Truths Belt, the Spirits Sword, the Buckler Love
Hopes Helmet, and the Shield of Faith kept fresh.   *40*
The Scutchons of thy Honour make my Sign
As Garland Tuns are badges made of Wine.

New mould, new make me thus, me new Create
Renew in me a spirit right, pure, true.

Lord make me thy New Creature, then new make   *45*
   All things to thy New Creature here anew,
   New Heart, New thoughts, New Words, New wayes likewise.
   New Glory then shall to thyselfe arise.

TEXT NOTES:

Line 1: *Draught,* stroke.
Line 4: *Under thy Hatch betwixt Decks here Contain'd,* suggestive of the conception
   of a three-level universe, with earth between heaven and hell.
Line 10: *Scutchon* (escutcheon), shield bearing coat of arms.
Line 15: *Sodder,* solder.
Line 21: *Flakes,* flames, flashes.
Line 32: *Orient,* precious.
Line 42: *Garland Tuns,* ceremonial or ornamental wine cups or chalices.

31. MEDITATION. 1 COR. 3.21.22.

ALL THINGS ARE YOURS.

17.12m [Feb.] 1688.

Begracde with Glory, gloried with Grace,
   In Paradise I was, when all Sweet Shines
Hung dangling on this Rosy World to face
   Mine Eyes, and Nose, and Charm mine Eares with Chimes.
   All these were golden Tills the which did hold   *5*
   My evidences wrapt in glorious folds.

But as a Chrystall Glass, I broke, and lost
   That Grace, and Glory I was fashion'd in
And cast this Rosy World with all its Cost
   Into the Dunghill Pit, and Puddle Sin.   *10*
   All right I lost in all Good things, each thing
   I had did hand a Vean of Venom in.

Oh! Sad-Sad thing! Satan is now turnd Cook:
   Sin is the Sauce he gets for ev'ry Dish.
I cannot bite a bit of Bread or Roote   *15*
   But what is sopt therein, and Venomish.
   Right's lost in what's my Right. Hence I do take
   Onely what's poison'd by th'infernall Snake.

But this is not the Worst: there's worse than this.
   My Tast is lost; no bit tasts sweet to mee,   *20*

But what is Dipt all over in this Dish
  Of Ranck ranck Poyson: this my Sauce must bee.
Hell Heaven is, Heaven hell, yea Bitter Sweet:
  Poison's my Food: Food poison in't doth keep.

What e're we want, we cannot Cry for, nay　　　　*25*
  If that we could, we could not have it thus.
The Angell's can't devise, nor yet Convay
  Help in their Golden Pipes from God to us.
  But thou my Lord, (Heart leape for joy and sing)
  Hast done the Deed: and't makes the Heavens ring.　　*30*

By mee all lost, by thee all are regain'd.
  All things are thus fall'n now into thy hande.
And thou steep'st in thy Blood what Sin had stain'd
  That th'Stains, and Poisons may not therein stand.
  And having stuck thy Grace all o're the same　　*35*
  Thou giv'st it as a Glorious Gift again.

Cleare up my Right, my Lord, in thee, and make
  Thy Name stand Dorst upon my Soule in print,
In grace I mean, that so I may partake
  Of what I lost, in thee, and of thee in't.　　*40*
  I'l take it then, Lord, at thy hand, and sing
  Out Hallelujah for thy Grace therein.

TEXT NOTES:
Line 2: *Shines,* displays.
Line 5: *Tills,* boxes for valuables.
Line 6: *My evidences,* proof or assurances of salvation.
Line 6: *Folds,* coverings.
Line 12: *Vean* (vein), vessel.
Line 38: *Dorst,* endorsed, signed on back of a bill or note; made payable to.

32. MEDITATION. 1 COR. 3.22.

WHETHER PAUL OR APOLLOS, OR CEPHAS.

28.2m [Apr.] 1689.

Thy Grace, Dear Lord's my golden Wrack, I finde
  Screwing my Phancy into ragged Rhimes,
Tuning thy Praises in my feeble minde
  Untill I come to strike them on my Chimes.
  Were I an Angell bright, and borrow could　　*5*
  King Davids Harp, I would them play on gold.

But plung'd I am, my minde is puzzled,
　When I would spin my Phancy thus unspun,
In finest Twine of Praise I'm muzzled.
　　My tazzled Thoughts twirld into Snick-Snarls run.   *10*
　　Thy Grace, my Lord, is such a glorious thing,
　　It doth Confound me when I would it sing.

Eternall Love an Object mean did smite
　Which by the Prince of Darkness was beguilde,
That from this Love it ran and sweld with spite   *15*
　　And in the way with filth was all defilde
　　Yet must be reconcild, cleansd, and begrac'te
　　Or from the fruits of Gods first Love displac'te.

Then Grace, my Lord, wrought in thy Heart a vent,
　Thy Soft Soft hand to this hard worke did goe,   *20*
And to the Milke White Throne of Justice went
　　And entred bond that Grace might overflow.
　　Hence did thy Person to my Nature ty
　　And bleed through humane Veans to satisfy.

Oh! Grace, Grace, Grace! this Wealthy Grace doth lay   *25*
　Her Golden Channells from thy Fathers throne,
Into our Earthen Pitchers to Convay
　　Heavens Aqua Vitae to us for our own.
　　O! let thy Golden Gutters run into
　　My Cup this Liquour till it overflow.   *30*

Thine Ordinances, Graces Wine-fats where
　Thy Spirits Walkes, and Graces runs doe ly
And Angells waiting stand with holy Cheere
　　From Graces Conduite Head, with all Supply.
　　These Vessells full of Grace are, and the Bowls   *35*
　　In which their Taps do run, are pretious Souls.

Thou to the Cups dost say (that Catch this Wine,)
　This Liquour, Golden Pipes, and Wine-fats plain,
Whether Paul, Apollos, Cephas, all are thine.
　　Oh Golden Word! Lord speake it ore again.   *40*
　　Lord speake it home to me, say these are mine.
　　My Bells shall then thy Praises bravely chime.

TEXT NOTES:
Line 1: *Wrack* (rack), frame on which cloth, wire, etc., is stretched.
Line 7: *Plung'd,* overwhelmed, embarrassed.
Line 10: *Tazzled,* tasseled? dazzled?

Line 10: *Snick-Snarls,* tangles.
Line 19: *Vent,* opening.
Line 31: *Wine-fats,* wine-vats.
Line 32: *Walkes . . . runs,* paths.

33. MEDITATION. 1 COR. 3.22.

LIFE IS YOURES.

7.5m [July] 1689.

My Lord my Life, can Envy ever bee
   A Golden Vertue? Then would God I were
Top full thereof untill it colours mee
   With yellow streaks for thy Deare sake most Deare,
   Till I be Envious made by't at myselfe,   *5*
   As scarcely loving thee my Life, my Health.

Oh! what strange Charm encrampt my Heart with spite
   Making my Love gleame out upon a Toy?
Lay out Cart-Loads of Love upon a mite?
   Scarce lay a mite of Love on thee, my Joy?   *10*
   Oh, Lovely thou! Shalt not thou loved bee?
   Shall I ashame thee thus? Oh! shame for mee!

Nature's amaz'de, Oh monstrous thing Quoth shee,
   Not Love my life? What Violence doth split
True Love, and Life, that they should sunder'd bee?   *15*
   She doth not lay such Eggs, nor on them sit.
   How do I sever then my Heart with all
   Its Powers whose Love scarce to my Life doth crawle.

Glory lin'de out a Paradise in Power
   Where e'ry seed a Royall Coach became   *20*
For Life to ride in, to each shining Flower.
   And made mans Flower with glory all ore flame.
   Hells Inkfac'de Elfe black Venom spat upon
   The same, and kill'd it. So that Life is gone.

Life thus abusde fled to the golden Arke,   *25*
   Lay lockt up there in Mercie's seate inclosde:
Which did incorporate it whence its Sparke
   Enlivens all things in this Arke inclosde.

Oh, glorious Arke! Life's Store-House full of Glee!
Shall not my Love safe lockt up ly in thee?   *30*

Lord arke my Soule safe in thyselfe, whereby
I and my Life again may joyned bee.
That I may finde what once I did destroy
Again Conferde upon my soul in thee.
Thou art this Golden Ark; this Living Tree   *35*
Where life lies treasurde up for all in thee.

Oh! Graft me in this Tree of Life within
The Paradise of God, that I may live.
Thy Life make live in mee; I'le then begin
To bear thy Living Fruits, and them forth give.   *40*
Give mee my Life this way; and I'le bestow
My Love on thee my Life, and it shall grow.

TEXT NOTES:
Date: Written the day of his wife's death.
Line 8: *Toy,* trifle.
Line 9: *Mite,* insect, minute particle.
Line 25: *The golden Arke,* Revelation 11:19, "And the temple of God was opened
in heaven, and there was seen in his temple the ark of his testament."

34. MEDITATION. 1 COR. 3.22.

DEATH IS YOURS.

25.9m [Nov.] 1689.

My Lord I fain would Praise thee Well but finde
Impossibilities blocke up my pass.
My tongue Wants Words to tell my thoughts, my Minde
Wants thoughts to Comprehend thy Worth, alas!
Thy Glory far Surmounts my thoughts, my thoughts   *5*
Surmount my Words: Hence little Praise is brought.

But seing Non-Sense very Pleasant is
To Parents, flowing from the Lisping Child,
I Conjue to thee, hoping thou in this
Will finde some hearty Praise of mine Enfoild,   *10*
But though my pen drop'd golden Words, yet would
Thy Glory far out shine my Praise in Gold.

Poor wretched man Deaths Captive stood full Chuffe
  But thou my Gracious Lord didst finde reliefe,
Thou King of Glory didst, to handy cuff   *15*
  With King of Terrours, and dasht out his Teeth,
  Plucktst out his sting, his Poyson quelst, his head
  To pieces brakest. Hence Cruell Death lies Dead.

And still thou by thy gracious Chymistry
  Dost of his Carkass Cordialls make rich, High,   *20*
To free from Death makst Death a remedy:
  A Curb to Sin, a Spur to Piety.
  Heavens brightsom Light shines out in Death's Dark Cave.
  The Golden Dore of Glory is the Grave.

The Painter lies who pensills death's Face grim   *25*
  With White bare butter Teeth, bare staring bones,
With Empty Eyeholes, Ghostly Lookes which fling
  Such Dread to see as raiseth Deadly groans,
  For thou hast farely Washt Deaths grim grim face
  And made his Chilly finger-Ends drop grace.   *30*

Death Tamde, Subdude, Washt fair by thee! Oh Grace!
  Made Usefull thus! thou unto thine dost say
Now Death is yours, and all it doth in't brace.
  The Grave's a Down bed now made for your clay.
  Oh! Happiness! How should our Bells hereby   *35*
  Ring Changes, Lord, and praises trust with joy.

Say I am thine, My Lord: Make me thy bell
  To ring thy Praise. Then Death is mine indeed
A Hift to Grace, a Spur to Duty; Spell
  To Fear; a Frost to nip each naughty Weede.   .   *40*
  A Golden doore to Glory. Oh I'le sing
  This Triumph o're the Grave! Death where's thy Sting?

TEXT NOTES:
Line 9: *Conjue* (congee), bow (Glossary, Stanford, ed., *Poems of E.T.*).
Line 13: *Chuffe,* swollen.
Line 15: *Handy cuff,* fisticuff, fight with fists.
Line 25: *The Painter lies,* reference to broadside, emblem, and gravestone art.
Line 26: *Butter Teeth,* buck'teeth.
Line 39: *Hift,* help.
Line 39: *Spell,* charm, exorcism.
Line 40: *Naughty,* evil.
Line 42: *Death* . . . I Corinthians 15:55.

35. MEDITATION. 1 COR. 3.22.

THINGS PRESENT.

19.11m [Jan.] 1689.

Oh! that I ever felt what I profess.
  'Twould make me then the happi'st man alive.
Ten thousand Worlds of Saints can't make this less
  By living on't, but it would make them thrive.
  These Loaves and Fishes are not lessened   *5*
  Nor Pasture over stock, by being fed.

Lord am I thine? art thou, Lord, mine? So rich!
  How doth thy Wealthy bliss branch out thy sweets
Through all things Present? These the Vent-holes which
  Let out those Ravishing Joys our Souls to greet?   *10*
  Impower my Powers sweet Lord till up they raise
  My 'Fections that thy glory on them blaze.

How many things are there now, who display'th?
  How many Acts each thing doth here dispense?
How many Influences each thing hath?   *15*
  How many Contraries each Influence?
  How many Contraries from Things do flow?
  From Acts? from Influences? Who can show?

How Glorious then is he that doth all raise
  Rule and Dispose and make them all Conspire   *20*
In all their Jars, and Junctures, Good-bad wayes
  To meliorate the self same Object higher?
  Earth, Water, Fire, Winds, Herbs, Trees, Beasts and Men,
  Angells, and Divells, Bliss, Blasts, advance one stem?

Hell, Earth, and Heaven with their Whole Troops come   *25*
  Contrary Windes, Grace, and Disgrace, Soure, Sweet,
Wealth, Want, Health, Sickness, to Conclude in Sum
  All Providences Works in this good meet?
  Who, who can do't, but thou, my Lord? and thou
  Dost do this thing. Yea thou performst it now.   *30*

Oh, that the Sweets of all these Windings, spoute
  Might, and these Influences streight, and Cross,
Upon my Soule, to make thy Shine breake out
  That Grace might in get and get out my dross!
  My Soule up lockt then in this Clod of Dust   *35*
  Would lock up in't all Heavenly Joyes most just.

But oh! thy Wisdom, Lord! thy Grace! thy Praise!
  Open mine Eyes to see the same aright.
Take off their film, my Sins, and let the Rayes
  Of thy bright Glory on my peepholes light.   *40*
  I fain would love and better love thee should,
  If 'fore me thou thy Loveliness unfold.

Lord, Cleare my Sight, thy Glory then out dart.
  And let thy Rayes beame Glory in mine eye
And stick thy Loveliness upon my heart,   *45*
  Make me the Couch on which thy Love doth ly.
  Lord make my heart thy bed, thy heart make mine.
  Thy Love bed in my heart, bed mine in thine.

TEXT NOTES:
Line 21: *Jars, and Junctures,* disharmony and harmony.
Line 40: *Peepholes,* eyes.

36. MEDITATION. 1 COR. 3.22.

THINGS TO COME YOURS.

16.1m [Mar.] 1689.

What rocky heart is mine? My pincky Eyes
  Thy Grace spy blancht, Lord, in immensitie.
But finde the Sight me not to meliorize,
  O Stupid Heart! What strang-strange thing am I?
  I many months do drown in Sorrows Spring   *5*
  But hardly raise a Sigh to blow down Sin.

To find thee Lord, thus overflowing kinde,
  And t'finde mee thine, thus overflowing vile,
A Riddle seems onrivetted I finde.
  This reason saith is hard to reconcile.   *10*
  Dost Vileness choose? Or can't thy kindness shown
  Me meliorate? Or am I not thine own?

The first two run thy glory would to Shame:
  The last plea doth my Soule to hell Confine.
My Faith therefore doth all these Pleas disdain.   *15*
  Thou kindness art, it saith, and I am thine.
  Upon this banck it doth on tiptoes stand
  To ken o're Reasons head at Graces hand.

But Did I say, I wonder, Lord, to spie
   Thy Selfe so kind; and I so vile yet thine?   *20*
I eate my Word: and wonder more that I
   No viler am, though all ore vile do shine.
   As full of Sin I am, as Egge of meate.
   Yet finde thy golden Rod my Sin to treate.

Nay did I say, I wonder t'see thy Store   *25*
   Of kindnesses, yet me thus vile with all?
I now Unsay my Say: I wonder more
   Thou dash me not to pieces with thy maule,
   But in the bed, Lord, of thy goodness lies
   The Reason of't, which makes my Wonders rise.   *30*

For now I wonder t'feele how I thus feele.
   My Love leapes into Creatures bosoms; and
Cold Sorrows fall into my Soule as Steel,
   When faile they, yet I kiss thy Love's White hand.
   I scarce know what t'make of myselfe. Wherefore   *35*
   I crave a Pardon, Lord, for thou hast Store.

How wondrous rich art thou? Thy Storehouse vast
   Holdes more ten thousand fold told ore and ore
Than this Wide World Can hold. The doore unhasp.
   And bring me thence a Pardon out therefore.   *40*
   Thou Stoughst the World so tite with present things
   That things to Come, though crowd full hard, cant in.

These things to Come, tread on the heels of those.
   The presents breadth doth with the broad world run.
The Depth and breadth of things to come out goes   *45*
   Unto Times End which bloweth out the Sun.
   These breadth and length meate out Eternity.
   These are the things that in thy Storehouse ly.

A Cockle Shell contains this World as well
   As can this World thy Liberallness contain.   *50*
And by thy Will these present things all fell
   Unto thy Children for their present gain;
   And things to Come too, to Eternity.
   Thou Willedst them: they're theirs by Legacy.

But am I thine? Oh! what strange thing's in mee?   *55*
   Enricht thus by thy Legacy? yet finde
When one small Twig's broke off, the breach should bee
   Such an Enfeebling thing upon my minde.

Then take a pardon from thy Store, and twist
  It in my Soule for help. 'Twill not be mist.   60

I am asham'd to say I love thee do.
  But dare not for my Life, and Soule deny't.
Yet wonder much Love's Springs should lie so low
  Thy loveliness its Object shines so bright.
  Shall all the Beams of Love upon me shine?   65
  And shall my Love Love's Object still make pine?

I'me surely made a Gazing Stock to all.
  The Holy Angells Wonder: and the Mock
Of Divells (pining that they misse it all)
  To see these beams gild me a Stupid Stock.   70
  Thy Argument is good, Lord point it, come
  Let't lance my heart, till True Loves Veane doth run.

But that there is a Crevice for one hope
  To creep in, and this Message to Convay
That I am thine, makes me refresh. Lord ope   75
  The Doore so wide that Love may Scip, and play.
  My Spirits then shall dance thy Praise. I'me thine.
  And Present things with things to come are mine.

TEXT NOTES:
Line 1: *Pincky,* squinty.
Line 2: *Blancht,* white.
Line 3: *Meliorize,* meliorate, improve.
Line 9: *Onrivetted,* unlocked, opened.
Line 17: *Banck,* ridge.
Line 18: *Ken,* gaze.
Line 39: *Unhasp,* unfasten.
Line 41: *Stoughst,* stow; or stuff.
Line 67: *Gazing Stock,* person at whom others stare.
Line 76: *Scip,* skip.

37. MEDITATION. 1 COR. 3.23.

YOU ARE CHRIST'S.

4.3m [May] 1690.

My Soule, Lord, quailes to thinke that I should bee
  So high related, have such colours faire

Stick in my Hat, from Heaven: yet should see
  My Soule thus blotcht: Hells Liveries to beare.
What Thine? New-naturizd? Yet this Relation   *5*
  Thus barren, though't 's a Priviledg-Foundation?

Shall I thy Vine branch be, yet grapes none beare?
  Grafft in thy Olive stand: and fatness lack?
A Shackeroon, a Ragnell, yet an Heire?
  Thy spouse, yet, oh! my Wedden Ring thus slack?   *10*
  Should Angel-Feathers plume my Cap, I should
  Be swash? but oh! my Heart hereat grows Cold.

What is my Title but an empty Claim?
  Am I a fading Flower within thy Knot?
A Rattle, or a gilded Box, a Flame   *15*
  Of Painted Fire, a glorious Weedy Spot?
  The Channell ope of Union, the ground
  Of Wealth, Relation: yet I'me barren found?

What am I thine, and thou not mine? or dost
  Not thou thy Spouse joyn in thy Glory Cleare?   *20*
Is my Relation to thee but a boast?
  Or but a blustring say-so, or spruice jeere?
  Should Roses blow more late, sure I might get,
  If thine, some Prim-Rose or sweet Violet?

Make me thy Branch to bare thy Grapes, Lord, feed   *25*
  Mee with thy bunch of Raisins of the Sun.
Mee stay with apples; let me eate indeed
  Fruits of the tree of Life: its richly hung.
  Am I thy Child, Son, Heir, thy Spouse, yet gain
  Not of the Rights that these Relations claim?   *30*

Am I hop't on thy knees, yet not at ease?
  Sunke in thy bosom, yet thy Heart not meet?
Lodgd in thine Arms? yet all things little please?
  Sung sweetly, yet finde not this singing sweet?
  Set at thy Table, yet scarce tast a Dish   *35*
  Delicious? Hugd, yet seldom gain a Kiss?

Why? Lord, why thus? Shall I in Question Call
  All my Relation to thyselfe? I know
It is no Gay to please a Child withall
  But is the Ground whence Priviledges flow.   *40*
  Then ope the sluce: let some thing spoute on me.
  Then I shall in a better temper bee.

TEXT NOTES:
Line 1: *Quailes,* faints, fails.
Line 9: *Shackeroon,* vagabond.
Line 9: *Ragnell,* bum.
Line 12: *Swash,* showy, swashbuckling.
Line 14: *Knot,* garden-plot.
Line 22: *Spruice* (spruce), lively, smart in appearance.
Line 31: *Hop't,* hopped, bounced.
Line 39: *Gay,* toy.

38. MEDITATION. 1 JOH. 2.1. AN ADVOCATE

WITH THE FATHER.

6.5m [July] 1690.

Oh! What a thing is Man? Lord, Who am I?
  That thou shouldst give him Law (Oh! golden Line)
To regulate his Thoughts, Words, Life thereby.
  And judge him Wilt thereby too in thy time.
  A Court of Justice thou in heaven holdst   5
  To try his Case while he's here housd on mould.

How do thy Angells lay before thine eye
  My Deeds both White, and Black I dayly doe?
How doth thy Court thou Pannellst there them try?
  But flesh complains. What right for this? let's know.   10
  For right, or wrong I can't appeare unto't.
  And shall a sentence Pass on such a suite?

Soft; blemish not this golden Bench, or place.
  Here is no Bribe, nor Colourings to hide
Nor Pettifogger to befog the Case   15
  But Justice hath her Glory here well tri'de.
  Her spotless Law all spotted Cases tends.
  Without Respect or Disrespect them ends.

God's Judge himselfe: and Christ Atturny is,
  The Holy Ghost Regesterer is founde.   20
Angells the sergeants are, all Creatures kiss
  The booke, and doe as Evidences abounde.
  All Cases pass according to pure Law
  And in the sentence is no Fret, nor flaw.

What saist, my soule? Here all thy Deeds are tri'de.   25
  Is Christ thy Advocate to plead thy Cause?

Art thou his Client? Such shall never slide.
  He never lost his Case: he pleads such Laws
As Carry do the same, nor doth refuse
  The Vilest sinners Case that doth him Choose.   *30*

This is his Honour, not Dishonour: nay
  No Habeas-Corpus gainst his Clients came
For all their Fines his Purse doth make down pay.
  He Non-Suites Satan's Suite or Casts the Same.
  He'l plead thy Case, and not accept a Fee.   *35*
  He'l plead Sub Forma Pauperis for thee.

My Case is bad. Lord, be my Advocate.
  My sin is red: I'me under Gods Arrest.
Thou hast the Hint of Pleading; plead my State.
  Although it's bad thy Plea will make it best.   *40*
  If thou wilt plead my Case before the King:
  I'le Waggon Loads of Love, and Glory bring.

TEXT NOTES:
Line 6: *Mould,* earth.
Line 15: *Pettifogger,* tricky, caviling lawyer.
Line 24: *No Fret, nor flaw,* no invalidating defect.
Line 36: *Sub Forma Pauperis,* under the law regarding paupers, entitling them to representation in court.

39. MEDITATION. FROM 1 JOH. 2.1. IF ANY
MAN SIN, WE HAVE AN ADVOCATE.

9.9m [Nov.] 1690.

My Sin! my Sin, My God, these Cursed Dregs,
  Green, Yellow, Blew streakt Poyson hellish, ranck,
Bubs hatcht in natures nest on Serpents Eggs,
  Yelp, Cherp and Cry; they set my Soule a Cramp.
  I frown, Chide, strik and fight them, mourn and Cry   *5*
  To Conquour them, but cannot them destroy.

I cannot kill nor Coop them up: my Curb
  'S less than a Snaffle in their mouth: my Rains
They as a twine thrid, snap: by hell they're spurd:
  And load my Soule with swagging loads of pains.   *10*
  Black Imps, young Divells, snap, bite, drag to bring
  And pick mee headlong hells dread Whirle Poole in.

Lord, hold thy hand: for handle mee thou may'st
  In Wrath: but, oh, a twinckling Ray of hope
Methinks I spie thou graciously display'st.   *15*
  There is an Advocate: a doore is ope.
  Sin's poyson swell my heart would till it burst,
  Did not a hope hence creep in't thus, and nurse't.

Joy, joy, Gods Son's the Sinners Advocate
  Doth plead the Sinner guiltless, and a Saint.   *20*
But yet Atturnies pleas spring from the State
  The Case is in: if bad its bad in plaint.
  My Papers do contain no pleas that do
  Secure mee from, but knock me down to, woe.

I have no plea mine Advocate to give: *25*
  What now? He'l anvill Arguments greate Store
Out of his Flesh and Blood to make thee live.
  O Deare bought Arguments: Good pleas therefore.
  Nails made of heavenly Steel, more Choice than gold
  Drove home, Well Clencht, eternally will hold.   *30*

Oh! Dear bought Plea, Deare Lord, what buy't so deare?
  What with thy blood purchase thy plea for me?
Take Argument out of thy Grave t'appeare
  And plead my Case with, me from Guilt to free.
  These maule both Sins, and Divells, and amaze   *35*
  Both Saints, and Angells; Wreath their mouths with praise.

What shall I doe, my Lord? what do, that I
  May have thee plead my Case? I fee thee will
With Faith, Repentance, and obediently
  Thy Service gainst Satanick Sins fulfill.   *40*
  I'l fight thy fields while Live I do, although
  I should be hackt in pieces by thy foe.

Make me thy Friend, Lord, be my Surety: I
  Will be thy Client, be my Advocate:
My Sins make thine, thy Pleas make mine hereby.   *45*
  Thou wilt mee save, I will thee Celebrate.
  Thou'lt kill my Sins that cut my heart within:
  And my rough Feet shall thy smooth praises sing.

TEXT NOTES:
Line 1: *Dregs,* sediment; feces, excrement; corrupt or defiling matter.
Line 3: *Bubs,* pustules.
Line 7: *Curb,* strap under lower jaw of horse.

Line 8: *Snaffle,* simple bridle-bit.
Line 9: *Thrid,* thread.
Line 10: *Swagging,* pendulous with weight.
Line 36: *Wreath their mouths,* open their mouths in the form of a circle to sing.
Line 48: *Feet,* verse; chorus of song.

40. MEDITATION. 1 JOH. 2.2. HE IS A PROPITIATION FOR OUR SIN.

12m [Feb.] 1690/1.

Still I complain; I am complaining still.
  Oh! woe is me! Was ever Heart like mine?
A Sty of Filth, a Trough of Washing-Swill
  A Dunghill Pit, a Puddle of mere Slime.
  A Nest of Vipers, Hive of Hornets; Stings.   *5*
  A Bag of Poyson, Civit-Box of Sins.

Was ever Heart like mine? So bad? black? Vile?
  Is any Divell blacker? Or can Hell
Produce its match? It is the very Soile
  Where Satan reads his Charms, and sets his Spell.   *10*
  His Bowling Ally, where he sheeres his fleece
  At Nine Pins, Nine Holes, Morrice, Fox and Geese.

His Palace Garden where his courtiers walke.
  His Jewells Cabbinet. Here his Caball
Do sham it, and truss up their Privie talk   *15*
  In Fardells of Consults and bundles all.
  His shambles, and his Butchers stale's herein.
  It is the Fuddling Schoole of every sin.

Was ever Heart like mine? Pride, Passion, fell.
  Ath'ism, Blasphemy, pot, pipe it, dance   *20*
Play Barlybreaks, and at last Couple in Hell.
  At Cudgells, Kit-Cat, Cards and Dice here prance.
  At Noddy, Ruff-and-trumpt, Jing, Post-and-Pare,
  Put, One-and-thirty, and such other ware.

Grace shuffled is away: Patience oft sticks   *25*
  Too soon, or draws itselfe out, and's out Put.
Faith's over trumpt, and oft doth lose her tricks.
  Repentance's Chalkt up Noddy, and out shut.
  They Post, and Pare off Grace thus, and its shine.
  Alas! alas! was ever Heart like mine?   *30*

Sometimes methinks the serpents head I mall:
   Now all is still: my spirits do recreute.
But ere my Harpe can tune sweet praise, they fall
   On me afresh, and tare me at my Root.
   They bite like Badgers now nay worse, although   *35*
   I tooke them toothless sculls, rot long agoe.

My Reason now's more than my sense, I feele
   I have more Sight than Sense. Which seems to bee
A Rod of Sun beams t'whip mee for my steele.
   My Spirits spiritless, and dull in mee   *40*
   For my dead prayerless Prayers: the Spirits winde
   Scarce blows my mill about. I little grinde.

Was ever Heart like mine? My Lord, declare.
   I know not what to do: What shall I doe?
I wonder, split I don't upon Despare.   *45*
   Its grace's wonder that I wrack not so.
   I faintly shun't: although I see this Case
   Would say, my sin is greater than thy grace.

Hope's Day-peep dawns hence through this chinck. Christs name
   Propitiation is for sins. Lord, take   *50*
It so for mine. Thus quench thy burning flame
   In that clear stream that from his side forth brake.
   I can no Comfort take while thus I see
   Hells cursed Imps thus jetting strut in mee.

Lord take thy sword: these Anakims destroy: *55*
   Then soake my soule in Zions Bucking tub
With Holy Soap, and Nitre, and rich Lye.
   From all Defilement me cleanse, wash and rub.
   Then wrince, and wring mee out till th'water fall
   As pure as in the Well: not foule at all.   *60*

And let thy Sun, shine on my Head out cleare.
   And bathe my Heart within its radient beams:
Thy Christ make my Propitiation Deare.
   Thy Praise shall from my Heart breake forth in streams.
   This reeching Vertue of Christs blood will quench   *65*
   Thy Wrath, slay Sin and in thy Love mee bench.

TEXT NOTES:
Line 6: *Civet-Box,* perfume container.
Line 11: *Sheeres his fleece,* dupes unskilled players whom he easily defeats.
Line 12: *Morrice,* a game.

Line 14: *Caball,* coterie (specifically, reference to certain ministers of Charles II).
Line 16: *Fardells,* bundles, packs.
Line 16: *Consults,* advisors.
Line 17: *Shamble,* meat counter.
Line 17: *Butchers stale's,* butcher's stall is.
Line 18: *Fuddling,* drinking, boozing.
Line 19: *Fell,* bitterness, animosity.
Line 20: *Pot,* pout? drink? mock?
Line 21: *Barlybreaks,* party game for three couples.
Line 22: *Kit-Cat,* boys' ball game.
Lines 23–24: *Noddy . . . One-and-thirty,* card games.
Line 29: *Shine,* lustre, worth.
Line 32: *Recreute,* reinvigorate.
Line 36: *Took them toothless sculls,* took them for toothless skulls.
Line 39: *Steele,* coldness, hardness.
Line 45: *Split,* suffer shipwreck.
Line 49: *Day-peep,* earliest dawn.
Line 54: *Strut,* contention.
Line 55: *Anakims,* giants in the Land of Canaan; see Joshua 11:21.
Line 56: *Bucking tub,* boiling tub for cloth.
Line 59: *Wrince,* rinse.
Line 65: *Reeching* (reeking), emanating.

41. MEDITATION. JOH. 14.2. I GO TO
PREPARE A PLACE FOR YOU.

24.3m [May] 1691.

A Clew of Wonders! Clusterd Miracles!
    Angells, come whet your sight hereon. Here's ground.
Sharpen your Phansies here, ye Saints in Spiricles.
    Here is enough in Wonderment to drownd's.
    Make here the Shining dark or White on which   *5*
    Let all your Wondring Contemplations pitch.

The Magnet of all Admiration's here.
    Your tumbling thoughts turn here. Here is Gods Son,
Wove in a Web of Flesh, and Bloode rich geere.
    Eternall Wisdoms Huswifry well spun.   *10*
    Which through the Laws pure Fulling mills did pass.
    And so went home the Wealthy's Web that was.

And why thus shew? Hark, harke, my Soule. He came
    To pay thy Debt. And being come most Just

The Creditor did sue him for the same,   *15*
    Did winn the Case, and in the grave him thrust.
Who having in this Prison paid the Debt.
    And took a Quittance, made Death's Velvet fret.

He broke her Cramping tallons did unlute
    The sealed Grave, and gloriously up rose.   *20*
Ascendeth up to glory on this Sute,
    Prepares a place for thee where glorie glowes.
    Yea yea for thee, although thy griefe out gush
    At such black Sins at which the Sun may blush.

What Wonder's here? Big belli'd Wonders in't   *25*
    Remain, though wrought for Saints as white as milk.
But done for me whose blot's as black as inke.
    A Clew of Wonders finer far than Silke.
    Thy hand alone that wound this Clew I finde
    Can to display these Wonders it unwinde.   *30*

Why didst thou thus? Reason stands gasterd here.
    She's overflown: this Soares above her Sight.
Gods onely Son for Sinners thus appeare,
    Prepare for Durt a throne in glory bright!
    Stand in the Doore of Glory to imbrace   *35*
    Such dirty bits of Dirt, with such a grace!

Reason, lie prison'd in this golden Chain.
    Chain up thy tongue, and silent stand a while.
Let this rich Love thy Love and heart obtain
    To tend thy Lord in all admiring Style.   *40*
    Lord screw my faculties up to the Skill
    And height of praise as answers thy good Will.

Then while I eye the Place thou hast prepar'de
    For such as I, I'le sing thy glory out
Untill thou welcome me, as 'tis declar'de   *45*
    In this sweet glory runing rounde about.
    I would do more but can't, Lord help me so
    That I may pay in glory what I owe.

TEXT NOTES:
Line 1: *Clew,* ball of thread or clustered things.
Line 3: *Spiricles,* minute coiled threads in the coating of certain seeds.
Line 4: *Drownd's,* drown us, sink or overwhelm us.
Line 9: *Web,* cloth.
Line 9: *Geere,* matter.

Line 18: *Quittance,* release.
Line 18: *Velvet,* position of ease or advantage.
Line 18: *Fret,* erode.
Line 19: *Unlute,* uncement, break open.
Line 21: *Sute,* suit; i.e. Christ's suit on our behalf.
Line 31: *Gasterd,* terrified; destroyed.

42. MEDITATION. REV. 3.22. I WILL GIVE HIM
TO SIT WITH ME IN MY THRONE.

2.6m [Aug.] 1691.

    Apples of gold, in silver pictures shrin'de
       Enchant the appetite, make mouths to water.
    And Loveliness in Lumps, tunn'd, and enrin'de
       In Jasper Cask, when tapt, doth briskly vaper:
       Brings forth a birth of Keyes t'unlock Loves Chest,   *5*
       That Love, like Birds, may fly to't from its nest.

    Such is my Lord, and more. But what strang thing
       Am I become? Sin rusts my Lock all o're.
    Though he ten thousand Keyes all on a string
       Takes out, scarce one, is found, unlocks the Doore.   *10*
       Which ope, my Love crincht in a Corner lies
       Like some shrunck Crickling: and scarce can rise.

    Lord ope the Doore: rub off my Rust, Remove
       My sin, And Oyle my Lock. (Dust there doth shelfe).
    My Wards will trig before thy Key: my Love   *15*
       Then, as enliven'd, leape will on thyselve.
       It needs must be, that giving handes receive
       Again Receivers Hearts furld in Love Wreath.

    Unkey my Heart; unlock thy Wardrobe: bring
       Out royall Robes: adorne my Soule, Lord: so,   *20*
    My Love in rich attire shall on my King
       Attend, and honour on him well bestow.
       In Glory he prepares for his a place
       Whom he doth all beglory here with grace.

    He takes them to the shining threashould cleare   *25*
       Of his bright Palace, cloath'd in Grace's flame.
    Then takes them in thereto, not onely there
       To have a Prospect, but possess the same.

The Crown of Life, the Throne of Glorys Place,
   The Fathers House blancht o're with orient Grace.   *30*

Can'an in golden print enwalld with jems:
   A Kingdome rim'd with Glory round: in fine
A glorious Crown pal'de thick with all the stems
   Of Grace, and of all Properties Divine.
   How happy wilt thou make mee when these shall   *35*
   As a bless't Heritage unto mee fall?

Adorn me, Lord, with Holy Huswifry.
   All blanch my Robes with Clusters of thy Graces:
Thus lead me to thy threashold: give mine Eye
   A Peephole there to see bright glories Chases.   *40*
   Then take mee in: I'le pay, when I possess,
   Thy Throne, to thee the Rent in Happiness.

TEXT NOTES:
Line 3: *Tunn'd,* stored.
Line 3: *Enrin'de,* preserved.
Line 11: *Crincht,* cringed.
Line 12: *Crickling,* dried apple (Glossary, Stanford, ed., *Poems of E.T.*).
Line 15: *Wards,* ridges on inside plate of lock.
Line 15: *Trig,* spring.
Line 30: *Blancht o're,* made white.
Line 30: *Orient,* precious.
Line 33: *Pal'de,* fenced.
Line 40: *Chases,* setting, enclosure.

43. MEDITATION. REV. 2.10.

A CROWN OF LIFE.

8.9m [Nov.] 1691.

Fain I would sing thy Praise, but feare I feign.
   My Sin doth keepe out of my heart thy Feare,
Damps Love: defiles my Soule. Old Blots new stain.
   Hopes hoppled lie, and rusty Chains worn cleare.
   My Sins that make me stand in need of thee,   *5*
   Do keep me back to hugge all Sin I see.

Nature's Corrupt, a nest of Passion, Pride,
   Lust, Worldliness, and such like bubs: I pray,

But struggling finde, these bow my Heart aside.
  A Knot of Imps at barly breaks in't play.   *10*
  They do inchant me from my Lord, I finde,
  The thoughts whereof proove Daggers in my minde.

Pardon, and Poyson them, Lord, with thy Blood.
  Cast their Curst Karkasses out of my Heart.
My Heart fill with thy Love: let Grace it dub.   *15*
  Make this my Silver Studs by thy rich art.
  My Soule shall then be thy sweet Paradise.
  Thou'st be its Rose, and it thy Bed of Spice.

Why mayn't my Faith now drinke thy Health, Lord, ore,
  The Head of all my Sins? And Cast her Eye,   *20*
In glorifying glances, on the Doore
  Of thy Free Grace, where Crowns of Life do lie?
  Thou'lt give a Crown of Life to such as bee
  Faithfull to Death. And shall Faith faile in mee?

A Crown of Life, of Glory, Righteousness,   *25*
  Thou wilt adorn them with, that will not fade.
Shall Faith in mee shrinke up for Feebleness?
  Nor take my Sins by th'Crown, till Crownless made?
  Breath, Lord, thy Spirit on my Faith, that I
  May have thy Crown of Life, and Sin may dy.   *30*

How Spirituall? Holy shall I shine, when I
  Thy Crown of Righteousness ware on my Head?
How Glorious when thou dost me glorify
  To ware thy Crown of Glory pollished?
  How shall I when thy Crown of Life I ware   *35*
  In lively Colours flowrish, fresh, and fair?

When thou shalt Crown me with these Crowns I'l bend
  My Shallow Crown to crown with Songs thy Name.
Angels shall set the tune, I'le it attend:
  Thy Glory'st be the burden of the same.   *40*
  Till then I cannot sing, my tongue is tide.
  Accept this Lisp till I am glorifide.

TEXT NOTES:
Line 4: *Hoppled,* hobbled.
Line 8: *Bubs,* storms; pustules; bubbles.
Line 10: *Barly breaks,* a party game.
Line 15: *Dub,* invest with honor; adorn.

44. MEDITATION. 2 TIM. 4.8.

A CROWN OF RIGHTEOUSNESS.

17.11m [Jan.] 1691.

A Crown, Lord, yea, a Crown of Righteousness.
  Oh! what a Gift is this? Give Lord I pray
An Holy Head, and Heart it to possess
  And I shall give thee glory for the pay.
    A Crown is brave, and Righteousness much more.   *5*
    The glory of them both will pay the score.

A Crown indeed consisting of fine gold
  Adherent, and Inherent Righteousness,
Stuck with their Ripe Ripe Fruits in every fold
  Like studded Carbuncles they do it dress.   *10*
    A Righteous Life doth ever ware renown
    And thrusts the Head at last up in this Crown.

A Milk whit hand sets't on a Righteous Head.
  An hand Unrighteous can't dispose it nay
It's not in such an hande. Such hands would bed   *15*
  Black Smuts on't should they fingers on it lay.
    Who can the Crown of Righteousness suppose
    In an Unrighteous hand for to dispose.

When once upon the head its ever green
  And altogether Usde in Righteousness,   *20*
Where blessed bliss, and blissfull Peace is seen,
  And where no jar, nor brawler hath access.
    Oh! blessed Crown what hold the breadth of all
    The State of Happiness in Heavens Hall.

A Crown of Righteousness, a Righteous Head,   *25*
  Oh naughty man! my brain pan turrit is
Where Swallows build, and hatch: Sins black and red.
  My head and heart do ach, and frob at this.
    Lord were my Turret cleansd, and made by thee
    Thy Graces Dovehouse turret much might bee.   *30*

Oh! make it so: then Righteousness pure, true
  Shall Roost upon my boughs, and in my heart
And all its fruits that in Obedience grew
  To stud this Crown like jems in every part.
    Ist then be garnisht for this Crown, and thou   *35*
    Shalt have my Songs to diadem thy brow.

Oh! Happy me, if thou wilt Crown me thus.
   Oh! naughty heart! What swell with Sin? fy, fy.
Oh! Gracious Lord, me pardon: do not Crush
   Me all to mammocks: Crown and not destroy.   *40*
   Ile tune thy Prayses while this Crown doth come.
   Thy Glory bring I tuckt up in my Songe.

TEXT NOTES:

Line 8: *Adherent Righteousness,* righteousness of Christ that is imputed to the be-
liever in justification. Taylor elsewhere describes this "imputed righteous-
ness" as "the righteousness of Christ's active and passive obedience made ours
by God's imputation" (Grabo, ed., *Taylor's Treatise Concerning the Lord's
Supper,* 29; for "active and passive obedience" see note on Meditation
II.160).

Line 8: *Inherent Righteousness,* also termed "implanted righteousness," right-
eousness of the believer through "the sanctifying graces of the Spirit com-
municated to the soul" (Grabo, ed., *Taylor's Treatise Concerning the Lord's
Supper,* 29).

Line 16: *Smuts,* smudges of sooty matter.

Line 22: *Jar,* discord.

Line 26: *Brain pan,* skull.

Line 28: *Frob,* throb.

Line 35: *Ist,* I would.

Line 40: *Mammocks,* broken pieces.

45. MEDITATION. 1 PET. 5.4. YE SHALL

RECEIVE A CROWN OF GLORY.

24.2m [Apr.] 1692.

A Crown of Glory! Oh! I'm base, its true.
   My Heart's a Swamp, Brake, Thicket vile of Sin.
My Head's a Bog of Filth; Blood bain'd doth spew
   Its venom streaks of Poyson o're my Skin.
   My Members Dung-Carts that bedung at pleasure,   *5*
   My Life, the Pasture where Hells Hurdloms leasure.

Becrown'd with Filth! Oh! what vile thing am I?
   What Cost, and Charge to make mee Meddow ground
To drain my Bogs? to lay my Frog-pits dry?
   To stub up all my brush that doth abound?   *10*
   That I may be thy Pasture fat and frim,
   Where thy choice Flowers, and Hearbs of Grace shine trim?

Vast charge thus to subdue me: Wonders play
  Hereat like Gamesters; 'bellisht Thoughts dresst fine,
In brave attire, cannot a finger lay   *15*
    Upon it that doth not besmut the Shine.
    Yet all this cost and more thou'rt at with me.
    And still I'm sad, a Seing Eye may see.

Yet more than this: my Hands that Crown'd thy Head
  With sharpest thorns, thou washest in thy Grace.   *20*
My Feet that did upon thy Choice Blood tread
    Thou makest beautifull thy Way to trace.
    My Head that knockt against thy head, thou hugg'st
    Within thy bosom: boxest not, nor lugg'st.

Nay more as yet: thou borrow'st of each Grace
  That stud the Hearts of Saints, and Angells bright   *25*
Its brightest beams, the beams too of the place
    Where Glory dwells: and all the Beames of Light
    Thy, and thy Fathers Glorious Face out spread,
    To make this Crown of Glory for my head.   *30*

If it was possible the thoughts that are
  Imbellisht with the riches of this tender
Could torment such as do this bright Crown Ware,
    Their Love to thee Lord's lac'de so streight, and slender.
    These beams would draw up Griefe to cloude this Glory,   *35*
    But not so then; though now Grace acts this Story.

My Pen enravisht with these Rayes out strains
  A sorry Verse: and when my gold dwells in
A Purse guilt with the glory bright that flames
    Out from this Crown, I'le tune an higher pin.   *40*
    Then make me Lord heir of this Crown. Ile sing
    And make thy Praise on my Heroicks ring.

TEXT NOTES:
Line 2: *Brake,* clump of bushes, thicket.
Line 3: *Bain'd,* burst.
Line 6: *Hurdloms,* whoredoms?
Line 10: *Stub up,* dig up by the roots.
Line 11: *Frim,* flourishing.
Line 24: *boxest,* cuffs.
Line 24: *lugg'st,* pulls, tugs.
Line 42: *Heroicks,* verses.

46. MEDITATION. REV. 3.5. THE SAME SHALL
BE CLOATHED IN WHITE RAIMENT.

17.5m [July] 1692.

Nay, may I, Lord, believe it? Shall my Skeg
  Be ray'd in thy White Robes? My thatcht old Cribb
(Immortal Purss hung on a mortall Peg,)
    Wilt thou with fair'st array in heaven rig?
    I'm but a jumble of gross Elements   *5*
    A Snaile Horn where an Evill Spirit tents.

A Dirt ball dresst in milk white Lawn, and deckt
  In Tissue tagd with gold, or Ermins flush,
That mocks the Starrs, and sets them in a fret
    To se themselves out shone thus. Oh they blush.   *10*
    Wonders stand gastard here. But yet my Lord,
    This is but faint to what thou dost afford.

I'm but a Ball of dirt. Wilt thou adorn
  Mee with thy Web wove in thy Loom Divine
The Whitest Web in Glory, that the morn   *15*
    Nay, that all Angell glory, doth ore shine?
    They ware no such. This whitest Lawn most fine
    Is onely worn, my Lord, by thee and thine.

This Saye's no flurr of Wit, nor new Coin'd Shape
  Of frollick Fancie in a Rampant Brain.   *20*
It's juyce Divine bled from the Choicest Grape
    That ever Zions Vinyarde did mentain.
    Such Mortall bits immortalliz'de shall ware
    More glorious robes, than glorious Angells bare.

Their Web is wealthy, wove of Wealthy Silke   *25*
  Well wrought indeed, its all brancht Taffity.
But this thy Web more white by far than milke
    Spun on thy Wheele twine of thy Deity
    Wove in thy Web, Fulld in thy mill by hand
    Makes them in all their bravery seem tand.   *30*

This Web is wrought by best, and noblest Art
  That heaven doth afford of twine most choice
All brancht, and richly flowerd in every part
    With all the sparkling flowers of Paradise
    To be thy Ware alone, who hast no peere   *35*
    And Robes for glorious Saints to thee most deare.

Wilt thou, my Lord, dress my poore wither'd Stump
  In this rich web whose whiteness doth excell
The Snow, though 'tis most black? And shall my Lump
  Of Clay ware more than e're on Angells fell?   *40*
  What shall my bit of Dirt be deckt so fine
  That shall Angelick glory all out shine?

Shall things run thus? Then Lord, my tumberill
  Unload of all its Dung, and make it cleane.
And load it with thy wealthi'st Grace untill
  Its Wheeles do crack, or Axletree complain.   *45*
  I fain would have it cart thy harvest in,
  Before its loosed from its Axlepin.

Then screw my Strings up to thy tune that I
  May load thy Glory with my Songs of praise.   *50*
Make me thy Shalm, thy praise my Songs, whereby
  My mean Shoshannim may thy Michtams raise.
  And when my Clay ball's in thy White robes dresst
  My tune perfume thy praise shall with the best.

TEXT NOTES:
Line 1: *Skeg,* nail.
Line 2: *Ray'd* (arrayed), hung.
Line 2: *Cribb,* cabin.
Line 6: *Snaile Horn,* snail shell.
Line 7: *Lawn,* fine linen.
Line 8: *Tissue,* rich cloth.
Line 8: *Tagd,* fringed.
Line 8: *Ermins flush,* white fur.
Line 9: *In a fret,* in an anxious state.
Line 11: *Gastard,* astonished.
Line 14: *Web,* woven fabric.
Line 19: *Saye,* fine-textured cloth.
Line 19: *Flurr,* flurry; flourish.
Line 19: *Wit,* fashion.
Line 26: *Brancht,* embroidered.
Line 30: *Bravery,* finery.
Line 30: *Tand,* brown, like leather.
Line 40: *Angells fell,* angel hair.
Line 43: *Tumberill,* dung-cart.
Line 51: *Shalm* (shawm), oboe-like instrument.
Line 52: *Mean,* poor.
Line 52: *Shoshannim,* stringed instrument mentioned in Psalms 45 and 69.
Line 52: *Michtams,* psalm tunes; see Psalms 57, 58, 59.

47. MEDITATION ON MATT. 25.21. ENTER THOU
INTO THE JOY OF THY LORD.

9.8m [Oct.] 1692.

Strang, strang indeed. It rowell doth my heart
    With pegs of Greefe, and tents of greatest joy:
When I wore Angells Glory in each part
    And all my skirts wore flashes of rich die
    Of Heavenly Colour, hedg'd in with rosie Reechs,   *5*
    A spider spit its Vomit on my Cheeks.

Thisranckling juyce bindg'd in its cursed stain
    Doth permeat both Soul and Body: soile
And drench each Fibre, and infect each grain.
    Its ugliness swells over all the ile.   *10*
    Whose stain'd mishapen bulk's too high, and broad
    For th'Entry of the narrow gate to God.

Ready to burst, thus, and to burn in hell:
    Now in my path I finde a Waybred spring
Whose leafe drops balm that doth this venom quell   *15*
    And juyce's a Bath, that doth all stains out bring
    And sparkling beauty in the room convay.
    Lord feed me with this Waybred Leafe, I pray.

My stain will out: and swelling swage apace.
    And holy Lusters on my shape appeare.   *20*
All Rosie Buds: and Lilly flowers of grace
    Will grace my turfe with sweet sweet glory here.
    Under whose shades Angells will bathing play
    Who'l guard my Pearle to glory, hous'd in clay.

Those Gates of Pearle, porter'd with Seraphims,   *25*
    On their carbuncle joynts will open wide.
And entrance give me where all glory swims
    In to the Masters Joy, e're to abide.
    O sweet sweet thought. Lord take this praise though thin.
    And when I'm in't Ile tune an higher pin.   *30*

TEXT NOTES:
Line 1: *Rowell,* spur.
Line 2: *Pegs,* pins, spikes.
Line 2: *Tents,* probes.
Line 5: *Reechs* (reeks), haziness.

Line 7: *Bindg'd,* soaked.
Line 10: *Ile,* guts.
Line 14: *Waybred,* plant by the wayside.
Line 14: *Spring,* spring up.
Line 17: *In the room,* in its place.
Line 19: *Swage,* reduce.
Line 22: *Turfe,* shadows; earthly life.
Line 25: *Porter'd,* verb formed from "porter," gate-keeper.
Line 30: *Tune an higher pin,* sing at a higher pitch.

48. MEDITATION ON MATT. 25.21.
ENTER INTO THE JOY OF THY LORD.

10m? [Dec.] 1692.

When I, Lord, eye thy Joy, and my Love, small,
  My heart gives in: what now? Strange! Sure I love thee!
And finding brambles 'bout my heart to crawl
  My heart misgives mee. Prize I ought above thee?
  Such great Love hugging them, such small Love, thee!   *5*
  Whether thou hast my Love, I scarce can see.

My reason rises up, and chides my Cup
  Bright Loveliness itselfe. What not love thee!
Tumbling thy Joy, Lord, ore, it rounds me up.
  Shall loves nest be a thorn bush: not thee bee?   *10*
  Set Hovells up of thorn kids in my heart!
  Avant adultrous Love. From me depart.

The Influences my vile heart sucks in
  Of Puddle Water boyld by Sunn beams till
Its Spiritless, and dead, nothing more thin   *15*
  Tasts wealthier than those thou dost distill.
  This seems to numb my heart to think that I
  Should null all good to optimate a toy.

Yet when the beamings, Lord, of thy rich Joys,
  Do guild my Soule, meethinks I'm sure I Love thee.   *20*
They Calcine all these brambly trumperys
  And now I'm sure that I prize naught above thee.
  Thy beams making a bonefire of my Stack
  Of Faggots, bring my Love to thee in'ts pack.

For when the Objects of thy Joy impress   *25*
  Their shining influences on my heart

My Soule seems an Alembick doth possess
   Love stilld into rich Spirits by thy Art.
And all my pipes, were they ten thousand would
   Drop Spirits of Love on thee, more rich than gold.   *30*

Now when the world with all her dimples in't
   Smiles on me, I do love thee more than all:
And when her glory freshens, all in print,
   I prize thee still above it all. And shall.
   Nay all her best to thee, do what she can,   *35*
   Drops but like drops dropt in a Closestoole pan.

The Castings of thy Joy, my Lord therefore
   Let in the Cabbin of my Joy rise high,
And let thy Joy enter in mee before
   I enter do into my masters joy.   *40*
   Thy joyes in mee will make my Pipes to play
   For joy thy Praise while teather'd to my clay.

TEXT NOTES:

Line 7: *My Cup,* Communion chalice, probably before Taylor in meditation.
Line 9: *Tumbling,* pouring.
Line 9: *Rounds,* gathers.
Line 11: *Hovells,* harvested stacks, as of corn.
Line 11: *Kids,* seed pods.
Line 18: *Optimate,* make noble.
Line 18: *Toy,* amorous sport; idle fancy; a trifle.
Line 21: *Calcine,* burn to ashes.
Line 21: *Trumperys,* deceit, trickery; weeds that hinder growth of valuable plants.
Line 27: *Alembick,* still, apparatus for distilling.
Line 33: *In print,* to a nicety.
Line 36: *Closestoole pan,* closet-stool pan, chamber pot?
Line 37: *Castings,* formation, raising.
Line 41: *Pipes to play,* voice to sing.

49. MEDITATION. MATT. 25.21.

THE JOY OF THY LORD.

26.12m [Feb.] 1692.

Lord, do away my Motes: and Mountains great.
   My nut is vitiate. Its kirnell rots:
Come, kill the Worm, that doth its kirnell eate
   And strike thy sparkes within my tinderbox.

Drill through my metall-heart an hole wherein   *5*
  With graces Cotters to thyselfe it pin.

A Lock of Steel upon my Soule, whose key
  The serpent keeps, I fear, doth lock my doore.
O pick't: and through the key-hole make thy way
  And enter in: and let thy joyes run o're.   *10*
    My Wards are rusty. Oyle them till they trig
    Before thy golden key: thy Oyle makes glib.

Take out the Splinters of the World that stick
  Do in my heart: Friends, Honours, Riches, and
The Shivers in't of Hell whose venoms quick   *15*
    And firy make it swoln and ranckling stand.
    These wound and kill: those shackle strongly to
    Poore knobs of Clay, my heart. Hence sorrows grow.

Cleanse, and enlarge my kask: It is too small:
  And tartarizd with worldly dregs dri'de in't.   *20*
It's bad mouth'd too: and though thy joyes do Call
    That boundless are, it ever doth them stint.
    Make me thy Chrystall Caske: those wines in't tun
    That in the Rivers of thy joyes do run.

Lord make me, though suckt through a straw or Quill,   *25*
    Tast of the Rivers of thy joyes, some drop.
'Twill sweeten me: and all my Love distill
    Into thy glass, and me for joy make hop.
    'Twill turn my water into wine: and fill
    My Harp with Songs my Masters joyes distill.   *30*

TEXT NOTES:
Line 1: *Motes,* mounds, embankments.
Line 6: *Cotters,* pins for fastening.
Line 11: *Wards,* inner works of lock.
Line 11: *Trig,* spring.
Line 12: *Glib,* slippery, easy to move.
Line 15: *Shivers,* splinters, chips.
Line 16: *Ranckling,* festering.
Line 20: *Tartarized,* deposited; consigned to hell.
Line 20: *Dri'de,* dried.
Line 22: *Stint,* cut short, cease flowing.
Line 23: *Tun,* store.

EDWARD TAYLOR:
FROM *PREPARATORY MEDITATIONS.*
SECOND SERIES

Of the 167 meditative poems Taylor wrote between 1693 and 1725, 19 are represented in this section. Readers will note the stability over time of both form and imagery. Taylor explored specific themes, however, in certain blocks of meditations, for example typology (II:1–30); the person of Christ (II:42–56); the meaning of the sacrament (II:102–111); and the book of Canticles or Song of Solomon (II:115–153) (see Introduction, pp. 55–56). In some cases the dated poems can be matched with extant sermons, making possible comparison of Puritan spirituality and homiletics. The poems express Taylor's overwhelming love for Christ, his passionate longing for union with Christ, and his desire to serve and praise Christ forever.

1. MEDITATION. COL. 2.17. WHICH ARE SHADDOWS
OF THINGS TO COME AND THE BODY IS CHRISTS.

[16] 93.

Oh Leaden heeld. Lord, give, forgive I pray.
   Infire my Heart: it bedded is in Snow.
I Chide myselfe seing myselfe decay.
   In heate and Zeale to thee, I frozen grow.
   File my dull Spirits: make them sharp and bright: *5*
   Them firbush for thyselfe, and thy delight.

My Stains are such, and sinke so deep, that all
   The Excellency in Created Shells

Too low, and little is to make it fall
   Out of my leather Coate wherein it dwells.   *10*
   This Excellence is but a Shade to that
   Which is enough to make my Stains go back.

The glory of the world slickt up in types
   In all Choise things chosen to typify,
His glory upon whom the worke doth light,   *15*
   To thine's a Shaddow, or a butterfly.
   How glorious then, my Lord, art thou to mee
   Seing to cleanse me, 's worke alone for thee.

The glory of all Types doth meet in thee.
   Thy glory doth their glory quite excell: *20*
More than the Sun excells in its bright glee
   A nat, an Earewig, Weevill, Snaile, or Shell.
   Wonders in Crowds start up; your eyes may strut
   Viewing his Excellence, and's bleeding cut.

Oh! that I had but halfe an eye to view   *25*
   This excellence of thine, undazled: so
Therewith to give my heart a touch anew
   Untill I quickned am, and made to glow.
   All is too little for thee: but alass
   Most of my little all hath other pass.   *30*

Then Pardon, Lord, my fault: and let thy beams
   Of Holiness pierce through this Heart of mine.
Ope to thy Blood a passage through my veans.
   Let thy pure blood my impure blood refine.
   Then with new blood and spirits I will dub   *35*
   My tunes upon thy Excellency good.

TEXT NOTES:
Line 1: *Heeld,* heeled, i.e. slow, weighed down.
Line 6: *Firbush* (furbish), remove rust by polishing.
Line 8: *Shells,* external things.
Lines 9–10: *Fall Out of,* be removed from.
Line 10: *Leather Coate,* skin.
Line 13: *Slickt up,* polished, made elegant; made plausible.
Line 13: *Type,* symbol, figure, emblem; specifically, Old Testament persons, events, objects that prefigure God's revelation in Jesus Christ and the Church.
Line 23: *Strut,* bulge.
Line 30: *Pass,* passage.
Line 35: *Dub,* drum; adorn.

7. MEDITATION. PS. 105.17. HE SENT A MAN

BEFORE THEM, EVEN JOSEPH,

WHO WAS SOLD ETC.

5.6m [Aug.] 1694.

All Dull, my Lord, my Spirits flat, and dead
   All water sockt and sapless to the skin.
Oh! Screw mee up and make my Spirits bed
   Thy quickening vertue For my inke is dim,
   My pensill blunt. Doth Joseph type out thee?   *5*
   Haraulds of Angells sing out, Bow the Knee.

Is Josephs glorious shine a Type of thee?
   How bright art thou? He Envi'de was as well.
And so was thou. He's stript, and pick't, poore hee,
   Into the pit. And so was thou. They shell   *10*
   Thee of thy Kirnell. He by Judah's sold
   For twenty Bits, thirty for thee he'd told.

Joseph was tempted by his Mistress vile.
   Thou by the Divell, but both shame the foe.
Joseph was cast into the jayle awhile.   *15*
   And so was thou. Sweet apples mellow so.
   Joseph did from his jayle to glory run.
   Thou from Death's pallot rose like morning sun.

Joseph layes in against the Famine, and
   Thou dost prepare the Bread of Life for thine.   *20*
He bought with Corn for Pharaoh th'men and Land.
   Thou with thy Bread mak'st such themselves Consign
   Over to thee, that eate it. Joseph makes
   His brethren bow before him. Thine too quake.

Joseph constrains his Brethren till their sins   *25*
   Do gall their Souls. Repentance babbles fresh.
Thou treatest sinners till Repentance springs
   Then with him sendst a Benjamin like messe.
   Joseph doth Cheare his humble brethren. Thou
   Dost stud with Joy the mourning Saints that bow.   *30*

Josephs bright shine th'Eleven Tribes must preach.
   And thine Apostles now Eleven, thine.
They beare his presents to his Friends: thine reach
   Thine unto thine, thus now behold a shine.

How hast thou pensild out, my Lord, most bright   *35*
Thy glorious Image here, on Josephs Light.

This I bewaile in me under this shine
    To see so dull a Colour in my Skin.
Lord, lay thy brightsome Colours on me thine.
    Scoure thou my pipes then play thy tunes therein.   *40*
    I will not hang my Harp in Willows by.
    While thy sweet praise, my Tunes doth glorify.

TEXT NOTES:
Line 2: *Sockt,* soaked.
Line 2: *Sapless,* barren.
Line 3: *Screw,* press; stretch; raise.
Line 3: *Bed,* embed.
Line 4: *Quickening,* life-giving.
Line 7: *Shine,* attributes; virtues; fame.
Line 7: *Type,* foreshadowing.
Line 9: *Pick't,* plundered.
Line 12: *Told* (tolled), collected.
Line 18: *Pallot* (pallet), bed.
Line 28: *Benjamin like messe,* feast Joseph provided when reunited with his broth-
    ers, the portion for Benjamin being the largest; Genesis 43:34.
Line 36: *Light,* bright example.
Line 40: *Scoure,* polish.

12. MEDITATION. EZEK. 37.24. DAVID MY SERVANT
SHALL BE THEIR KING.

7.5m [July] 1695.

Dull, Dull indeed! What shall it e're be thus?
    And why? Are not thy Promises, my Lord,
Rich, Quick'ning things? How should my full Cheeks blush
    To finde mee thus? And those a lifeless Word?
    My Heart is heedless: unconcernd hereat: *5*
    I finde my Spirits Spiritless, and flat.

Thou Courtst mine Eyes in Sparkling Colours bright,
    Most bright indeed, and soul enamoring,
With the most Shining Sun, whose beames did smite
    Me with delightfull Smiles to make mee spring.   *10*
    Embellisht knots of Love assault my minde
    Which still is Dull, as if this Sun ne're shin'de.

David in all his gallantry now comes,
 Bringing to tende thy Shrine, his Royall Glory,
Rich Prowess, Prudence, Victories, Sweet Songs,   *15*
 And Piety to Pensill out thy Story;
  To draw my Heart to thee in this brave shine
  Of typick Beams, most warm. But still I pine.

Shall not this Lovely Beauty, Lord, set out
 In Dazzling Shining Flashes 'fore mine Eye,   *20*
Enchant my heart, Love's golden mine, till't spout
 Out Streames of Love refin'd that on thee lie?
  Thy Glory's great: Thou Davids Kingdom shalt
  Enjoy for aye. I want and thats my fault.

Spare me, my Lord, spare me, I greatly pray,   *25*
 Let me thy Gold pass through thy Fire untill
Thy Fire refine, and take my filth away.
 That I may shine like Gold, and have my fill
  Of Love for thee; untill my Virginall
  Chime out in Changes sweet thy Praises shall.   *30*

Wipe off my Rust, Lord, with thy wisp me scoure,
 And make thy Beams pearch on my Strings their blaze.
My tunes Cloath with thy Shine, and Quavers poure
 My Cursing Strings on, loaded with thy Praise.
  My Fervent Love with Musick in her hand,   *35*
  Shall then attend thyselfe, and thy Command.

TEXT NOTES:
Line 18: *Typick,* prefiguring, symbolic.
Line 29: *Virginall,* small spinet-like keyed instrument without legs.
Line 30: *Chime out in Changes,* go through the variations in ringing a peal of bells.
Line 31: *Wisp,* bundle of straw for cleaning.
Line 32: *Pearch,* place upon
Line 33: *Quavers,* musical notes; trills.

18. MEDITATION. HEB. 13.10.

WEE HAVE AN ALTAR.

Westfield 18.8m [Oct.] 1696.

A Bran, a Chaff, a very Barly yawn,
 An Husk, a Shell, a Nothing, nay yet Worse,
A Thistle, Bryer prickle, pricking Thorn

A Lump of Lewdeness, Pouch of Sin, a purse
Of Naughtiness, I am, yea what not Lord?   *5*
And wilt thou be mine Altar? and my bord?

Mine Heart's a Park or Chase of sins: Mine Head
  'S a Bowling Alley. Sins play Ninehole here.
Phansy's a Green: sin Barly breaks in't led.
    Judgment's a pingle. Blindeman's Buff's plaid there   *10*
    Sin playes at Coursey Parke within my Minde.
    My Wills a Walke in which it aires what's blinde.

Sure then I lack Atonement. Lord me help.
    Thy Shittim Wood ore laid With Wealthy brass
Was an Atoning altar, and sweet smelt: *15*
    But if ore laid with pure pure gold it was
    It was an Incense Altar, all perfum'd
    With Odours, wherein Lord thou thus was bloom'd.

Did this ere during Wood when thus orespread
    With these erelasting Metalls altarwise   *20*
Type thy Eternall Plank of Godhead, Wed
    Unto our Mortall Chip, its sacrifice?
    Thy Deity mine Altar. Manhood thine.
    Mine Offring on't for all men's Sins, and mine?

This Golden Altar puts such weight into   *25*
    The sacrifices offer'd on't, that it
Ore weighs the Weight of all the sins that flow
    In thine Elect. This Wedge, and beetle split
    The knotty Logs of Vengeance too to shivers:
    And from their Guilt and shame them cleare delivers.   *30*

This Holy Altar by its Heavenly fire
    Refines our Offerings: casts out their dross
And sanctifies their Gold by its rich 'tire
    And all their steams with Holy Odours boss.
    Pillars of Frankincense and rich Perfume   *35*
    They 'tone Gods nosthrills with, off from this Loom.

Good News, Good Sirs, more good than comes within
    The Canopy of Angells. Heavens Hall
Allows no better: this atones for sin,
    My Glorious God, Whose Grace here thickest falls.   *40*
    May I my Barly yawn, Bran, Bryer Claw,
    Lay on't a Sacrifice? or Chaff or Straw?

Shall I my sin Pouch lay, on thy Gold Bench
  My Offering, Lord, to thee? I've such alone
But have no better. For my sins do drench   *45*
  My very best unto their very bone.
  And shall mine Offering by thine Altars fire
  Refin'd, and sanctifi'd to God aspire?

Amen, ev'n so be it. I now will climb
  The stares up to thine Altar, and on't lay   *50*
Myselfe, and services, even for its shrine.
  My sacrifice brought thee accept I pray.
  My Morn, and Evning Offerings I'le bring
  And on this Golden Altar Incense fling.

Lord let thy Deity mine Altar bee   *55*
  And make thy Manhood, on't my sacrifice.
For mine Atonement: make them both for mee
  My Altar t'sanctify my gifts likewise
  That so myselfe and service on't may bring
  Its worth along with them to thee my king.   *60*

The thoughts whereof, do make my tunes as fume,
  From off this Altar rise to thee Most High
And all their steams stufft with thy Altars blooms,
  My Sacrifice of Praise in Melody.
  Let thy bright Angells catch my tune, and sing't   *65*
  That Equalls Davids Michtam which is in't.

TEXT NOTES:
Line 1: *Yawn* (awn), bristle.
Line 6: *Bord,* table.
Line 7: *Chase,* hunting-ground.
Line 9: *Barly breaks,* a game.
Line 14: *Shittim,* acacia.
Line 19: *During,* enduring.
Line 28: *Beetle,* mallot.
Line 29: *Shivers,* splinters.
Line 34: *Boss,* embellishment.
Line 36: *'Tone,* atone.
Line 41: *Bryer Claw,* thornbush.
Line 63: *Stufft,* full, complete.
Line 63: *Blooms,* beauty.
Line 66: *Michtam,* psalm tune.

33. MEDITATION. JOH. 15.13.
GREATER LOVE HATH NO MAN THAN THIS,
THAT A MAN LAY DOWN HIS LIFE
FOR HIS FRIEND.

1.8m [Oct.] 1699.

Walking, my Lord, within thy Paradise
 I finde a Fruite whose Beauty smites mine Eye
And Taste my Tooth that had no Core nor Vice.
  An Hony Sweet, that's never rotting, ly
  Under a Tree, which view'd, I knew to bee   5
  The Tree of Life whose Bulk's Theanthropie.

And looking up, I saw its boughs all bow
 With Clusters of this Fruit that it doth bring,
Nam'de Greatest LOVE. And well, For bulk, and brow,
  Thereof, of th'sap of Godhood-Manhood spring.   10
  What Love is here for kinde? What sort? How much?
  None ever, but the Tree of Life, bore such.

Who is the Object of this Love? and in
 Whose mouth doth fall the Apple of this tree?
Is't Man? A Sinner? Such a Wormhol'de thing?   15
  Oh! matchless Love, Laid out on such as Hee!
  Should Gold Wed Dung, should Stars Wooe Lobster Claws,
  It would no wonder, like this Wonder, cause.

Is sinfull Man the Object of this Love?
 What then doth it for this its Object doe,   20
That doth require a purging far above
  The whiteness, Sope and Nitre can bestow,
  (Else Justice will its Object take away
  Out of its bosome, and to hell't convay?)

Hence in it steps, to justice saith, I'll make   25
 Thee satisfaction, and my Object shine.
I'l slay my Humane Nature for thy sake
  Fild with the Worthiness of thy Divine
  Make pay therewith. The Fruite doth sacrifice
  The tree that bore't. This for its object dies.   30

An Higher round upon this golden scale
 Love cannot Climbe, than to lay down the Life
Of him that loves, for him belov'd to bale,
  Thereby to satisfy, and end all strife.

Thou lay'st, my Lord, thy Life down for thy Friend   *35*
And greater Love than this none can out send.

Then make me, Lord, thy Friend, I humbly pray
    Though I thereby should be deare bought by thee.
Not dearer yet than others, for the pay
    Is but the same for others as for mee.   *40*
    If I be in thy booke, my Life shall proove
    My Love to thee, an Offering to thy Love.

TEXT NOTES:
Line 3: *Core,* corruption (in ref. to apple supposed to have stuck in Adam's throat).
Line 6: *Bulk,* trunk.
Line 6: *Theanthropie,* union of divine and human natures in Christ.
Line 9: *Bulk, and brow,* possible readings: (a) torso and head; (b) cargo and profit
    (prow); (c) hull and prow; (d) bread and wine (brew).
Line 11: *Kinde,* birth; nature.
Line 22: *Sope,* soap.
Line 22: *Nitre,* saltpeter, white crystalline substance.
Line 31: *Round,* rung.
Line 31: *Scale,* ladder.
Line 33: *Bale,* bail, deliver from jail.

36. MEDITATION. COL. 1.18.

HE IS THE HEAD OF THE BODY.

19.3m [May] 1700.

An Head, my Lord, an honourable piece;
    Nature's high tower, and wealthy Jewelry;
A box of Brains, furld up in reasons fleece:
    Casement of Senses: Reason's Chancery:
    Religions Chancell pia-mater'd ore   *5*
    With Damask Roses that Sweet wisdom bore.

This is, my Lord, the rosie Emblem sweet,
    Blazing thyselfe out, on my mudd wall, fair,
And in thy Palace, where the rosy feet
    Of thy Deare Spouse doth thee her head thus ware.   *10*
    Her Head thou art: Head glory of her Knot.
    Thou art her Flower, and she thy flower pot.

The Metall Kingdoms had a Golden head,
    Yet had't no brains, or had its brains out dasht.

But Zions Kingdome fram'd hath better sped,   15
   Through which the Rayes of thy rich head are lasht.
   She wares thee Head, thou art her strong defence
   Head of Priority, and Excellence.

Hence art an head of Arguments so strong
   To argue all unto thyselfe, when bent   20
And quickly tongue ty, or pluck out the tongue
   Of all Contrary pleas or arguments.
   It makes them weake as water, for the tide
   Of Truth and Excellence rise on this Side.

Lord, let these barbed Arrows from thy bow   25
   Fly through mine Eyes, and Eares to strike my heart.
And force my Will, and Reason to thee so
   And stifle pleas made for the other part
   That so my Soule, rid of their Sophistry
   In rapid flames of Love to thee may fly.   30

My Metaphors are but dull Tacklings tag'd
   With ragged Non-Sense. Can such draw to thee
My stund affections all with Cinders clag'd,
   If thy bright beaming headship touch not mee?
   If that thy headship shines not in mine eyes,   35
   My heart will fuddled ly with wordly toyes.

Lord play thy Excellency on this pin
   To tongue ty other pleas my gadding heart
Is tooke withall. Chime my affections in
   To serve thy Sacred selfe with Sacred art.   40
   Oh! let thy Head stretch ore my heart its wing
   And then my Heart thy Headships praise shall sing.

TEXT NOTES:
Line 3: *Furld*, rolled.
Line 3: *Fleece*, covering.
Line 4: *Chancery*, courthouse.
Line 5: *Pia-mater*, membrane enveloping the brain.
Line 11: *Knot*, garden.
Line 13: *Head*, god.
Line 15: *Sped*, speed.
Line 16: *Lasht*, let fly.
Line 17: *Wares*, heeds? wears?
Line 19: *Head*, main point.
Line 31: *Tacklings*, furnishings, baggage.
Line 33: *Clag'd*, clogged.

Line 36: *Toyes,* trifles.
Line 38: *Gadding,* wandering.
Line 39: *Chime,* summon by chiming.

43. MEDITATION. ROM. 9.5.

GOD BLESSED FOREVER.

26.8m [Oct.] 1701.

When, Lord, I seeke to shew thy praises, then
  Thy shining Majesty doth stund my minde,
Encramps my tongue and tongue ties fast my Pen,
  That all my doings, do not what's designd.
    My Speeche's Organs are so trancifide   5
    My words stand startld, can't thy praises stride.

Nay Speeches Bloomery can't from the Ore
  Of Reasons mine, melt words for to define
Thy Deity, nor t'deck the reechs that sore
  From Loves rich Vales, sweeter than hony rhimes.   10
    Words though the finest twine of reason, are
    Too Course a web for Deity to ware.

Words Mentall are syllabicated thoughts:
  Words Orall but thoughts Whiffld in the Winde.
Words Writ, are incky, Goose quill-slabbred draughts,   15
  Although the fairest blossoms of the minde.
    Then can such glasses cleare enough descry
    My Love to thee, or thy rich Deity?

Words are befould, Thoughts filthy fumes that smoake,
  From Smutty Huts, like Will-a-Wisps that rise   20
From Quaugmires, run ore bogs where frogs do Croake,
  Lead all astray led by them by the eyes.
    My muddy Words so dark thy Deity,
    And cloude thy Sun-Shine, and its Shining Sky.

Yet spare mee, Lord, to use this hurden ware.   25
  I have no finer Stuff to use, and I
Will use it now my Creed but to declare
  And not thy Glorious Selfe to beautify.
    Thou art all-God: all Godhead then is thine
    Although the manhood there unto doth joyne.   30

Thou art all Godhead bright, although there bee
  Something beside the Godhead in thee bright.
Thou art all Infinite although in thee
  There is a nature pure, not infinite.
  Thou are Almighty, though thy Humane tent   *35*
  Of Humane frailty upon earth did sent.

He needs must be the Deity most High,
  To whom all properties essensiall to
The Godhead do belong Essentially
  And not to others: nor from Godhead go   *40*
  And thou art thus, my Lord, to Godhead joynd.
  We finde thee thus in Holy Writ definde.

Thou art Eternall; Infinite thou art;
  Omnipotent, Omniscient, Erywhere,
All Holy, Just, Good, Gracious, True, in heart,   *45*
  Immortal, though with mortall nature here.
  Religious worship hence belongs to thee
  From men and angells: all, of each degree.

Be thou my God, and make mee thine Elect
  To kiss thy feet, and worship give to thee: *50*
Accept of mee, and make mee thee accept.
  So I'st be safe, and thou shalt served bee.
  I'le bring thee praise, buskt up in Songs perfum'de,
  When thou with grace my Soule hast sweetly tun'de.

TEXT NOTES:

Line 7: *Bloomery,* the first forge in an iron-works, through which metal passes after
    separation from ore.
Line 9: *Deck,* adorn.
Line 9: *Reechs* (reeks), odors.
Line 9: *Sore,* soar.
Line 10: *Vales,* valleys.
Line 12: *Web,* cloth.
Line 12: *Ware,* wear.
Line 14: *Whiffld,* blown in puffs.
Line 15: *Draughts,* marks, strokes.
Line 17: *Glasses* (glosses), poems based on a text.
Line 17: *Descry,* proclaim.
Line 20: *Smutty Huts,* smoke-houses.
Line 20: *Will-a-Wisps,* marsh gas.
Line 25: *Hurden ware,* coarse fabric.
Line 35: *Tent,* dwelling; intent, purpose.

Line 36: *Sent,* scent, smell.
Line 53: *Buskt,* dressed.

44. MEDITATION. JOH. 1.14.
THE WORD WAS MADE FLESH.

28.10m [Dec.] 1701.

The Orator from Rhetorick gardens picks
   His Spangled Flowers of sweet-breathd Eloquence
Wherewith his Oratory brisk he tricks
   Whose Spicy Charms Eare jewells do commence.
   Shall bits of Brains be candid thus for eares?   *5*
   My Theme claims Sugar Candid far more cleare.

Things styld Transcendent, do transcende the Stile
   Of Reason, reason's stares neere reach so high.
But Jacob's golden Ladder rounds do foile
   All reasons Strides, wrought of THEANTHROPIE.   *10*
   Two Natures distance-standing, infinite,
   Are Onifide, in person, and Unite.

In Essence two, in Properties each are
   Unlike, as unlike can be. One All-Might
A Mite the other; One Immortall fair.   *15*
   One mortall, this all Glory, that all night.
   One Infinite, One finite. So for ever:
   Yet ONED are in Person, part'd never.

The Godhead personated in Gods Son
   Assum'd the Manhood to its Person known,   *20*
When that the Manhoods essence first begun
   That it did never Humane person own.
   Each natures Essence e're abides the same.
   In person joynd, one person each do claim.

Oh! Dignifide Humanity indeed: *25*
   Divinely person'd: almost Deifide.
Nameing one Godhead person, in our Creed,
   The Word-made-Flesh. Here's Grace's 'maizing stride.
   The vilst design, that villany e're hatcht
   Hath tap't such Grace in God, that can't be matcht.   *30*

Our Nature spoild: under all Curses groans
   Is purg'd, tooke, grac'd with grace, united to

A Godhead person, Godhead-person owns
  Its onely person. Angells, Lord its so.
This Union ever lasts, if not relate   *35*
Which Cov'nant claims Christs Manhood, separate.

You Holy Angells, Morning-Stars, bright Sparks,
  Give place: and lower your top gallants. Shew
Your top-saile Conjues to our slender barkes:
  The highest honour to our nature's due.   *40*
  Its neerer Godhead by the Godhead made
  Than yours in you that never from God stray'd.

Here is good anchor hold: and argument
  To anchor here, Lord, make my Anchor stronge
And Cable, both of holy geer, out sent   *45*
  And in this anch'ring dropt and let at length.
  My bark shall safely ride then though there fall
  On't th'strongest tempests hell can raise of all.

Unite my Soule, Lord, to thyselfe, and stamp
  Thy holy print on my unholy heart.   *50*
I'st nimble be when thou destroyst my cramp
  And take thy paths when thou dost take my part.
  If thou wilt blow this Oaten Straw of mine,
  The sweetest piped praises shall be thine.

TEXT NOTES:
Line 3: *Brisk,* sharp-witted; finely dressed.
Line 3: *Tricks,* dresses up.
Line 4: *Eare jewells,* earrings.
Line 5: *Candid,* candied.
Line 6: *Cleare,* completely.
Line 7: *Stile,* arrangement of steps.
Line 9: *Rounds,* rungs.
Line 10: *Theanthropie,* union of divine and human natures in Christ.
Line 12: *Onifide,* one-i-fied.
Line 15: *Mite,* insect; object of little or no value.
Line 28: *'Maizing,* amazing.
Line 38: *Gallants,* flags flown from mizzenmast.
Line 38: *Shew,* show.
Line 39: *Conjues* (congees), bows.
Line 39: *Barkes,* small ships, rowboats.
Line 45: *Geer,* rigging material.
Line 51: *I'st,* I would.

48. MEDITATION. REV. 1.8.

THE ALMIGHTY.

13.7m [Sept.] 1702.

O! What a thing is Might right mannag'd? 'Twill
  That Proverb brain, whose face doth ware this paint.
(Might ore goe's Right) for might doth Right fulfill
  Will Right revive when wrong makes Right to faint.
    Might hatches Right: Right hatches Might, they are   5
    Each Dam, and Chick, to each: a Lovely paire.

Then Might well mannag'd riseth mighty: yet
  Doth never rise up to Almightiness.
Almightiness nere's in a mortall bit.
    But, Lord, thou dost Almightiness possess.   10
    Might in it's fulness: all mights Fulness bee
    Of ery Sort and Sise stow'd up in thee.

But what am I, poor Mite, all mightless thing!
  That cannot rive a rush, that I should e're
Adventure t'dress Almighty up, or bring   15
  Almightiness deckt in its mighty geere?
    Then spare my Stutting Stamring, inky Quill,
    If it its bowells on thy Power distill.

My Mite (if I such Solicisms might
  But use) would spend its mitie Strength for thee   20
Of Mightless might, of feeble stronge delight.
    Its little ALL thy Sacrifice showld bee.
    For thee't would mock at all the Might and Power
    That Earth, and Hell possess: and on thee shower.

A Fig for Foes, for Divells, Hell, and all   25
  The powres of darkness, thou now on my Side
Their Might's a little mite, Powers powerless fall.
    My Mite Almighty will not let down slide.
    I will not trust unto this Might of mine:
    Nor in my Mite distrust, while I am thine.   30

Thy Love Almighty is, to Love mee deare,
  Thy Grace Almighty mee to save: thy Truth
Almighty to depend on. Justice cleare
  Almighty t'justify, and judge. Grace shewth.
    Thy Wisdom too's Almighty all to eye,   35
    And Holiness is such to sanctify.

If thy Almightiness, and all my Mite
   United be in sacred Marriage knot,
My Mite is thine: Mine thine Almighty Might.
   Then thine Almightiness my Mite hath got.   *40*
   My Quill makes thine Almightiness a String
   Of Pearls to grace the tune my Mite doth sing.

TEXT NOTES:

Line 2: *Brain,* kill by dashing out brains.

Line 3: *Might ore goe's Right,* "might overcomes right" (Morris Palmer Tilley, *A Dictionary of the Proverbs in England in the Sixteenth and Seventeenth Centuries,* University of Michigan, Ann Arbor, 1950, p. 460, entry M922).

Line 6: *Dam* (dame), mother.

Line 12: *Sise,* size.

Line 14: *Rive,* tear apart; or possibly (reave) carry away.

Line 14: *Rush,* plant growing in marshy ground; or possibly a thing of no value (as in "not worth a rush").

Line 16: *Geere,* armor, apparel.

Line 17: *Stutting,* stuttering.

Line 18: *Distill,* drip.

Line 19: *Solicisms* (solecisms), ungrammatical combinations of words.

Line 25: *Fig,* poisoned fig; contemptuous gesture made by thrusting thumb between two closed fingers.

69. MEDITATION. CANT. 2.2.

THE LILLIE OF THE VALLIES.

30.4m [June] 1706.

Dull! Dull! my Lord, as if I eaten had
   A Peck of Melancholy: or my Soule
Was lockt up by a Poppy key, black, sad:
   Or had been fuddled with an Hen bane bowle.
   Oh, Leaden temper! my Rich Thesis Would   *5*
   Try metall to the back, sharp, it t'unfold.

Alas! my Soule, Thy Sunburnt Skin looks dun:
   Thy Elementall jacket's Snake like pi'de.
I am Deform'd, and Uggly all become.
   Soule Sicknesses do nest in mee: and Pride.   *10*
   I nauseous am: and mine iniquites
   Like Crawling Worms doe worm eat on my joys.

All black though plac'de in a White lilly Grove:
   Not sweet, though in a bed of Lillies rowle,
Though in Physicians shop I dwell, a Drove   *15*
   Of Hellish Vermin range all ore my Soul.
   All Spirituall Maladies play rex in mee,
   Though Christ should Lilly of my Vally bee.

But, Oh! the Wonder! Christ alone the Sun
   Of Righteousness, that he might do the Cure   *20*
The Lilly of the Vallies is become
   Whose Lillie properties do health restore.
   It's glory shews I'm filthy: yet must spring
   Up innocent, and beautifull by him.

Its Vally State and Bowing Head declare   *25*
   I'm Haughty but must have a Humble minde.
Its Healing Virtue shew I'm sick: yet rare
   Rich Remedies I'st in this Lilly finde.
   Yea Christ the Lilly of the Vallies shall
   Be to mee Glory, Med'cine, Sweetness, all.   *30*

The Lillies Beautie, and its Fragrancy
   Shews my ill-favourdness, and Nauseous Stinck:
And that I must be beautifull, fully,
   And breath a Sweetness that the aire must drink.
   This Beauty, Odour, Med'cin, Humble Case   *35*
   This Vallys Lilly shall my Soul begrace.

Lord, make me th'Vally where this Lilly grows.
   Then I am thine, and thou art mine indeed.
Propriety is mutuall: Glorious shows
   And Oderif'rous breath shall in me breed,   *40*
   Which twisted in my Tunes, thy praise shall ring
   On my Shoshannim's sweetest Well tun'de string.

TEXT NOTES:
Line 3: *Poppy,* narcotic.
Line 4: *Hen bane,* plant with narcotic properties.
Line 7: *Dun,* dull brown.
Line 8: *Pi'de* (pied), multi-colored, blotched.
Line 14: *Rowle* (roll), wander; envelop.
Line 17: *Rex,* pranks; king.
Line 42: *Shoshannim,* stringed instrument mentioned in Psalms 45, 69.

72. MEDITATION. MAR. 16.19. SAT DOWN
ON THE RIGHT HAND OF GOD.

15.10m [Dec.] 1706.

Enoculate into my mentall Eye
  The Visive Spirits of the Holy Ghost
My Lord, that I may see the Dignity
  Of thy bright Honour in thy heavenly Coast
  Thou art deckt with as Sunshine bright displaid   *5*
  That makes bright Angells in it, cast a Shade.

Enrich my Phansy with Seraphick Life,
  Enquicknd nimbly to catch the Beams
Thy Honour flurs abroad: in joyous Strife
  To make sweet Musick on such Happy Themes.   *10*
  That in such Raptures, and Transports of joy,
  To Honour kings I may my Phansy 'ploy.

At God's Right Hand! Doth God mans parts enjoy?
  This with Infinity can never stande.
Yet so God sayes, His Son to Dignify   *15*
  In manhood, said, sit at my right hand.
  The manhood thus a brighter Honour bears
  By Deity than Deity ere wares.

The Splendor of the matter of each Story
  Of th'Heavenly Palace Hall all brightend cleare,   *20*
The Presence Chamber of the King of Glory
  Common with thee, to Saints and Angells there.
  They share with thee in this Celestiall Shine.
  Although their Share is lesser far than thine.

Yet they in all this glorious Splendor bright,   *25*
  So many Suns like, shining on each other,
Encreasing each's glory, fall down right
  To kiss thy feet, whose Shine this glorie Covers.
  Their brightest Shine, in Glory's highest Story,
  Is t'stand before thee in thy bright-bright glory.   *30*

Thy Honour brightens theirs, as't on theirs falls.
  Its Royall Honour thou inheritst, Cleare,
A Throne of Glory in bright glories Hall:
  At Gods right Hand thou sits enthroned there.
  The Highest Throne in brightest glory thou   *35*
  Enjoyest. Saints, and Angels 'fore thee bow.

Come down, bright Angells, Now I claim my place.
  My nature hath more Honour due, than yours:
Mine is Enthron'de at Gods Right-Hand, through Grace.
    This Grace for mine and not for yours, endures.   *40*
    Yours is not there, unless in part of mine,
    As Species in their Genus do combine.

Hence make my Life, Lord, keep thine Honour bright.
  And let thine Honour brighten mee by grace.
And make thy Grace in mee, thee honour right.   *45*
    And let not mee thy Honour ere deface.
    Grant me the Honour then to honour thee
    And on my Bells thine Honour chimed shall bee.

TEXT NOTES:
Line 1: *Enoculate,* engraft.
Line 2: *Visive,* sight-giving.
Line 4: *Coast,* region.
Line 7: *Seraphick,* ecstatically adoring; contemplative.
Line 9: *Flurs,* scatters.
Line 9: *Strife,* striving.
Line 18: *Ere,* earlier? ever?
Line 18: *Wares,* wears; heeds; lays out.
Line 46: *Ere,* ever.

79. MEDITATION. CAN. 2.16. MY BELOVED
IS MINE AND I AM HIS.

8.12m [Feb.] 1707.

Had I Promethius' filching Ferula
  Filld with its sacred theft the stoln Fire:
To animate my Fancy lodg'd in clay,
    Pandora's Box would peps the theft with ire.
    But if thy Love, My Lord, shall animate   *5*
    My Clay with holy fire, 'twill flame in State.

Fables fain'd Wonders do relate so strange
  That do amuse when heard. But oh! thy Fame
Pend by the Holy Ghost, (and ne'er shall Change
    Nor vary from the truth) is wonders flame   *10*
    Glazde o're with Heavens Embelishments, and fan'd
    From evry Chaff, Dust, Weedy Seed, or Sand.

What wilt thou change thyselfe for me, and take
  In lew thereof my sorry selfe; whereby,
I am no more mine own, but thine, probate,   *15*
    Thou not so thine, as not mine too thereby?
    Dost purchase me to be thine own, thyselfe
    And be'st exchange for mee, thyselfe, and wealth?

I'm Thine, Thou Mine! Mutuall propriety:
  Thou giv'st thyselfe. And for this gift takst mee   *20*
To be thine own. I give myselfe (poore toy)
    And take thee for myne own, and so to bee.
    Thou giv'st thyselfe, yet dost thyselfe possess,
    I give and keep myselfe too neretheless.

Both gi'n away and yet retain'd aright.   *25*
  Oh! Strange! I have thee mine, who hast thyselfe,
Yet in possession Thou hast mee as tite,
    Who still enjoy myselfe, and thee my wealth.
    What strang appropriations hence arise?
    Thy Person mine, Mine thine, even weddenwise?   *30*

Thine mine, mine Thine, a mutuall claim is made.
  Mine, thine are Predicates unto us both.
But oh! the Odds in th' purchase price down laid:
    Thyselfe's thy Price, myselfe my mony go'th.
    Thy Purchase mony's infinitly high;   *35*
    Of Value for me: mine for thee, 's a toy.

Thou'rt Heir of Glory, dost Bright image stand
  Ev'n of the God of Glory. Ownest all.
Hast all Wealth Wisdom Glory, Might at hand
    And all what e're can to mans Glory fall.   *40*
    And yet thou givst thyselfe to purchase mee
    Ev'n of myselfe, to give myselfe to thee.

And what am I? a little bit of Clay.
  Not more, nor better thing at all I give.
(Though give myselfe) to thee as Purchase pay.   *45*
    For thee, and for thy all, that I may live.
    What hard terms art thou held unto by me.
    Both in thy Sale, and Purchase, laid on thee?

But yet this thing doth not impov'rish thee
  Although thou payest down thy glorious selfe.   *50*
And my down laying of myselfe I see
    For thee,'s the way for mee to blessed wealth.

Thou freely givst what I buy Cheape of thee.
I freely give what thou buyst deare of mee.

The Purchasd Gift, and Given Purchase here   *55*
  (For they're both Gifts, and Purchases) by each
For each, make each to one anothers deare,
  And each delight t'heare one anothers Speech.
  Oh! Happy Purchase. And oh! Happy Sale:
  Making each others joye in joyous gales.   *60*

Let this dash out the snarling teeth that grin,
  Of that Damnd Heresy, calld SHERLOSISM,
That mocks, and scoffs the UNION (that blesst thing)
  To Christs Blesst Person, Happy Enkentrism.
  For if thats true, Christs Spouse spake false in this   *65*
  Saying My Beloved's Mine, and I am his.

Hence, Oh! my Lord, make thou mee thine that so
  I may be bed wherein thy Love shall ly,
And be thou mine that thou mayst ever show
  Thyselfe the Bed my Love its lodge may spy.   *70*
  Then this shall be the burden of my Song
  My Well belov'de is mine: I'm his become.

TEXT NOTES:
Line 1: *Filching,* pilfered, stolen.
Line 1: *Ferula,* fennel-stalk.
Line 4: *Peps* (pepse), pelt, throw at; or perhaps "pepst," intoxicate.
Line 9: *Pend* (penned), written (in Scripture).
Line 14: *Lew,* lieu.
Line 15: *Probate,* proven.
Line 19: *Propriety,* ownership.
Line 21: *Toy,* thing of little or no value.
Line 25: *Gi'n,* given.
Line 27: *Tite,* title.
Line 32: *Predicates,* appellations, titles.
Line 33: *Odds,* difference.
Line 60: *Gales,* songs; mirth.
Line 62: *Sherlosism,* controversial doctrine put forth by William Sherlock (1641?–
    1707), Dean of St. Paul's, that the Trinity is composed of three distinct sub-
    stances and that mystical union between Christ and believers is impossible. In
    his sermons *Upon the Types of the Old Testament,* Taylor charged Sherlock
    with the heresy of Socinianism, which denies the divinity of Christ and is the
    root of Unitarianism (Rowe, *Saint and Singer,* 97, 311 n. 9). Stanford notes
    that the Calvinist Edward Polhill's work, *An Answer to the Discourse of Wil-*

liam Sherlock Touching the Knowledge of Christ, was in Taylor's library (Stanford, ed., *Poems of Taylor*, 228).
Line 64: *Enkentrism*, probably a reference to the Christocentric theology expressed in lines 63–66.

81. MEDITATION. JOH. 6.53. UNLESS YE EAT THE FLESH OF THE SON OF MAN, AND DRINK HIS BLOOD, YOU HAVE NO LIFE IN YOU.

2.3m [May] 1708.

I fain would praise thee, Lord, but often finde
  Some toy or trinket slipping in between
My heart and thee, that whiffles hence my minde
  From this I know not how, and oft unseen.
    That such should interpose between my Soule   5
    And thee, is matter for mee to Condole.

I finde thou art the Spring of Life, and Life
  Is up Empon'd in thee, that's Life indeed.
Thou art Lifes Fountain and its Food. The Strife
  Of Living things doth for Life Sake proceed.   10
    But he that with the best of Lifes is spic'te
    Doth eate, and drinke the Flesh, and blood of Christ.

What feed on Humane Flesh and Blood? Strang mess!
  Nature exclaims. What Barbarousness is here?
And Lines Divine this sort of Food repress.   15
  Christs Flesh and Blood how can they bee good Cheer?
    If shread to atoms, would too few be known,
    For ev'ry mouth to have a single one?

This Sense of this blesst Phrase is nonsense thus.
  Some other Sense makes this a metaphor.   20
This feeding signifies, that Faith in us
  Feeds on this fare, Disht in this Pottinger.
    Faith feeds upon this Heavenly Manna rare
    And drinkes this Blood. Sweet junkets: Angells Fare.

Christs works, as Divine Cookery, knead in   25
  The Pasty Past, (his Flesh and Blood) most fine
Into Rich Fare, made with the rowling pin
  His Deity did use. (Obedience prime)
    Active, and Passive is the Food that all
    That have this Life feed on within thy Hall.   30

Here's Meate, and Drinke for Souls to use: (Good Cheer,)
  Cookt up, and Brewd by Pure Divinity
The juyce tund up in Humane Casks that ne'er
  Were musty made by any Sluttery.
  And tapt by Graces hand whose table hold   *35*
  This fare in Dishes far more rich than Gold.

Thou, Lord, Envit'st me thus to eat thy Flesh,
  And drinke thy blood more Spiritfull than wine.
And if I feed not here on this rich mess,
  I have no life in mee: no life Divine.   *40*
  The Spirituall Life, the Life of God, and Grace
  Eternall Life, obtain in me no place.

The Naturall Life the Life of Reason too
  Are but as painten Cloths to that I lack
The Spirituall Life, and Life Eternall View.   *45*
  If none of mine, my Glorys face grows black.
  And how should I upon this food ere feed,
  If thou give unto me no vitall Seed?

Those Fruits (the Works) that gloriously do shine
  Upon thy Humane Nature Flesh and Blood   *50*
From thy Divine, are th'Purchase price, and th'Fine
  Set on our heads, and made our Spirituall Food.
  Faith thats the feeding on these pleasant flowers,
  Incorporates thy Flesh and Blood with ours.

Thy Flesh, and Blood and Office Fruites shall bee   *55*
  My Souls Plumb Cake it eates, as naturally,
In Spirituall wise mixt with my soul, as wee
  Finde food doth with the body properly.
  So that my life shall be mentain'd and thrive
  Eternally when Spiritually alive.   *60*

Oh! feed mee, Lord, on thy rich Florendine.
  Made of the Fruites which thy Divinity
As Principall did beare, (more sweet than wine)
  Upon thy Manhood, meritoriously.
  If I be fed with this rich fare, I will   *65*
  Say Grace to thee with Songs of holy Skill.

TEXT NOTES:
Line 3: *Whiffles,* puffs, trifles.
Line 6: *Condole,* lament.
Line 8: *Empon'd,* dammed up (from "pond," to dam); impounded.

Line 11: *Spic'te,* spiced.

Line 13: *Mess,* food; slop; also a pun on Mass, the Catholic Eucharist.

Line 22: *Pottinger,* porringer, bowl.

Line 24: *Junkets,* delicacies; sweetmeat cakes; confections.

Line 26: *Pasty,* meat-pie; or like paste.

Line 26: *Past* (paste), flour moistened with water or milk and kneaded into dough.

Line 33: *Tund,* stored.

Line 34: *Sluttery,* impurity.

Line 39: *Mess,* food, meal.

Line 44: *Painten* (painted), colored; or perhaps "painting cloths" or "painting clothes."

Line 61: *Florendine,* meat-pie, tart.

104. MEDITATION. MATTH. 26.26.27.

HE TOOKE BREAD.—

AND HE ALSO TOOKE THE CUP:

30.7m [Sept.] 1711.

What? Bread, and Wine, My Lord! Art thou thus made?
   And made thus unto thine in th'Sacrament?
These are both Cordiall: and both displai'd
   Food for the Living. Spirituall Nourishment.
   Thou hence art food, and Physick rightly 'pli'de   *5*
   To Living Souls. Such none for dead provide.

Stir up thy Appetite, my Soule, afresh,
   Here's Bread, and Wine as Signs, to signify
The richest Dainties Cookery can Dress
   Thy Table with, filld with felicity.   *10*
   Purge out and Vomit by Repentance all
   Ill Humours which thy Spirituall Tast forestall.

Bread, Yea substantiall Bread dresst daintily
   Gods White bread made of th'kidnie of Wheate
Ground in his Mill to finest Flowre, we spy,   *15*
   Searc'de through his strict right Bolter, all compleate
   Moulded up by Gods hand and baked tite
   In Justices hot oven, Gods Cake-bread white.

It is Gods Temple bread; the fine Flower Cake.
   The pure Shew Bread on th'golden Table set,   *20*

Before the Mercy-Seate in golden Plate,
   Thy Palate for this Zions Simnill whet.
   If in this oyled Wafer thou dost eate
   Celestiall Mannah, Oh! the Happy meate.

But that's not all. Here's wine too of brave State.   *25*
   The Blood, the pure red blood of Zions Grape
Grounde in the Mill of Righteousness to 'bate
   Gods firy wrath and presst into the Shape
   Of Royall Wine in Zion's Sacred bowles
   That Purges Cleanse and Chearish doth poore Soules.   *30*

This Bread, and Wine hold forth the selfe same thing
   As they from their first Wheat and Vine made flow
Successively into their Beings, bring
   The manner of Christs Manhood and forth show
   It was derived from th'head Humanity   *35*
   Through Generations all successively.

And as this Bread and Wine receive their forms
   Not fram'd by natures acting, but by Art.
So Christs Humanity was not ere born
   By natures Vertue which she did impart.   *40*
   But by Almighty power which acted so
   Transendently, did nature overdoe.

These two are of all food most Choice indeed
   Do Emblemise Christ's Elementall frame
Most Excellent and fine, of refinde Seed,   *45*
   With Sparkling Grace deckt, and their Works in flame
   As grafted in and flowing from his Nature
   And here is food of which his are partaker.

Bread must be broke and Eate Wine pourd out too
   And drunke and so they feed and do delight.   *50*
Christ broken was upon Gods wheele (its true)
   And so is spirituall bread that feeds aright
   And his Choice blood shead for our Sins is made
   Drinke for our Souls: a Spirituall Drinke displaid.

Food though its ne're so rich, doth not beget   *55*
   Nor make its Eaters; but their Lives mentain.
This Bread and Wine begets not Souls; but's set
   'Fore spirituall life to feed upon the Same.
   This Feast is no Regenerating fare.
   But food for those Regenerate that are.   *60*

Spit out thy Fur, my Tongue; renew thy Tast.
   Oh! whet thine Appetite, and cleanly brush
Thy Cloaths and trim thy Soule. Here food thou hast
   Of Royall Dainties, that requires thee thus
   That thou adorned be in Spirituall State: *65*
   This Bread ne're moulds, nor wine entoxicate.

They both are Food, and Physick, purge out Sin
   From right Receivers. Filth, and Faults away:
They both are Cordialls rich, do Comfort bring.
   Make Sanctifying Grace thrive ery day,   *70*
   Making the spirituall man hate spirituall sloath
   And to abound in things of Holy growth.

Lord, feed me with th'Bread of thy Sacrament:
   And make me drinke thy Sacramentall Wine:
That I may Grow by Graces nourishment   *75*
   Wash't in thy Vinall liquour till I shine,
   And rai'd in Sparkling Grace unto thy Glory,
   That so my Life may be a gracious story.

TEXT NOTES:

Line 3: *Cordiall,* of the heart.
Line 5: *'Pli'de,* applied.
Line 14: *Kidnie of Wheate,* finest wheat; see Deuteronomy 32:14 (KJV only).
Line 16: *Searc'de* (searced), sifted.
Line 17: *Tite,* immediately.
Line 19: *Flower,* flour.
Line 20: *Shew Bread,* offering bread in Old Testament worship; Exodus 25:30, 1
   Chronicles 28:16, and elsewhere.
Line 22: *Simnill,* bread of fine flour, boiled, then sometimes baked.
Line 22: *Whet,* white.
Line 23: *Oyled,* anointed.
Line 44: *Elementall,* material; also in reference to Communion elements.
Line 56: *Mentain,* maintain.
Line 57: *This Bread and Wine begets not Souls,* in refutation of the view of the
   sacrament put forth by Solomon Stoddard (1643–1729), Taylor's contempo-
   rary and theological adversary in Northampton, who held that it was a con-
   verting ordinance and should thus be open to all. Taylor and most of New
   England believed that the Lord's Supper served to nourish spiritually those who
   were already members of the church covenant and were therefore in Christ.
Line 76: *Vinall,* produced by, originating in, wine.
Line 77: *Rai'd,* arrayed.

119. MEDITATION. CAN. 5.12. HIS EYES ARE AS

THE EYES OF DOVES BY RIVERS OF WATERS

WASHED WITH MILK, AND FITLY SET.

9.3m [May] 1714.

My Lord, (my Love,) what loveliness doth ly,
    In this pert percing fiery Eye of thine?
Thy Dove like Eyes ore varnish gloriously
    Thy Face till it the Heavens over shine.
    No Eye did ever any face bedight   *5*
    As thine with Charming Beauty and Delight.

No Eye holes did at any time enjoy,
    An apple of an Eye like this of thine
Nor ever held an Apple of an Eye
    Like that thine held. Apple and Eye hole fine   *10*
    Oh! How these Apples and these Eye holes fit,
    Its Eye Omniscient on its fulness sits!

Never were Eyeballs so full trust with might
    With such rich, sharp, quick visive Spirits tite
Nor gave such glances of such beauty bright   *15*
    As thine, my Lord, nor wore so smart a Sight.
    All bright, All Right, all Holy, Wise, and Cleare
    Or ere discover did such beauty here.

Look here, my Soule, thy Saviours Eye most brisk
    Doth glaze and make't most Charming beauty weare   *20*
That Ever Heaven held or ever kisst.
    All Saints, and Angells at it Gastard stare.
    This Eye with all the beauties in his face
    Doth hold thy heart and Love in a blesst Chase.

Lord let these Charming Glancing Eyes of thine   *25*
    Glance on my Souls bright Eye its amorous beams
To fetch as upon golden Ladders fine
    My Heart and Love to thee in Hottest Steams.
    Which bosom'd in thy brightest beauty cleare
    Shall tune the glances of thy Eyes Sweet Deare.   *30*

TEXT NOTES:
Line 2: *Pert,* beautiful, open.
Line 3: *Varnish,* invest with bright, glossy appearance.

Line 5: *Bedight,* array.
Line 8: *Apple of an Eye,* pupil, eyeball.
Line 10: *Fine,* make for beauty.
Line 13: *Trust* (trussed), compactly formed.
Line 14: *Tite,* tight (in reference to "trust," as "tightly formed").
Line 15: *Glances,* flashes.
Line 16: *Smart,* neat, elegant in appearance.
Line 17: *Cleare,* pure.
Line 22: *Gastard,* astonished.
Line 24: *Chase,* setting of a gem.

120. MEDITATION. CAN. 5.13.
HIS CHEEKS ARE AS A BED OF SPICES,
AS SWEET FLOWERS ETC.

4.4m [June] 1714.

My Deare-Deare Lord! What shall my speech be dry?
    And shall I court thee onely with dull tunes?
When I behold thy Cheekes like brave beds ly
    Of Spices and sweet flowers, reechs of Perfumes?
    Sweet beauty reeching in thy Countenance   5
    Oh! amorous Charms: that bring't up in a Trance!

Oh! brightest Beauty, Lord, that paints thy Cheeks
    Yea sweetest Beauty that Face ere did ware,
Mans Clayey Face ne're breathd such ayery Reechs
    Nor e're such Charming Sweetness gave so fair.   10
    If otherwise true Wisdoms voice would bee,
    That greater Love belong'd to these than thee;

If so, Love to thyselfe might slacke its pin
    And Love to Worldly Gayes might screw up higher
Its rusty pin, till, that her Carnall String   15
    Did raise Earths Tunes above the Heavenly Quire.
    Shall Vertue thus descend, and have Disgrace?
    Shall brightest beauty have the lowest place?

Shall dirty Earth out shine the Heavens bright?
    Our Garden bed out shine thy Paradise?   20
Shall Earthy Dunghills yield more sweet Delight?
    Be sweeter than thy Cheeks like beds of Spice?

Are all things natur'de thus and named wrong?
Hath God that made them all made all thus run?

Where is the thought that's in such dy pot di'de?   *25*
    Where is the mouth that mutters such a thing?
Where is the Tongue that dare such Speech let slide?
    As Cramps the Aire that doth such ditties ding
    Upon the Ear that wound and poison doe?
    Thy Auditory Temple where they goe?   *30*

Such things as these indeed are Hells black Smoke
    That pother from its Chimny tunnells vile
To smut thy perfect beauty, Damps thence broke
    Out of the Serpents Smokehole, to defile
    And Choake our Spirituall Smell and so to Crush   *35*
    Thy sweet perfum out of these briezes thus.

But Oh! my Lord, I do abhorr such notes
    That do besmoot thy Beautious Cheeks like Spice.
Like Pillars of perfume; thy Cheeks rich Coats,
    Of purest Sweetness, decke't in's beauty Choice.   *40*
    My bliss I finde lapt in my Love that keeps
    Its Station on thy sweet and Beautious Cheeks.

Lord lodge my Eyes upon thy Cheekes that are
    Cloathd ore with orient beauty like as't were
A Spice bed shining with sweet flowers all fair,   *45*
    Enravishing the very Skies so Cleare
    With their pure Spirits breathing thence perfumes
    Orecoming notes that fill my Harpe with tunes.

TEXT NOTES:
Line 3: *Brave,* excellent.
Line 3: *Beds,* flower-beds.
Line 4: *Reechs* (reeks), smells.
Line 9: *Ayery,* airy.
Line 14: *Gayes,* toys.
Line 32: *Pother,* pour out in a cloud.
Line 33: *Damps,* noxious gas.
Line 37: *Notes,* things; marks; stigma.
Line 41: *Lapt,* embraced, enwrapped.
Line 44: *Orient,* precious; radiant.

121. MEDITATION. CANT. 5.13.

HIS LIPS ARE LIKE LILLIES,

DROPPING SWEET SMELLING MYRRH.

28.9m [Nov.] 1714.

Peart Pidgeon Eyes, Sweet Rosie Cheeke of thine
　My Lord, and Lilly Lips, What Charms bed here?
To spiritualize my dull affections mine
　Until they up their heads in Love flames reare.
　The flaming beames sent from thy beautious face　　　　*5*
　Transcend all other beauties, and their grace.

Thy Pidgen Eyes dart piercing, beames on Love.
　Thy Cherry Cheeks sende Charms out to Loves Coast.
Thy Lilly Lips drop myrrh down from above
　To medicine our spirituall ailes, greate host.　　　　*10*
　These spirituall maladies that do invest
　The spiritual man are by thy myrrh redresst.

Art thou the Myrrh tree Lord? Thy mouth the Sorce,
　Thy Lilly Lips the bancks, the rivers too
Wherein thy Myrrhie Juyce as water-Course　　　　*15*
　Doth glide along? And like Choice waters flow?
　Lord make thy lilly Lips to ope the Sluce
　And drop thy Doctrine in my Soule, its juyce.

These golden Streams of Gospell Doctrine glide
　Out from thy Lilly Lips aright, my Lord,　　　　*20*
Oh! Spirituall myrrh! and raise a Holy Tide
　Of flowing Grace, and graces Sea afford.
　This is the Heavenly Shoure of Myrrh that flows
　Out of this Cloude of Grace thy Lips disclose.

That Grace that in thy lips is powered out　　　　*25*
　So that these lillie Lips of thine ere bee
The graceous Flood gate whence thy graces spout.
　My Lord, distill these drops of Myrrh on mee,
　If that thy lilly Lips drop on my heart
　Thy passing myrrh, twill med'cine ev'ry part.　　　　*30*

If that these Lilly Lips of thine drop out
　These Myrrhie drops into mine hearts dim Eye
And are to mee rich Graces golden Spout
　That poure out Sanctifying Grace Oh! joy.

This myrrh will medicine my heart that falls   *35*
Out of thy Lilly Lips, on graces Hall.

When these thy Lips poure out this myrrh on mee,
I shall be medicinde with myrrhed Wine
And purifide with oyle of Myrrh shall bee
And well perfumde with Odours rich divine.   *40*
And then my life shall be a Sacrifice
Perfum'de with this sweet incense up arise.

TEXT NOTES:
Line 1: *Peart* (pert), beautiful.
Line 1: *Pidgeon* (pigeon), sweetheart.
Line 8: *Coast,* side; countryside.
Line 11: *Invest,* clothe.
Line 23: *Shoure,* shower.
Line 25: *Powered,* poured.
Line 28: *Distill,* drip.
Line 36: *Hall,* residence.

150. MEDITATION. CANT. 7.3.

THY TWO BREASTS ARE LIKE

TWO YOUNG ROES THAT ARE TWINS.

6.7m [Sept.] 1719.

My Blessed Lord, how doth thy Beautious Spouse
In Stately Stature rise in Comliness?
With her two breasts like two little Roes that browse
Among the lillies in their Shining dress
Like stately milke pailes ever full and flow   *5*
With spirituall milke to make her babes to grow.

Celestiall Nectar Wealthier far than Wine
Wrought in the Spirits brew house and up tund
Within these Vessells which are trust up fine
Likend to two pritty neate twin Roes that run'd   *10*
Most pleasently by their dams sides like Cades
And suckle with their milk Christs Spirituall Babes

Lord put these nibbles then my mouth into
And suckle me therewith I humbly pray,
Then with this milk thy Spirituall Babe I'st grow,   *15*
And these two milke pails shall themselves display

Like to these pritty twins in pairs round neate
And shall sing forth thy praise over this meate.

Line 1: *Spouse,* in this poem not the individual soul but the Church is the Bride of
Christ, with Taylor as the spiritual infant nourished by the Church as mother.
Line 8: *Tund,* stored.
Line 9: *Trust,* (trussed), dressed.
Line 11: *Dam,* mother; mistress.
Line 11: *Cade,* cask; young animal cast off by mother and brought up as a domestic
pet.
Line 13: *Nibbles,* nipples.
Line 17: *Round neate,* completely pure; nicely plump.

160. MEDITATION. CANT. 2.1.
I AM THE LILLY OF THE VALLIE.

Westfield 22.10m [Dec.] 1722.

My Lord my Love I want words fit for thee.
  And if't were otherwise, affections want
To animate the words that they might bee
  A mantle to send praise to praises camp
  But want I word and Spirits for the Same;   5
  If I omit thy praise I sure have blame.

Lord make my heart in mee an humble thing
  The humble hearts thy Habitation bright.
Its fatted then by thee and thou therein
  Enrich it will with thy Celestiall Light.   10
  Thyselfe, dear Lord, shall be its gloryous Shine
  Wherewith it shall adorned be and fine.

I being thus, become thy Vallie low.
  O plant thyselfe my lilly flower there.
Sure then my lilly in it up will grow   15
  In beauty. And its fragrancy will fleer.
  My heart thy spirituall valie all divine
  Thyselfe the lilly of the Vally thine.

I am thy Vally where thy lilly grows
  Thou my White and Red blesst lilly fresh;   20
Thy Active and thy Passive 'bedience do
  Hold out Active and Passive Right'ousness.

Pure White and Red making a lovely grace,
Present thee to our Love to hug and 'brace.

The Medicinall Virtue of the lilly speake   *25*
That thou my Lilly are Physician who
Healst all Diseased Souls both small and greate.
None dy of any Spirituall Sores that to thee goe.
The Vally lilly then doth Emblemize
Thy fitness for thy Mediatoriall guise.   *30*

Shall Heaven itselfe with all its glorious flowers
Stick them as feathers in thy Cap my king
And in this glory bow to plant in, power
Them as a lilly flower my Vally in,
Which is not onely deepe but durty too,   *35*
What wonders this? What praise and thanks hence due?

But oh! alas my pin box is too small
To hold praise meet for such praiseworthiness.
The Angells and Archangells in Gods hall
Mee your Shoshannim tend then to adress   *40*
My Lord with praises bright in highest tunes
And though they are Stuttings they are sweet perfumes.

If thou the Lilly of my Vally bee
My Vally shall then glorious be and shine
Allthough it be a barren Soile for thee: *45*
The Lilly of my Vally is divine.
I'le borrow heavenly praise for thee my king
To sacrifice to thee on my Harps sweet string.

TEXT NOTES:
Lines 1 and 2: *Want,* lack.
Line 4: *Mantle,* cape, covering.
Line 9: *Fatted,* enriched.
Line 16: *Fleer,* flare, spread out.
Line 21: *Thy Active and thy Passive 'bedience,* the obedience of Christ to the Father
    while on earth; "obedience Active, to the Duties required: and Passive unto
    the Penaltie inflicted which is the price of our Redemption" (Grabo, ed., *Tay-
    lor's Christographia,* 185).
Lines 20 and 23: *White and Red,* symbolic of active or inherent righteousness (pu-
    rity) and passive or adherent righteousness (through the blood of Christ).
Line 22: *Active and Passive Right' ousness,* the "evangelical righteousness" of
    saints in Christ, also termed inherent and adherent righteousness (Grabo, ed.,
    Taylor's Treatise Concerning the Lord's Supper, 29. See note to I:44, l. 8
    above). Elsewhere, Taylor speaks of the Church being filled with "Fulness of

Christ as an Active, and in a Passive Sense.'' In an active sense, Christ pours saving and sanctifying grace into the Church. In a passive sense, ''Christ is filld up with the Church'' as the saints join together as his ''Mystical Body'' (Grabo, ed., *Taylor's Christographia*, 304–307).

Line 30: *Guise,* manner, behavior.

Line 40: *Shoshannim,* stringed instrument, mentioned in Psalms 45 and 69.

Line 42: *Stuttings,* stutterings.

INDEX TO INTRODUCTION

INDEX TO TEXTS

Other Volumes in This Series